William Henry Thomes

The Gold hunters in Europe

The dead alive

William Henry Thomes

The Gold hunters in Europe
The dead alive

ISBN/EAN: 9783743301368

Manufactured in Europe, USA, Canada, Australia, Japa

Cover: Foto ©ninafisch / pixelio.de

Manufactured and distributed by brebook publishing software (www.brebook.com)

William Henry Thomes

The Gold hunters in Europe

THE GOLD HUNTER'S LIBRARY.

THE GOLD HUNTERS IN EUROPE;

OR,

THE DEAD ALIVE.

BY

WILLIAM H. THOMES,

AUTHOR OF "THE GOLD HUNTER'S ADVENTURES, OR LIFE IN AUSTRALIA,"
"THE BUSHRANGERS," ETC.

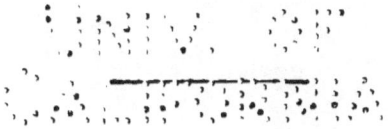

BOSTON:
LEE AND SHEPARD, PUBLISHERS.
NEW YORK:
LEE, SHEPARD AND DILLINGHAM.
1875.

Entered, according to Act of Congress, in the year 1868, by
LEE AND SHEPARD,
In the Clerk's Office of the District Court of the District of Massachusetts.

Stereotyped at the Boston Stereotype Foundry,
No. 19 Spring Lane.

INTRODUCTION.

A WORD OF EXPLANATION TO THE GENERAL READER

THOSE who have perused "THE GOLD HUNTERS, OR ADVENTURES IN AUSTRALIA," and "THE BUSHRANGERS, OR LIFE IN AUSTRALIA," will recollect several prominent persons who were conspicuous in all encounters with desperate robbers in Victoria and in other sections of that province. These characters will figure quite extensively in this volume. Daring, cool, collected Fred, the favorite of man, woman, and child, once more appears upon the stage, and with him our old Australian friend, the commissioner of the mounted police, the terror of bushrangers and ticket-of-leave men; Murden, the bold and rash, thorough English in all his habits and ideas, yet a man to be relied upon in every emergency, and who would have died rather than desert a comrade in distress; Hezekiah Hopeful, of Hillsboro' County, New Hampshire, the mechanical genius, who invented a quartz-crusher, and by its aid made a fortune in Australia — a genuine representative of the Yankee, prompt to fall in love with a pretty face, full of pluck and all the dogged energy of his race, —

he, too, will contribute his share for the entertainment of the reader; and, lastly, the writer of "THE GOLD HUNTERS" and "THE BUSHRANGERS," the historian of the party, will tell you what we saw, what adventures we encountered in foreign countries, and other matters of interest.

All these things will be told in a straightforward matter-of-fact manner. In the campaigns which we are about to commence, we shall always be accompanied by a four-footed friend, whose fidelity has been tested, and whose courage is above suspicion. Rover (his name is familiar to the reader) is not too old to do valuable service for his master; for his eyes are as bright and his teeth as strong as when we first met him on the dry, parched plains of Australia, on that terrible night when the bushrangers maltreated his mistress and killed his master. Age sits lightly on his massive head, and although the dear old hound seldom relaxes his dignity for the purpose of joining in the sports of the field, yet he is as fleet of foot and as untiring as ever.

With these explanations, brief but necessary for a perfect understanding of the characters which are to appear in the volume, the writer will commence unfolding his series of adventures, and hopes to hold the reader's attention to the end.

CONTENTS.

CHAPTER I.
Reminiscences of the Past. — Widowers condoling with each other. — Strange Visitors. — The Dead alive. — Plans for the Future. 9

CHAPTER II.
In which Fred relates a few Particulars of his Resurrection from a Tomb, and what happened to him afterwards. . . 17

CHAPTER III.
All aboard. — The Thunderer under Steam. — The first Adventure. — Child overboard. — To the Rescue. — In the Water and on the Ship. 28

CHAPTER IV.
Dripping wet. — Heroes for the Hour. — A Pair of bright Eyes. — An Introduction. — An Earl's Thanks. — A Promise. . 38

CHAPTER V.
A Father's Story. — In a Convent. — We promise Aid. — The Earl and Countess. — A Coquette. — Queenstown and a Surprise. 48

CHAPTER VI.
A strong Escort. — Suspected of being Fenians. — The attempted Rescue. — The Flight after the Fight. . . . 58

CHAPTER VII.
A secret underground Retreat. — Whiskey Stills and Fenianism. — The Attack and Defence. — A Blow for Liberty. . 69

CHAPTER VIII.
An Attempt to escape. — Rover and the Fenian's Leg. — A Game that was blocked. — Storming the Cellar. — A familiar Voice. 79

CONTENTS.

CHAPTER IX.
A strange Meeting. — An old Acquaintance. — Pat and his Accusations. — In the Street. — The Barracks. — The Despatch. 90

CHAPTER X.
Ordered to Dublin. — The Warning. — The mysterious Voice. — Off for Dublin. — Drunken Soldiers. — The Fenians again. 101

CHAPTER XI.
Surrounded by Fenians. — The Search for Gold. — A Disappointment. — Maurice in Danger. — Fred to the Rescue. — A Signal. 112

CHAPTER XII.
A long Tramp. — A Cave in the Mountains. — A Proposition. — The Refusal. 122

CHAPTER XIII.
A Plan for an Escape. — Sentinels and Whiskey. — Securing Muskets. — A Struggle. — A Sentinel on the Watch. . 132

CHAPTER XIV.
Capturing an Outpost. — On the Mountains. — The Hut in the Valley. — The Still and its Owner. — A Surprise. . . 143

CHAPTER XV.
A Surprise. — A Proposition. — Death or Gold. — Heavy Demands. — The Rope and the Victim. — Terms accepted. — An Interruption. 154

CHAPTER XVI.
Surprised Fenians. — The Pursuit. — An Acquaintance. — For Dublin. — Another Arrest. 164

CHAPTER XVII.
Champagne and Whiskey Punch. — On our Way to the Castle. — An Audience with his Lordship. 173

CHAPTER XVIII.
A convinced Lord. — Hez and his Hand-shaking. — Discharged. — An Explanation. — A Ruse to escape Attentions. 183

CHAPTER XIX.
The Serenade. — A grand Row. — Off for Liverpool. — Hez and a pretty Girl. — Disappearance of Hopeful. — A Request for Money. 193

CONTENTS.

CHAPTER XX.

Hopeful in a bad Way. — His Messengers. — Rover undertakes a difficult Task, and accomplishes it. — A Proposal. . . 202

CHAPTER XXI.

A Proposition. — It is accepted. — In Search of Hopeful. — The Saloon, and what we saw there. — Daisy appears. . . 212

CHAPTER XXII.

A Struggle. — A Prisoner. — Search for Hopeful. — The lost One found. — A Surprise. 222

CHAPTER XXIII.

A wretched Lover. — A little Prudence and Reason. — A Resolution. — An Escape. — A Gang of Roughs. — The Officers of the Police. 232

CHAPTER XXIV.

Another Surprise. — A Retreat. — A Demand. — Murden's Point. — Daisy and her future Life. 241

CHAPTER XXV.

What to do with a fainting Girl. — Rover and the Landlord. — Murden and his Protégée. — An awkward Meeting. . 250

CHAPTER XXVI.

An Explanation, and one that is satisfactory. — An Interview with Daisy. — Her Consent. — Another Surprise. . . 260

CHAPTER XXVII.

Daisy and her Voyage. — Explanations. — Off for London. — The Pride of England. — A Caller. — A Landlord's Astonishment. 270

CHAPTER XXVIII.

An Invitation for Lancaster from a live Earl. — Meeting with Relatives. — A Bit of Advice. — A Scene unexpected. . 280

CHAPTER XXIX.

A Declaration of Love on the Part of Hopeful. — The Departure for Paris. — Our Plans. — An Arrest in the Name of the Emperor. 289

CHAPTER XXX.

Under Arrest. — An Examination. — A remarkable Man. — An Edict. — A Surprise. — The Emperor. 300

CHAPTER XXXI.

Hopeful and the Emperor. — The Hopper Gun. — An Interview appointed. — Convents. — A Dinner. — An Appointment. 310

CHAPTER XXXII.

The Interior of a French Hotel. — How a Countess can plot and plan to rob those who have Money. — An Interruption. 321

CHAPTER XXXIII.

Death in the Midst of Life. — An astonished Group. — Grumbling Companions. — An Interview with Miss Josie. . . 330

CHAPTER XXXIV.

The Emperor Napoleon and Family. — A kind Reception. — An Explanation. — The Leave-taking. 339

CHAPTER XXXV.

The Garden Mabille. — A pretty Girl. — A Flirtation. — A Dance. — An Invitation. — A Graybeard. — The Iron Gate. 349

CHAPTER XXXVI.

In a Convent. — A dangerous Position. — A Confession. — The Effect of a Sneeze. — Face to Face. 358

CHAPTER XXXVII.

A fallen Priest. — A Reënforcement. — An Advance. — A Retreat. — A deadly Agent. — A Surprise and a Rescue. . 367

CHAPTER XXXVIII.

Safe Advice. — A surprised Father. — A Proposal. — Off for England. — Weddings. — Finishing up. — The End. . . 375

THE
GOLD HUNTERS IN EUROPE;

OR,

THE DEAD ALIVE.

CHAPTER I.

REMINISCENCES OF THE PAST. — WIDOWERS CONDOLING WITH EACH OTHER. — STRANGE VISITORS. — THE DEAD ALIVE. — PLANS FOR THE FUTURE.

ONE evening Hezekiah Hopeful, my old companion in arms, was seated in my library, smoking a cigar, and looking as mournful as a man should look who had lost a dear wife six months before. At my feet, on a velvet rug, reposed Rover, a noble hound, that winked and wagged his tail every time Australia was mentioned, as though he knew that he had seen some stirring times in that land of gold, kangaroos, and bushrangers.

"I'll tell you what it is," said Hopeful, after a moment's silence, sending out a volume of smoke, " darned ef I don't wish I was back in Australia agin. We did have fun thar — now didn't we? O Lord, how we did make them ere bushrangers run when once we struck their trails! And then, how we raked in the gold! — solid, yellow gold, and not sich stuff as we has to handle and call it money."

"You miss your wife, Hopeful," I said; "I can see it in your face, and by every word that you utter. Take another, and be contented with the wealth that you have got, for you know you are the richest man in Hillsboro' County."

"I know that, but I'll be gol darned ef I can forget my Martha quite so soon. I shall never love another gal as I loved her; and to think that she should die jist at this time is a little too hard on me. I must do somethin' to occupy my time, or I shall go near about ravin' distracted. Come, let's make a trip to Australia, and look at old friends. They'll be glad to see us, I knows."

The hound started to his feet and uttered a prolonged howl, that rattled the windows and called forth a severe reprimand from me.

"You see," Hopeful continued, after quiet was restored, "even old Rover would like to see Australia once more. Wouldn't you, old dog?"

The hound laid his head for a second on Hez's knee, and then stalked to the door, sniffed for a moment, and once more uttered a deep bay — a bark that told of joy and sorrow; and I could only quiet him by throwing a slipper at his head, and then compelling him to bring it to me.

"The dog misses the tender care of his mistress," I said. "Since Jenny died he has seemed sad and mournful, and is uneasy if I am out of his sight for a moment."

"That's what I came here for," cried Hopeful. "I want to have a square talk with you, and I mean to afore I leaves the house. Here you is a mopin' yerself to death ever since the death of yer wife. Now, 'tain't no use to go on in this way. You is a young man, only thirty years of age, and can see lots of happy days if yer is a mind to think so."

"Take the advice to yourself," I remarked. "You have been as mournful as an owl since you were a widower."

"I know; but then I lost Martha, and she —"

"Wouldn't compare for a moment with my Jenny."

Hopeful was about to utter an indignant protest when some one knocked at the door. Once more Rover manifested symptoms of restlessness, and paced up and down the library like a caged tiger, growling and uttering subdued bays.

"What in the devil is the matter with the dog?" exclaimed Hez, a little impatiently. "One can't hear himself think while he's goin' on at this rate. I should say we was in the bush, and Black Darnley and all his gang was round us. Lay down, old dog, and be a good fellow."

But Rover paid no attention to the blandishments of Hez, for he remained at the door and snuffed at the threshold as though he would like to leave us for a few minutes on important business.

"Come in," I shouted, as some one again knocked at the door.

The head of my reliable housekeeper, the lady who had taken charge of my establishment since I was left a widower, now appeared and uttered an apology for disturbing me.

"I shouldn't have ventured to do so," she said, "if the gentlemen were not so persistent in seeing you. They said that they must see you this night, and that they would not leave the house until they had spoken with you."

"What names did they give?" I inquired.

"They said they couldn't give any names, for you wouldn't know them if they did. They look as though they came from foreign parts, for they are so tanned that all the lotions in the city couldn't made them white."

"Some of your naval friends," suggested Hez. "They want a lark, and have come to see ef you wouldn't jine 'em. Don't do it; 'coz, if you do, I shan't have any one to talk to about my lost and gone Martha."

"Show them up," I said; and as I gave the order, Rover dashed from the room, and uttered the most joyful bays. The dog seemed to have lost all his usual self-possession and staid dignity — something unusual on his part.

"Confound 'em, couldn't they have let me have one evenin' with yer all alone?" muttered Hez. "It's jist my luck. Well, I haven't bin in the city afore for three months, and now some cusses happen along and spile my visit."

"They won't stay long," I said, and then waited for my visitors to be shown to the library; but somehow, there appeared to be a most unaccountable delay in their appearing, for five minutes elapsed before I heard footsteps approaching the room.

Then my housekeeper, with a flushed face, and an air of the deepest agitation, threw open the door and admitted a gentleman who was so much muffled up that I could not see his face, for he had on a cloak with a large standing collar, and was so impolite as to wear on his head a slouched hat, that was drawn down deep over his eyes.

I glanced at the figure as it entered the doorway, and saw that it was about five feet eight inches, and that was all I could discern, for the cloak hid the rest.

"Some darned beggar, I'll bet," muttered Hez. "Don't give him even a piece of currency, for I'll warrant that he don't need it."

Even while Hez was speaking, I could hear Rover, in the lower part of the house, utter certain howls, in a subdued tone, as though some one was attempting to gag him, and prevent his giving expression to the joy that filled his doggish heart.

"Will you take a seat?" I asked the stranger, and pointed to a chair.

The intruder shook his head, but remained silent.

"I knew he was a darned beggar. I can read men like a book. Don't give him nothin', and keep an eye on yer silver spoons, or ye will miss some of 'em," Hopeful whispered across the table; and I feared that the stranger heard the words, for I noticed that his form shook as though with suppressed indignation.

"Hush," I replied. "Let me deal with my own company as I see fit."

Another growl from Hopeful, and then I turned to the stranger.

"Have you business with me?" I demanded. "If you have, state it as soon as possible, for I am engaged."

"Will you give me a drink?" the stranger asked, in a gruff voice, that did not sound like anything I had heard before.

"Certainly. Throw off your hat and cloak, and help yourself to a glass of wine." I pointed to the decanters and glasses that were on a side-table.

The stranger followed my instructions as far as the wine was concerned, for he poured out a goblet nearly full, and then said, —

"A long life and a merry one to all true-hearted Australian adventurers."

I sprang to my feet, and so did Hez. We rushed towards the stranger with one accord, tore from his head the slouched hat, stripped him of his cloak, and then there stood revealed before us our old, esteemed, brave-hearted friend, Murden, the commissioner of the mounted police for the province of Victoria, Australia — the very man who had fought with us, starved with us, made money with us, and would have died for us if it had been necessary.

With a great cry of delight I caught my friend in my arms, and then Hez caught us both in his arms, and for a moment we danced around the library, to the great danger of furniture and pictures.

"In the name of all that is most welcome and cheerful, tell me where you came from, and how did you get here?" I demanded, as soon as I could find breath and voice.

We forced the Australian into a chair, made him drink another glass of wine, and took some ourselves for the purpose of keeping him company.

Hez, as though it would assist the commissioner in explaining matters, commenced patting him on the back, as he had seen mothers do when their infants were inclined to strangle.

"Let me have a moment to breathe, and I'll tell you all," Murden said. "D—n it, let my back alone, old fellow! I'm all right, and don't need that kind of treatment. Now, then, one more drink, and then I'm with you on all that you need for explanations."

"Yes, yes; go on," we said, impatiently.

"Well, in the first place, I'm here."

"We know that."

"And in the next place, you must know that I left Melbourne over two months ago."

"Go on."

"I wanted to see you, boys; so I packed up my luggage and started. I came by the way of California, and this night have arrived in Boston. Now, are you glad to see me?"

A shout was the reply, and then followed a grand handshaking, that must have assured Murden he was indeed welcome to our home.

"Some one is with you," I said, as soon as the excitement had subsided. "We must have him up here. Any friend of yours is a friend of ours. Up he must come!"

For a moment Murden looked a little embarrassed, and then said:

"A servant of mine. Let him alone for the present. He will do well enough until we have finished our conference. Now tell me how you do."

"Well; but we have met with misfortunes. Our wives are lost to us forever."

"So is mine. She died a year ago. Let us sympathize with each other; although, to tell you the truth, I don't intend to break my heart for my loss. My wife had the best of a good bargain the last few years of her life. But then she had a temper — a devil of a temper it was! Well, peace to her ashes; I shall never marry again."

"That is what all widows and widowers say; but they forget the sainted departed after sleeping alone through one cold winter," I remarked.

The young widowers shook their heads as though they had no longer any hope; so, as I saw the conversation was disagreeable to them, I changed it.

"Tell us how it happens that you are here, old friend," I asked, after a moment's pause, and a sharp examination of the commissioner's face, to notice if there were any changes.

"It is a long story," was the answer.

"Let us have it; and while you are spinning a yarn, and telling us of absent friends, my housekeeper shall prepare dinner; for I have no doubt but that you can eat something."

"I have a regular Ballarat appetite. I could eat an ox, I believe. I was so impatient to see you, that I did not stop for refreshments after arriving in the city."

"Glad of it. We will talk over past adventures while discussing oysters and ducks. I am so rejoiced to see you, that I haven't words to express all that I feel; but questions will pour in upon you before morning."

"The more the better. But now let me tell you what has transpired since you left Australia. Two months after your departure for home, I resigned my position as commissioner in the mounted police force."

"We know all that. Your letters informed us of the fact."

"I thought that it was better for me to do so," the ex-commissioner continued, " for the cursed bushrangers swore that I was the worst enemy they had in Victoria, and so they were bound to kill me if they could. I have no doubt they would have done so if they could have had a fair show for success. As I had saved a little money —"

Ironical laughter from Hez and myself, in which Murden joined most heartily. We knew that he had salted down many thousands of pounds in the course of his career.

"Well, well, we won't quarrel over a word," Murden continued. "I had so much money that I wished to live and enjoy it, and not run any more risks. The governor and council begged me to remain in office; but I was firm, and refused; and then the Parliament voted me a gift of one thousand pounds in money, and fifty thousand acres of land on the banks of the Lodden, which I have stocked with sheep and cattle, and in the course of a few years it will make me some returns. You see government did not behave mean to me."

"Thunder. I should think not," ejaculated Hez.

"As soon as I received the grants," continued Murden, "I started business with a young and active American, whom I had long known and loved as a brother."

"Hey? What?" Hez and I cried, in tones of amazement.

"An American, Jack, whom you know, but Hopeful does not. I think that he never saw him."

I could only sit and stare at the commissioner, while he upset his wine, blushed, and acted as nervous as a girl who is receiving her first proposal.

"In Heaven's name, whom do you mean?" I asked, and almost started to my feet; for I had a presentiment that I was to hear some startling news.

"Jack," Murden said, and his stern face lost all its coldness, and I saw that the strong man was trembling like a frightened child.

"Yes," I answered, but did not remove my eyes from his face, for it seemed as though I was incapable of exertion. A dull beating of the heart was all that I could feel.

"Jack," my Australian friend continued, "I told you that I went into business with an American whom I loved and esteemed. Can't you guess whom I mean?"

"No," I answered, in a mechanical manner. And I could not have uttered another word to have saved my life.

Murden got up from his seat, and came and stood near me, one hand resting on my shoulder.

"My dear old friend," he said in a sad tone, yet with a cheerful smile, "do you believe that the dead can be alive?"

I should have sprung from my chair, but Murden held me down, and I saw him motion to Hopeful to hand me a glass of wine, which he did. I swallowed the liquor, and once more fixed my eyes on Murden's face, awaiting further developments.

"The dead alive!" I murmured. "What terrible mystery have you to relate? For God's sake, don't keep me in suspense."

"Can you hear something more wonderful than any adventure through which you have passed in Australia?"

"Yes," I managed to gasp.

"Then be firm; for the dead is alive!"

He threw open the door of the library and whistled — a shrill, policeman's whistle, such as we had used in Australia when danger was near, or help was wanted.

There was a sharp response, and then up the stairs bounded Rover, and then into the apartment stalked Fred Button, whom I had seen buried three years before, a few miles from Boston.

I gave one wild look, uttered one wild cry, and then fell into Murden's arms insensible; for the shock was too much for me. I could not realize that the dead was alive.

CHAPTER II.

IN WHICH FRED RELATES A FEW PARTICULARS OF HIS RESURRECTION FROM A TOMB, AND WHAT HAPPENED TO HIM AFTERWARDS.

WHEN I recovered my senses I was lying on a lounge, with shirt collar unbuttoned, face and hair wet with iced water, and Murden and Hopeful chafing my hands, and at the same time endeavoring to force a little wine down my throat.

"He's all right," the commissioner said, when he saw my eyes opened. "I knew he'd come round, but cuss me if I 'sposed he'd go off like that."

"You was too quick for him," Hez replied. "Human natur can't stand everythin'. When they told me that Martha was goin' to leave me, I felt jest as though I should go too; but I rallied, and still drag through existence like a harrow :ver a rocky field."

"What did you play such a trick on me for?" I asked, sitting up and looking around the library for the strange face that I had last seen in a coffin.

"We have not played a trick of any kind on you," Murden answered. "All that you have seen has been real live flesh and blood, as noble a specimen of a Yankee as can be found in this section of the country, or on any cattle range in the States."

I looked at the commissioner's face while speaking, and saw that he was as grave as a church deacon. There was no sign of merriment in his eyes. The man was serious, if he never was before.

"What does it all mean?" I asked. "Give me some explanation, and as soon as possible."

"Can you endure it? Are you able to stand another surprise?"

"Yes."

"Be sure of your strength, for you are to hear something more marvellous than romance."

"Is the dead really alive?" I asked, in a whisper, endeavoring to suppress a shudder.

"Yes; will you see your old friend, or will you wait until you are more composed, and have gathered your scattered senses?"

"I will see him at once. Reality is less painful than this suspense. Let him come in and convince me that his form is composed of flesh and blood."

The door opened, and in came Fred, with a smile upon his lips, but a serious, anxious expression upon his face.

"Jack, my dear old friend," he said, coming towards me with extended hand, "take me to your heart once more, and forgive the trick which has been practised upon you."

I touched his hand and found it warm. The next instant our arms were around each other's neck, while Murden and Hez danced a species of Australian jig, to show how much affected they were, and Rover howled and barked in chorus, and seized our coat tails in the exuberance of his joy at the reunion.

At this instant my housekeeper, who had been let into the secret by Fred, while Murden was preparing me for the interview, showed her honest face at the door, her eyes looking rather red, as though they had recently been acquainted with tears.

"O, what a blessed hour this is!" she said. "O, what a happy meeting! But don't talk any more jest now, 'cos dinner is ready, and I'm afeard it will get cold and spile if yer don't set down to the table at once. You can talk and eat at the same time, I know."

No one paid the least attention to the old lady, except Rover, and he seemed inclined to obey the summons, for he cared more for his dinner than he did for sentiment. But when he found that no one was inclined to follow his lead to the dining-room, he uttered one or two growls of disappointment, and then lay down near the door to await events.

"Fred," I said, as soon as I could find words for utterance, "how could you deceive me for so many years?"

"You shall have a full explanation, old fellow, although I will not warrant that it shall be satisfactory. But you see me before you, alive and well, and just from Australia."

"Yes," interrupted Murden, "we have been in partnership in Melbourne for the past three years, and when he longed for home I resolved to come with him and see my friends in this part of the world."

"But why did you not write, and let me know that you were alive?" I asked.

"For reasons which I will give as soon as I have had my dinner, for I assure you that I am quite hungry for a dead man."

"The soup, gentlemen, is spilin'," the housekeeper once more said, thrusting in her jolly-looking face, and beaming at the group in the library.

"Then over the dinner-table you shall tell me your singular story," I cried, and led the way to the dining-room, to the great delight of Rover.

We were soon seated, and for half an hour only the most

commonplace remarks were indulged in; but as appetite became satisfied, questions were asked and answered, until the dessert was placed on the table, and then, over our coffee and wine, Fred, who looked as natural and as young, as bold and as noble, as when we worked together in the mines of California, or tramped through the bush and over the sterile plains of Australia, told me the great secret of his life, and to it we listened with wondering ears.

"I never had but one secret which I kept from your ears," Fred said, as he lighted a cigar. "It was of no great importance; but it worried me until I was nearly distracted. At one time I thought of confiding it to you, but feared that you would laugh at me. So I kept my own counsel, and determined to bear my own sorrows without a confederate."

"Was that like you, Fred? Did you fear to trust me with your sorrows or joys?" I asked.

"No common ones; but this was so serious, and yet so laughable, that I feared ridicule."

"A woman was at the bottom of it, I'll bet," Hez said. "They is the critters to raise the devil with a man! They is weak; but I tell yer they is strong when they nas a mind to put a feller over the road."

"You are right," said Fred, with one of his cheerful laughs. "A woman caused me all my uneasiness, and ultimately my death; and she was not a young woman either."

"I vow, I'll bet she was a widow," Hez muttered.

"She was a widow, and had three children," Fred said, with a face that attempted to be grave, but did not succeed. "She had determined, somehow, to have me take the dear departed's place, and be a father to her sons; but I objected to this nice little arrangement; and then commenced a struggle, in which woman's tears and man's natural obstinacy were pitted against each other. I was firm, and swore that I did not want a wife, and she was firm, and swore that she wanted a husband, and that I was the man she had selected, and that I must yield my opinions for her convenience. She said that I had kissed her, and talked love, and love meant marriage with her."

"Had you kissed her?" asked Hez, in an eager tone.

Fred laughed, blushed a little, and said,—

"I'm a man; and when a widow makes love to a person like me, she most generally gets kissed; but kissing does not mean marriage, although some women seem to think so."

"I don't know as I should have done any different if I had bin in yer place," Hez remarked, in a musing tone. "I allers had a weakness for widders."

Fred did not notice the interruption, but continued his narrative:—

"All this time I kept the matter from your knowledge, for I knew that you would scold me for getting involved in so serious a combination as a widow and three children. I also feared your ridicule, and all the sensible preaching which you would utter for my sake. But at last my sufferings became unendurable, and I determined to die, so that I could escape my persecutor. This I kept to myself until I had arranged all my plans. I made a will, and left a portion of my property to you, Jack, and I have no doubt but that you thought it singular that the amount was so small."

"Yes, I wondered what you had done with all your money, as I knew that you had not lived fast while in Boston."

"I invested more than one half in stock in a fictitious name, and left the widow five thousand dollars; but I sent the money to her in a letter, and told her that I was dying, and she would never see me more. I need not say to you that I had no thoughts of stepping out. I meant to get up a mock funeral, and for that purpose arranged with an undertaker and his family to do all the honors; but, faith, while I was laying out plans, I awoke one morning to the consciousness of being unable to move hand or foot, or even to open my eyes. The fact of it is, I was in a state of trance, with no more motion or feeling than if I was dead, with the exception of being able to hear and understand all that was going on. This interfered with my plans, for I intended to have written a letter to you, explaining what I had done, and asking you to meet me in New York and proceed to California, where we could stay a year or two, or until the widow gave up all thoughts of law or matrimony; and I assure you that death was preferable to either, for you know what a horror I have of law, and am not enthusiastic on the subject of marriage.

"But there I was, in a state of trance, and in the hands of a fellow who had agreed to bury me, or get up a mock funeral, for so many hundred dollars; and I could not help thinking that the scamp would chuckle at the idea of earning his money so easily. I strove to burst the bonds that held me, to call out for help, but I could not move even a finger; and when my host came into the room and saw me dead, he really appeared to feel rejoiced that all his troubles were over, and that he could clap me into a coffin and put me away, as he had done hundreds of others before.

"For two days I remained in the trance. You arrived, and shed tears, and uttered such words of grief that I strove to speak to you, and could not; and then I was put into a coffin, and I felt your hand on my brow, and felt your tears on my face; and that was the last until the lid of the coffin was screwed down."

"Devilish uncomfortable position for a live man," muttered Hez, with a shudder, while I was too interested to speak, for he had brought up the scene so vividly before me that I remembered to have spoken to the undertaker about the warmth of the body, while my hand rested on my friend's brow, even after his remains were enclosed in the coffin, and had been told that it was a common thing where death was so sudden, which I had believed, but in a half-doubting manner. O, why had I not insisted upon a proper examination by a skilful surgeon, instead of the country noodle who pronounced my friend dead!

Fred wet his lips with wine, and then continued his story.

"I remember, when the coffin was closed, how you told the undertaker that I should be placed in a tomb, and not buried in the ground, for that you meant to erect over my remains a monument worthy of my merits as a man and a friend; and those words, old fellow, saved my life." And here Fred extended his hands, and took both of mine in his usual hearty manner, as though his deep love had not been lost by years of separation.

"Go on," I said, "or you will kill me through anxiety to learn how you escaped from the tomb to which we consigned you."

Fred took a deep respiration, a fresh cigar, a glass of wine, and then resumed.

"I was placed in the tomb, and my escape from it was through the ardent desire of some half dozen H. medical students to acquire science in a short space of time, by cutting up such bodies as fell in their way in an illegitimate manner. The dear and rather wild youths of the medical class of old H. heard that a man had died suddenly, without visible cause, and they were determined to investigate, and see if they could learn a little something by an autopsy of my body; and for this purpose they visited the tomb in which I was placed. They found no trouble in getting an entrance, for the scamps had been there before, and had false keys to the locks. Perhaps the undertaker knew this, and received something to keep quiet about it; but at any rate, while I was wondering how many days it would take to starve me to death, I heard a slight noise; and then a screwdriver was set at work, and in a few minutes the lid of the coffin was raised, and a dark lantern was flashed in my face.

"'This is the cove,' said the fellow who held the lantern. 'He ain't altered a bit. Out with him at once, for we have no time to lose. He'll cut up splendid, I know, for his flesh is so firm.'

"The scamps rolled me out of the coffin, and were not

gentle in their work. I was struck on the head, and the blow started my blood to flowing, and broke the spell that bound me in fetters like death. For a moment I waited until I could get the kinks out of my cramped limbs, and then, while the students were about to take a drink in celebration of their triumph, and while they were remarking that I must have been quite a hard hitter in a general muss, I slowly rose to my feet, without their notice, and startled the fellow who was just about putting a bottle of whiskey to his lips."

"Egad, I should think so," remarked Hopeful, who had sat staring at Fred while he was relating his experience. "Darn if I don't think I should have hopped some, if I had bin thar. I don't call myself a coward —"

"That you ain't," cried Murden. "I've seen you in some tight places, but I never saw you show the white feather, even if the odds were two to one."

Hez looked gratified, and then continued, —

"No, I ain't a coward; but I tell you I can't stand ghosts, and if there is anything I would run from, 'tis one of 'em. I can face a bushranger, but not a feller what prowls round the airth arter he is put under ground."

"As the student placed the bottle to his lips," continued Fred, "I reached over his shoulder and snatched it from his hand. He turned round and gave me one look, and then uttered a yell that could have been heard half a mile. His companions caught sight of me, by the aid of the lantern, and with shrieks of terror rushed from the tomb, tumbling over each other in their haste to escape.

"I let them depart without further molestation; for I was too well satisfied at my release to frighten the fellows out of their senses. I heard them jump over the cemetery wall, enter their wagon, and drive off as fast as their horse could run; leaving several coats behind, which I needed, for the night was cold, and my blood was thin, and stomach empty. The first thing that I did was to take a drink, and the next to put on an overcoat, and, lastly, I returned thanks to Heaven for a wonderful escape from a terrible death.

"The liquor revived me, and gave me some strength. Then, by the aid of the dark lantern, I replaced the cover of the coffin, screwed it down, had a drink, and left the tomb with as thankful a heart as man could desire. I had been laid out in a suit of dark clothes, boots, and stockings, which was quite kind on your part, Jack, and very thoughtful, and, I assure you, quite useful, as I found, for there was no danger of attracting attention as I walked through the streets of Cambridge, on my way to some restaurant where I could get a square meal, for I was almost frantic with hunger, having been without food for several days.

"I was fortunate in finding a cellar that was kept open all night for the accommodation of market-men and stragglers, who needed food in the course of the night. As I entered the cellar, the person who had charge of it stared at me in a bewildered manner, and rubbed his eyes as though he could not trust them. I gave him an order for half a dozen different dishes; but still the fellow stared at me, and did not stir.

"What do you see to look at in me?" I asked.

"'Beg pardon, sir,' the man answered, 'but you does look jest as though the trumpet had blown, and you had come out of a graveyard. I should take yer for a ghost if I should meet yer anywhere but in a cook-shop. Ghosts don't eat, I believe; so I 'spose yer is flesh and blood.'

"'You may be assured of it by my orders,' I replied; 'so hurry up some steak, eggs, and coffee.'

"The man gave one more look at my face, and then waked up one of his assistants, and set him to work on my early breakfast; for I saw by the clock that it was just three, and daylight would not appear until six, and I could do nothing until I had thought of my position, and studied it in all its various phases.

"While the waiter was looking after my meal, I stole

a glance at a glass, and saw the reason why I had astonished the fellow. My face was deadly pale, and about my throat was a lace band, which did not improve my appearance. I tore it off, for it was too tomb-like to be pleasant; and when the waiter appeared I told him that I had been to a masquerade ball, and was on my way home on foot.

"'I should say, sir,' the fellow remarked, 'that you took the part of a corpse quite well, and I hopes, sir, that you didn't frighten the young ladies.'

"I pretended to laugh, and then remained in a thoughtful mood until after breakfast; and with food came resolution. I was dead to the widow and the world, and dead I intended to remain until she got married, or was buried. I would leave this part of the country, and go to California for a year or two; and, after writing you a long letter —"

"Which I never received," I said.

"I know that you did not, or you would have met me in New York, as I desired and dearly hoped. I waited for you, and again wrote to you; and, receiving no answer, went to California, from there to China, and from China to Australia, where I learned you had been for some years, but had sailed for home, with pockets full of money, just one month before I arrived. I felt terrible to think that I had missed you, but could not explain to you by letter all that I desired; so resolved, at Murden's solicitations, to remain in Melbourne, and enter some business with him, hoping that you would again pay Australia a visit."

"So I would if I had known that you were there. But, my dear old fellow, are you aware that I never received your letters, and that in Mount Auburn stands a monument erected to your memory?"

"Let it stand there. I shall want it some day, I suppose. The undertaker must have cheated you when he removed my remains."

"I rather think he did, for he told me I must not look at you, such an alteration had taken place. I did not, so was sold. He imagined that your body was stolen, and kept the news from me for fear of a row, and losing a good job. But there is one thing you have not told me How dare you venture home?"

"Because the widow is married, thank Heaven, and her children, present and future, are provided for. I am safe from her arts and temper."

"But the fortune that you left me I shall immediately restore."

"Bah! I have money enough to last us both a lifetime. Come, old fellow, come to my arms, and welcome a brother who has been dead, but is now alive, and who will never again separate from you, unless real death steps in and takes one of us."

We almost squeezed the breath from each other, and then I asked, —

"How are all our friends in Australia?"

"Smith is a member of Parliament and an aristocrat. He is one of the wealthiest men in Victoria. All the rest of our friends are well, and some of them are rich, and some none too well off."

"And now what are your plans?" I asked.

"I'm bound for England and Europe," answered Murden. "I want to see the old country once more. I have money and time enough."

"Let us all go with him," I cried. "What is to detain us? We are free men, and need new adventures to inspire us with energy and enterprise."

All of the company uttered a cheer.

"We will go together," was the cry; and after a glass of wine, we sat down and laid out our plans.

CHAPTER III.

ALL ABOARD.—THE THUNDERER UNDER STEAM.—THE FIRST ADVENTURE.—CHILD OVERBOARD.—TO THE RESCUE.—IN THE WATER AND ON THE SHIP.

WE were in no hurry to settle our proposed trip to Europe. After we had decided to go, there was no backing down, or desire to originate excuses for staying at home; so we sat over our coffee and cigars, and laid out our plans.

"We will first go to England," said Murden. "I have business in London with the government, that will take me a week or two to look after, and then I'm free for Ireland, Scotland, or Wales."

"Or France," suggested Hez. "I've bin told that them Paris women is stunners for show."

"Hear him! A widower talking about the female beauties of Paris!" was the general cry, which caused Hez to blush, and to stammer out that he felt so lonely that he must talk about something, and his sainted Martha was always uppermost in his mind.

"By the way," cried Fred, "let me propose a toast, which I know you will all join. Here is health, long life, and happiness to our friend Murden, who has risen from the police ranks to be inspector, captain, commissioner, member of Parliament for Victoria, and, lastly, a member of the governor's cabinet."

This was news to Hez and myself; so we cheered, as in duty bound, and drank the toast with all the honors.

"To tell the truth," cried Murden, while a flush of pride spread over his face, "I was a member of the cabinet for two months, and then the house voted that it had no confidence in us; so we resigned. I was secretary of agriculture, and had just commenced a system of tilling the earth that would have told on our exports, when I was forced out. All great men have their ups and downs, and I'm not exempted from the common lot."

We all laughed at the ex-minister, but he took it in such good part that we were disarmed, and at length forced to let him alone.

"We can take a look at Paris," Fred said, in a pause of the conversation.

"Blast it, we'll go everywhere," cried Murden. "We have money enough, and can afford to do as we like for a year or two."

"We'll come across some rare adventures, I have no doubt," Fred suggested, all enthusiasm. "We'll look for them, like knight errants of old; and I know that there is not a man of us who will shrink from rescuing and aiding maidens in distress."

"Leave 'em to me," that wretched Hopeful remarked. "I'll 'tend to 'em, and you look arter the men. The maidens comes more in my line, you see."

One would not have supposed that such was the case, to have looked at Hez's sandy hair and freckled face; but no one took the trouble to contradict the gentleman from Hillsborough; so he was satisfied, and the rest of us were.

The night was well advanced before we had concluded what to do, and had arranged all our plans. I was to take my child, a smart boy of four years, to England, and leave him with his grandparents, Sir William Byefield and lady, while I was travelling. They had desired me to visit them for more than a year, and I knew that they would be delighted to keep the boy while I was in Europe or out of it. We also resolved that we would take our Australian weapons, revolvers and knives, but leave our rifles at home, as too cumbersome to transport all over the continent; and, lastly, we determined to secure passage for England the next day, and sail just as soon as we could, after seeing to our bills of exchange, letters of credit, and other matters of interest.

"And what shall we do with Rover?" asked Fred, laying a hand on the dog's head, and patting him — an attention which the noble animal responded to by a dismal howl, as though he knew the subject of our discourse, and mourned for our determination.

There was a moment's silence. All looked at the dog with loving eyes. No one wanted to propose that he should be left behind, yet no one was bold enough to suggest that he should be taken with us. While we were thinking of the matter, Rover came to me, and placed both paws on my shoulders, and tried to give my face a lick with his huge tongue — an act of kindness on his part which I declined to accept just at that time; but the look which the noble brute assumed quite touched my heart. My resolution was formed in an instant.

"Rover goes with us," I said, in a tone that did not admit of argument.

My friends gave a shout of delight, and Rover, who understood me as well as if he had been a human being, and familiar with the English language, uttered such a series of joyous barks, and performed such a variety of gambols, that he tumbled against Hez, who was leaning back in his chair, and down they both went to the floor, with a crash that jarred the house.

"Gol darn yer," said Hez, picking himself up, "yer needn't go in sich conniptions jist 'cos yer is goin' with us. Ye has got to behave better than that, now I tell yer, when ye find yerself in the presence of all the kings and queens and nobility of Europe."

We roared at Hez's idea of the company which we were to meet; but Hopeful was not in the least disturbed.

"You jist wait," he said, "till them kings and emperors and sich hear that we is with 'em, and then you'll see if they don't send for us, and ax us to lend 'em a helpin' hand, or want to borrer money of us. Jist mark my words, now I tell yer."

We let Hez have his own ideas on the subject, thinking that he might discover his error in the course of his travels; and so, after a little more talk, and another glass of wine all round, we separated for the night, and went to our respective rooms.

The next morning we went and engaged cabin passage in the first-class steamer Thunderer, Captain Catall, to touch at some port in Ireland, and then go into dock at Liverpool. My friend Fred and I and Rover occupied one of the large family state-rooms, while Murden and Hez roomed together, and promised to be jolly all the passage.

The rest of the day we spent in getting ready for our journey. We bought bills of exchange, made visits, and showed Murden all the sights of Boston and vicinity; and while we were dodging from place to place, I found a gentleman, just married, who wanted a furnished house for a year or two, and so agreed to take mine at a fair price, and to use the furniture as though it was of some value to the owner.

In two days' time we had completed all our business, and on the third day we were on board the Thunderer, and steaming slowly down the harbor; and as I stood on the quarter-deck, holding my little boy's hand, and taking a quiet survey of my fellow-passengers, with Fred, Hez, and Murden near me, while Rover wandered up and down the deck, delighted at some signs of activity, I saw a little toddling girl, not more than three years of age, run up to the dog, and put her arms around his neck, and kiss the animal's nose and face, as though she rather liked her new acquaintance, while Rover suffered such liberties without remonstrance, being fond of children, and accustomed to pulling and hauling at the hands of Master Willie, my son, named after his grandfather.

"Take the child away from the dog," said a gentleman who stood near me, speaking to a servant who seemed to have charge of the little girl.

Just at that moment a handsome and distinguished-looking lady, who was seated on the quarter-deck, turned her head, and saw the position of the child and dog.

"O, my darling child!" exclaimed the lady, with a little scream. "The huge brute will bite you. Bring her to me, Eliza. Who could have brought so large an animal on board? I am sure a steamer is no place for a dog."

"I quite agree with you," replied the gentleman, whom I supposed to be her husband, and the father of her child. "None but Americans would take such a gross liberty."

"Halloo," whispered Fred; "we have already met with an adventure."

The girl, who seemed to have charge of the child, started to obey orders, and succeeded in separating the parties; but the child, not relishing such treatment, jerked away from the nursery-maid, ran towards the rail, and before any one could stop her, she had crawled under, and stood on the very edge of the quarter-deck, without the slightest protection from the water, that was foaming and bubbling beneath, stirred up by the propeller.

I saw the danger, and so did others. Her mother gave a piercing shriek, and exclaimed, —

"O, Heavens! my child, my child!"

The little girl uttered a crow of delight at her position, clapped her hands, and laughed at her mother's outstretched arms. The next moment the ship rolled a little, the child lost her balance, and over she went into the water, twenty feet beneath.

"Child overboard!" cried out a dozen men, as loud as they could yell.

"Stop her!" shouted a dozen others.

"Lower a boat!" exclaimed a few, and rushed towards one of the cutters that hung at the davits.

I heard, above the noise and confusion, a loud shriek, and saw that the mother of the child had fallen to the deck, quite insensible.

"Here is a chance for an adventure," I said to myself, and ran to the stern of the steamer, caught a glimpse of the child, twenty fathoms off, struggling in the water, its little arms tossing wildly about, as though seeking for something to grasp.

I gave my shoes a kick, tore off my jacket, and, with a strong jump, struck the water clear of the propeller. I went down some two fathoms, but came up like a rocket, and headed for the little girl.

"Fair play; give us a show with you," a familiar voice said; and, looking over my shoulder, I saw Fred a fathom or two behind me, and just in advance of him was Rover, both of them swimming like fishes for the child.

"Come on, old fellow," I cried; "I am glad of your company. Do your best, and we'll save the girl."

Rover uttered a bark of delight at the prospect of having a lark, and in a few seconds was up even with me, and in a moment we were on the spot where I had last seen the child.

The dog glanced around as though he did not understand her disappearance, and looked at me for an explanation, which, as I was in a hurry, I did not stop to give him. The child had sunk, and I had got to find her, if possible, before life was extinct.

With a sudden movement of my body, I disappeared beneath the surface of the water, and commenced my search. I swam along with the tide, looking to the right and left, up and down, and, as the water was clear, could see some distance. Thank God, my efforts were not in vain; for, just as I was about to give up, and rise for the purpose of getting a breath of fresh air, I caught sight of the child, hurried along by the tide, its long hair streaming in every direction, and several perch apparently eager for a feast.

With a desperate effort, although I felt as if my eyes would burst from their sockets, I swam forward, and succeeded in grasping the child by the arm, and then struck upwards; and when I reached the surface, there was but little breath left in my body, and I felt as though I could hardly sustain my own weight.

"Here I am, old fellow," cried a cheerful voice. "Give me the girl. I can manage her while you get your wind. You have done enough for one day; now let me and Rover do our share."

Fred, who was a bold swimmer, while speaking, grasped

the child in his strong arms, and Rover seized a portion of her dress, and thus they floated along, waiting for the boat which was just lowered from the steamer.

"Can you keep up?" asked Fred, who had an eye on me, as though anxious to see that I was all right.

"Yes, I guess so. I shall regain my strength in a moment. Look to the child, and be sure that she is taken care of."

"O, she is all right. Rover has got his eyes on her and you too. Hadn't you better let the dog help you a little? I can take care of the girl for ten minutes to come, and longer if necessary."

But I found I did not need help. A few minutes' floating on my back restored my strength so that I had no fear of drowning, and could turn my attention to the steamer, and noticed that the quarter-deck was crowded with passengers, and that the wildest excitement prevailed; for the captain of the vessel was urging the crew of the boat to renewed exertions, although it seemed to me that the men were doing all that they could to reach us.

"Can you hold out a little while longer?" I asked, as I swam towards Fred and Rover. "We shall soon be picked up."

"Yes, we are all right, and I hope the child is; but she looks awful white about the gills, and is as near death as is comfortable for one to contemplate."

"What made you follow me?" I asked, as I floated near the group.

"Well, when I saw Rover go after you, I thought it was but fair that I should jump, and superintend the whole lot; for you must know that I have not had an adventure for a year or more. Something tells me that I shall see quite a number while we are together. May they all be as useful as this one."

"Amen; for if the child survives, it will be another case of the dead alive."

"So it will."

There was a moment's silence. Rover released his hold

of the child, and licked the face that looked so corpse-like.
I trembled for fear he would utter a death-howl, which he
always did when the king of terrors was near; but he
only whined, which was conclusive proof to my mind that
life was not extinct.

"Bravo, old dog!" I said. "You encourage us to think
that all our efforts are not in vain."

"Thank Heaven for that. I wouldn't have the little
thing lose her life for all that I'm worth. But, I say," continued Fred, "what prompted you to jump after the child?"

"Well, because the dog was in some measure to blame
for the accident; and then, again, I heard the father of
the child utter a sneer against Americans. We'll put him
to shame for the words that he spoke. You see if he is
not sorry for them when we get on board."

"I have no doubt but that he will be; but recollect that
hereafter I must have an even chance when danger is to
be encountered. Don't think that I'm disposed to submit
to imposition of this kind. Fair play is all that I want
or ask."

"Can you hold out a minute longer?" hailed those in the
boat; and they were pulling like good fellows, although,
through excitement, they were not making as much progress through the water as they would have done had they
been cool and collected. In fact, I saw one man who was
so anxious to pick us up that he was glancing continually
over his shoulders, like a greenhorn pulling on to his first
whale, and thereby caught numberless crabs and some few
oaths, which the boat's crew hurled at his head for his
clumsiness.

"O, yes, we can hold out for an hour or two yet," I answered, and then gave Fred a little spell, so that he could
rest; and as I put an arm round the child's waist, I glanced
at its face, and saw that it continued deadly pale, and
showed no sign of life.

"Poor little thing!" I said; "I fear that it is past human aid."

"Never say die," was Fred's reply. "While there is

life there is hope; and I know that life is in that little casket."

"Here we are," cried the crew of the boat; and in went their oars, and then stout hands were thrust over the side of the cutter, and the little girl was raised from the water, and placed on cushions in the stern-sheets, while willing hands helped Fred and myself to crawl over the gunwale; and then Rover received his share of attention, and repaid it by shaking his huge form the instant he was in the boat, sending showers of water over the crew, and then darting aft and licking the pale face of the child.

"Give way, men!" cried the officer who was in charge of the boat. "Let us lose no time in getting back to the ship. The life of the child depends upon your efforts."

As the men shipped their oars, Fred and I passed aft, and my companion took the child in his arms, and let its little curly head rest upon his broad breast.

"I tell you what it is, gentlemen," said the officer who had charge of the boat, the first lieutenant of the steamer, "I've seen some smart things done in my sea-going experience, blast me if I haven't; but for two first-class passengers to jump overboard after a strange child is a little more than I ever heard of before, now I tell you; and I hope you will honor me with taking a drink with me as soon as you change your clothes. In fact, I want you to promise me to drink with me regularly every day through the passage. I can honor courage, even if an Englishman is not the one to show it."

"O, we will take a drink with you, never fear," replied Fred; and while he spoke he chafed the limbs of the little girl, and looked anxiously towards the ship, as if he wished that we were there, and the child was in the hands of the surgeon of the vessel.

"Thank you," said the officer; "I thought you would. Give way, men. Stretch your backs and make your oars bend. I suppose, gentlemen, you know who are the parents of the little girl."

"No, I am sure we don't," I replied.

"You don't?" cried the officer. "Why, you surprise me. I supposed that you knew the honored parents of that precious little piece of humanity, and that you jumped overboard to show your respect for his lordship."

"His what?" demanded Fred, looking up in surprise.

"Why, the Earl of Buckland. This is his child, and the mother is the Countess of Buckland, the daughter of the Duke of Boxborough. They were passengers with us when they came to this country, so that I got quite well acquainted with them. You will like them, I assure you; for they ain't like some of the nobility — too proud to speak to us plebeians."

Fred's lips curled while the officer was talking.

"We care as much for his lordship as he does for us, let me assure you. We should have made the attempt to save the child if she had been owned by steerage passengers, instead of a noble earl. What we have done is mere play to men like us, and we hope that his lordship will not feel that we must be noticed because we jumped overboard."

The lieutenant looked a little puzzled, as if he did not quite comprehend the reason of Fred's haughtiness; but before we had a chance for more words, the cutter shot alongside, and a hundred eager voices and two hundred willing hands were ready to ask questions and to assist in taking the girl up the steps and down into the cabin.

"My child! O, my child!" I heard the countess say, as she rushed towards us; but her husband was before her, and snatched the girl from Fred's arms, and disappeared in the cabin.

CHAPTER IV.

DRIPPING WET. — HEROES FOR THE HOUR. — A PAIR OF BRIGHT EYES. — AN INTRODUCTION. — AN EARL'S THANKS. — A PROMISE.

OF course there was an immense commotion on board the steamer, for a nobleman and his wife can't meet with a great misfortune without finding many sympathizers. The falling overboard of their child was well calculated to make the passengers open their mouths and their hearts at the same time.

"I tell you what it is, sirs," cried a red-faced Englishman, with a square body, and a silk hat that was frightful in its ugliness; "you did that devilish well. I couldn't have done better. No, sirs, not even if I had tried, and I wanted to, sirs; but I ain't as springy as I used to be, sirs, or I should have led you all, sirs, in going over after that precious little lamb. Besides, sirs, I don't know but that I have forgotten how to swim, for I haven't been in the water since I was a boy. You see the reason why I didn't plunge in after the treasure — don't you?"

The red-faced man did not give us time to speak, for he continued, —

"But, sirs, although I ain't much on water, I'm death on brandy, and I shall be proud to drink with you, sirs, at any time you are disposed; and as I'm willing just at this moment, suppose you come to my state-room and taste some of my vintage of thirty-one."

We declined the offer with all the civility that we could muster, under the circumstances, for men don't like long harangues when they are shivering in wet clothes, and feel that a change of dress is needed as soon as possible.

I glanced over the quarter-deck and saw that my son was in the arms of a matronly-looking woman, one who appeared quite competent to take charge of him; and after the little fellow had run to me and given me a kiss, and called me a "blessed dear papa," and told me that I was wet, and naughty to leave him the way that I did, Murden and Hez dragged us through the crowd of passengers, all anxious to get a glimpse of us, after the earl and his countess had left the deck. Among those who regarded us with interest were several young ladies, whose bright eyes and handsome faces rather made the scene flattering than otherwise; for I heard two or three of them whisper to each other, as we passed along, —

"They are unmarried Americans, immensely rich, and have passed years of their lives in Australia. They are perfectly splendid, and I mean to get an introduction just as soon as possible."

I received the flash of a pair of eyes that made me shiver, — but not with cold, — for I mentally thought that I had never seen anything so attractive as those dark eyes, which were full of merriment and sentiment.

But in a few minutes we were in our state-room, and had shed our clothes, were rubbed dry, had taken a little brandy and water, to keep out the cold, and then felt as well as ever.

"I tell you what it is, old fellows," said Murden, as he helped himself to a glass of brandy and water; "this is commencing adventures rather early. You have saved the life of an earl's child, and he won't forget it; now you can believe it."

"I am sure I don't care whether he does or not," returned Frank. "You know us well enough to be aware that we don't care whose child it is."

"Yes, yes, I know all that; but don't you fly in the face of luck or chance! Meet the earl with that courtesy which is so characteristic of my American friends, and he may do you a favor, and me also, for I have a mission to accomplish for Australia, and his lordship can help me."

Just at this moment, some one knocked at the door of our state-room, and the captain of the Thunderer, followed by a servant bearing glasses and two bottles of champagne, entered the apartment, and sat down in one of the berths.

"Gentlemen," said the bluff commander, "I'm d—d glad to know that I've got such perfect bricks on board the steamer, and I'm blasted glad to tell you that the child is all right and tight, and that his lordship is pumping tears out of his eyes as fast as though he was worked by a donkey-engine, while her ladyship, the countess, is so rejoiced at the safety of her darling, that she can't do anything but tack up and down the cabin and shuffle her hands."

The captain paused for a moment, after this long speech, and then took a long breath, and continued, —

"I come here to say that I must drink with you, gentlemen, and I have but little time to spare, before the pilot is discharged. Open the champagne, Sam, and let us imbibe. Now, then, here we go, all of us. A good passage and a merry one, and when you return to the States, don't fail to come with me, for I know how to make people comfortable. I ain't such a d—d stuck-up cuss as some of the captains of the line, although I say it, who shouldn't. Here we go!" And the wine went down his throat, hissing like water thrown on hot iron.

Luckily for us, the pilot sent for the captain; so we missed losing our heads with wine, for the commander could take an awful share of liquor and never show that he had wet his lips.

As soon as the captain was gone, we finished our toilets, gave our wet clothes to the steward for drying, and then went on deck to take a last, fond look at our own native land, and to smoke our cigars with some comfort. To do this, we went forward and passed up the fore-hatchway, and were thus enabled to escape notice from the passengers, who still crowded the quarter-deck, undisturbed by seasickness.

But Rover had suddenly risen to the rank of a hero, and betrayed us. He had been petted, and made much of by the ladies and gentlemen, so wandered around while we were in the cabin; but when we reached the deck, the animal seemed to be aware of the fact, and came bounding towards us, uttering his joy in lively barks.

"Down, Rover, and keep still," I said; and the dog obeyed without the least hesitation.

"This must be the gentleman who owns the hound," I heard a sweet voice say; and turning around, I saw the young girl with the dark, glorious eyes and beautiful face — the same one I had noticed when I was entering the cabin dripping wet.

She was leaning on the arm of an elderly gentleman, who looked enough like her to be her father. At any rate, I hoped that he was, for if he had said that he was her husband, I should have kicked him overboard, and taken good care that Rover remained on deck.

I turned to the fair speaker and raised my hat, which she acknowledged by a bow and a smile that displayed a row of teeth even and dazzlingly white.

"If you mean the fellers what went overboard arter the gal, these is the ones," cried that wretched Hez, who thought that he saw a chance to make the acquaintance of a pretty girl and display some of his fascinations at the same time. He pointed to Fred and myself, and we acknowledged the notice by a smile, but not the least feeling of shame for Hopeful's impulsiveness, even if it was a little out of place just at that moment.

"I was comrade and partner with this one," continued Hez, slapping me on the back. "We was like brothers to each other in Australia, and many is the time he has saved my life and put gold dust in my pockets at the same time. He is one of nature's noblemen, he is; and so is the other one, although I ain't so much acquainted with him."

The young lady smiled, although she tried to prevent doing so; but I saw lots of mirth in her bright eyes, so knew that she had a happy and joyous disposition.

"Hush, Hez, for Heaven's sake," I whispered to my friend. "Don't make me ridiculous."

"I shan't stop, either!" cried Hez, the champagne having made him bold. "I has a right to praise my friends, and will, when they is jolly good fellows."

Thank Heaven, Ma·den, who was always on hand, and

ready to do the right thing and at the right time, saw that I wanted to speak to the owner of the black eyes (he knew my weakness, as well as Fred), so pretended that he saw a whale, and got Hez to the forward part of the ship, and out of our way.

"Gentlemen," said the elderly person, on whose arm the lady was leaning, "this is my daughter, Miss Josephine Goldthwaite."

Once more we raised our hats and bowed low, and seriously considered if we should throw away our cigars, although we were on smoking-ground.

"My daughter," the father continued, "is desirous of testifying to you, gentlemen, in person, the esteem in which she holds your gallant deed in saving the life of the little girl. It was a brave action, and merits brave words of praise."

We introduced ourselves, and were soon chatting on terms of familiarity with the father and daughter; and then Fred, the kindest hearted fellow in the world, saw that I liked the lady a little better than I did the parent, so resolved to give me a chance. In a few words he interested Mr. Goldthwaite in matters connected with Australia; and then the old gentleman dropped his daughter's arm and walked off with Fred, leaving Miss Josephine in my company.

"Is your wife with you, Mr. Jack?" the lady asked, as soon as we were alone.

"I have no wife," I answered, and turned away my head, for the question awakened recollections which I did not wish disturbed.

"Forgive me," she said, "for speaking so thoughtlessly; but I saw your child, and so supposed that his mother was with him."

"I hope that she is," I replied, only by a powerful effort. "I trust that her spirit is hovering near him and me, day and night, and that its presence will make us purer and better."

The lady did not rep'y, although I could see that she felt

sorry for having awakened painful recollections in my breast. For a few minutes we remained silent, and then, as the ship rolled a little, rendering the lady slightly unsteady, I offered her my arm, which she accepted without a moment's hesitation, and we walked up and down the deck, with as much precision as two old sailors.

"You have been on the ocean before," I said, noting how firm was her step, and yet how light, in spite of the heavy swell that began to meet the steamer, and caused her to roll and pitch — a foretaste of what was to come.

"O, yes; I have crossed the ocean three or four times, and have resided in Paris several years. In fact, I completed what little education I received in that city."

"And you are now on your way there?" I asked.

"Yes; father has some business there which is of great importance. I wish that I dared to tell you what it is;" and the lady looked up in my face to see if it was a trusting one.

"Perhaps he will think me worthy of his confidence before the passage is over," I remarked.

"O, I know he will," cried the impulsive lady. "While you were saving the child, he remarked to me that those young gentlemen had courage and dash, and might help him if you were in Paris."

"Good," I said. "We will be in Paris several months, and nothing would delight me more than the opportunity to be of service to yourself or father."

"O, I am so pleased to hear you say that!" Miss Josie replied; and then, for fear that she had gone too far in her frankness, blushed and hesitated.

"I am sure you cannot be more pleased than myself at the opportunity of meeting in Europe, only I fear that in Paris you will forget your steamship acquaintances."

"Never fear," was the laughing response. "Brave deeds are not so easily forgotten, and I know that you and your friend are brave men."

"Thank you. I shall tell him of your opinion. We will treasure it as valuable."

"Don't laugh at me," the lady said, and her dark eyes began to look serious; so I hastened to assure her that I never thought of such a thing as smiling at her words, and in an instant the cloud passed from her beautiful face.

"Come," she said, at length, "I hear that you have quite a romantic history. Some one tells me that you have passed years in the bush, and gold mines of Australia, and that you were in continual danger while there. Is such the case?"

"Yes; we met with danger, and overcame it, in Australia," I replied.

"Do tell me all about it — won't you?" the lady asked. "If you don't, my father will take me to the quarter-deck, for I see that he is looking this way, as though he feared you were tired of me."

"Heaven forbid!" I exclaimed, most fervently; so serious, in fact, that the lady laughed, and then tried to look grave, but did not succeed. I was in the hands of a gay coquette, and she was giving me her first instructions in the great art of making herself agreeable, so that I should follow in her train of admirers, and worship her as others had done.

"We shall see," I muttered to myself, as I read her thoughts, plain as words spoken aloud; and then I commenced an account of my experiences in Australia, and told her how we had suffered and fought, and had at last succeeded, although the odds were against us.

"You must be a persevering gentleman," she remarked, as I concluded a history of a struggle that I had been engaged in at Gulchtown, Victoria, where the odds were so great against us, that it seemed as though we must fail in our efforts to secure the release of two young girls who had been captured by some bushrangers.

"I am firm in the right cause," I replied. "I would not be weak if justice was on my side."

She mused on the answer, and I saw that it did not please her; yet she did not know how to reply to it, and still keep up her character for good nature; but luckily just at this moment we saw approaching us the father of the child, the little girl whom we had saved.

"Here comes the Earl of Buckland," Miss Josie said. "He is about to thank you for what you have done. Perhaps I had better join my father, and let him talk to you without being restrained by my presence."

"And thereby deprive me of a greater pleasure than his words can convey. Please remain with me, and hear what he has to utter."

"Do you sincerely wish it?" asked the little coquette, with a look that was perfectly irresistible; and it seemed to me that I never saw so much fun in a woman's eyes.

"Certainly I do. Let us hear what his lordship has to say."

"Well, I will; for I want to know how an earl will express himself when grateful."

His lordship came towards me, and extended his hand, and, as he did so, said,—

"I think you are one of the gentlemen who saved the life of my child."

I bowed, and the earl continued,—

"I cannot find words to express to you the gratitude which I feel for your kindness and bravery; and my wife desires me to say that she wishes to thank you in person for what you have done, and that your name will be remembered in her prayers."

"The child has quite recovered, I hope;" for I saw that the earl expected me to say something, and that seemed the most appropriate.

"Nearly recovered, thanks to the skill of the surgeon of the ship;" and then the earl turned to Miss Josie, who was leaning on my arm, and addressed her.

"Ah, madam," he said, with a most courtly bow, "you should be proud of your husband, for he has shown himself capable of noble deeds."

I felt the blood rush to my face; and then the little coquette, who was clinging to my arm, had the impudence to laugh, and cover her eyes with her hands.

His lordship looked a little surprised, and for a moment was embarrassed, although he little suspected how he had blundered. I saw that he wanted an explanation, so hastened to give him one.

"You compliment me too highly when you assign me the position of husband to this lady. She has no mate, and I fear does not want one."

The earl smiled, and then I introduced him to Miss Josie in due form. Fred and Mr. Goldthwaite at this moment joined us, and conversation became general, and rather pleasant; for we found the earl did not manifest that haughtiness which we expected, was well informed on all matters, and deeply interested in Australia, so that Murden had an opportunity to lay before his lordship some plans and expectations which he had formed, and the earl promised his influence in carrying them out. Hez, who had never seen a live earl before, did nothing but walk around the great man and examine him from every point, as though he was desirous of contrasting him with other men, and making a note of the difference; and so well satisfied was he of the survey, that he could not help exclaiming, —

"I'll be gol darned ef he ain't as much like me as a piece of cheese!"— a remark that caused Miss Josie to cover her mouth with her handkerchief, to prevent exploding with laughter.

"Yes," said the earl, with a pleasant smile, "I am, like you, but a man, and have done nothing to entitle me to a better position in the world than yourself. Fortune favored my ancestors, however, and they were created nobles. I believe they performed some chivalrous actions in the reign of Henry the Eighth, and you see I am reaping the benefit of it."

The earl rather underrated his talents, for he was noted as a statesman all through Europe, and had served as governor-general of C. for several years.

We promised to grant the countess, his wife, an interview in the course of the day; and then his lordship left us to chat without feeling the reserve of his presence.

"Jack," said Fred, as his lordship left us, "I have undertaken an adventure on account of us four, which I think will occupy some of our time."

"Good. Let us hear what it is."

At this moment Miss Josie whispered me to remember her, and then left me for the quarter-deck, as though she feared to hear what was to come.

"Mr. Goldthwaite can afford all explanations," Fred said; and we looked to him for them.

"Gentlemen," Mr. Goldthwaite remarked, "I want to enlist your services for a noble object, or I should not ask your aid. Will you promise me such assistance as you can command, in case I call upon you in Paris or in Germany?"

"We will," was the response from all four.

"There will be danger to encounter; but if you are successful, you will have the satisfaction of knowing that you have brought peace to a parent's heart and rest to a lady's mind. I have a daughter a year older than the one on board. Through the machinations of an aunt, a devout Catholic, she is incarcerated in a convent; but where I have not learned."

"We must discover her retreat," we all cried, with one accord.

"And you will aid me in rescuing her, even if force is necessary?" asked Mr. Goldthwaite.

"We will."

We shook hands on the promise, and then the father told us the history of his daughter.

CHAPTER V.

A FATHER'S STORY.—IN A CONVENT.—WE PROMISE AID.—THE EARL AND COUNTESS.—A COQUETTE.—QUEENSTOWN AND A SURPRISE.

WE were much interested in Mr. Goldthwaite, and prepared to listen to his story with great interest. He had excited our curiosity by stating that one of his children was imprisoned in a convent, through the arts of a relative, and we had promised to assist in the lady's rescue at every hazard. Perhaps Miss Josie's bright eyes had been the means of predisposing me in favor of butting my head against a stone wall, or any other obstacle, so that I could win a smile from her, or a glance of gratitude for whatever I undertook. For this reason I paid much deference to the father, and my companions, seeing that such was the case, followed my example.

"Two years ago," commenced Mr. Goldthwaite, "I left my eldest daughter in Paris, in charge of her aunt, while I returned home with my other child, the youngest. I expected to return to Paris in the course of six months, but business detained me, so that I was unable to get away; but that circumstance did not cause me anxiety until six months since, when I received letters from France stating that my child and her aunt were under considerable Catholic influence, and that I had better pay some attention to the matter if I disapproved of such intimacy. I thought that there was needless alarm, and considered my sister strong-minded enough to take care of her religious principles as well as those of my child; but here I made a common mistake; for the mind which I supposed strong was the very element that was worked upon, and with such force that my daughter was carried away by entreaties and tears, and, as she informed me in a letter, the good of her soul required that she should enter a convent, and so end her days by dedicating the remainder of her existence to God, renouncing the pomp and vanities of the world as so much dross."

"Did she inform you what convent she should enter?" I asked.

"She did not; and gave as a reason that she knew I would seek for her and her aunt, but that both of them were so resolved that their future happiness depended upon a convent life, that they should not intimate where they were, or in what country they had sought seclusion. Any attempts to discover them would be fruitless, and only lead to expense and vexation."

For a moment we thought of the communication, each of us debating the points of the story, and the probabilities of discovering whether the ladies were in a French, German, or Italian convent.

"Did the ladies possess much money?" I asked.

"My sister had some ready money at her banker's, but most of her property is in Boston, and I have so managed it by attachments, that no one can get possession of it without a lawsuit, which is just what I want; for I desire to see the men who have been instrumental in producing so much unhappiness in my family."

"My opinion is, that the ladies are in one of the Parisian convents," I remarked, for I noticed that all looked to me for an opinion.

"If such is the case, how can we discover their retreat, and how can I recover my daughter?" Mr. Goldthwaite asked, in an anxious tone.

"That we are not prepared to answer just at present," was the reply. "Time, and a few weeks' residence in Paris, will enable us to mature some plan that shall lead to the rescue of your child."

"You think, then, that there is a chance to hope for the best?" and I saw the father brush a tear from his eye as he asked the question.

"To be sure there is. We have been in worse cases, and more difficult ones, and never yet failed. Be prudent, and make no more confidants, and we will act as your friends, and second all your efforts."

"I thank you, gentlemen, a thousand times for your kindness, and trust that I shall live to repay it. Only *bring the dead to life*, and you will indeed be benefactors to the poor and oppressed. As far as expenses are concerned, I will bear all that you incur. I am rich, and able to do so without being in the least embarrassed."

"Thank you," we said; "but while we don't claim to be rich, we assure you that we are not poor, and can afford our own expenses. If we worked for pay, one half the pleasure of an adventure would be lost to us. Let us pursue the course that seems most agreeable to us, and hereafter do not mention rewards or money."

"There is one reward you wouldn't object to," whispered Hez, who had eyes like a cat, and could see as far as most people.

He spoke so low that no one but myself heard him.

"What kind of a reward do you mean?" I asked.

"The reward of a pretty girl's hand;" and then the wretched fellow laughed in the most ridiculous manner, as though he had said something witty.

"What do you mean?" I asked, with an expression of surprise.

"O, I can see a hole through a ladder, I can, and ef you ain't makin' up yer mouth fer that gal, then no one is; that's all. Say, ef we find her sister, and she is as handsome as this one, I shouldn't mind steppin' up to her, I shouldn't; and ef she should fancy me, what's to prevent us from hitchin', hey?"

"Wait until we find her, Hez, before we lay out many plans for the future," I said.

"Yes," was the response, "and then let that good-lookin' Fred jist cut me out in less than no time. No, ye don't. We must have a bargain, and a fair one at that, ef yer want me to work."

"Selfish as ever," I replied. "O, Hez, why will you let a woman so warp your natural good judgment?"

"'Cos," was the confidential reply, "I likes a pretty face jist as well as you does; but you know that there ain't many pretty faces as likes me; so I must look out for myself, and take all the advantages that I can"— a fact that I could not help admitting; but before we could further discuss the matter, the announcement was made that dinner was ready, and at Mr. Goldthwaite's request, I waited upon Josie to the table, while Fred and her father were seated near each other, and talked in low and earnest tones on the topic that was nearest their hearts. But if I was proud of my position as Miss Josie's partner at the table, I received punishment as I went along; for the young lady was just as joyous as she would have been on the land, manifesting no sign of sickness, and partaking of the viands on the well-laden table with so hearty a relish that she caused several delicate-stomached females, ladies who were destined for sickness, yet held off as long as possible in hope that they could conquer the malady, to look at her knife-and-fork exercises with a certain amount of horror that was amusing to an old salt like myself.

"Well," Miss Josie whispered, as the stewards were bringing on the dessert, "you have concluded to help my father in his undertaking. I am so glad! for I don't know how he could succeed alone. He is getting old, and does not possess the resolution of former years."

"Yes, we have promised our aid. There is one great advantage in it — I shall be enabled to see more of you, by this arrangement."

"O, indeed! That is what you are congratulating yourself upon — is it? Well, I admire your audacity and assurance, I must say."

"And I hope that you will admire me, in the course of time, as much as you do my audacity," I replied, in a cool, self-satisfied tone.

"I hope you have a good opinion of yourself," Miss Josie cried. "I like modest men — some such man as your friend, Mr. Fred, who is splendid, I think. He is good-looking, too, which is more than —"

She hesitated as though to choose a word.

"Than you can say for myself. Is that what you mean?"

She smiled and nodded, and then shrugged her white shoulders.

"How good you are for guessing! I know you are a Yankee;" and she looked me in the face, and laughed.

"I am the most unfortunate man in the world," I said, seeing that she was acting a part, and determined to humor her to the utmost. "Just as I was flattering myself that you and I would be good friends, I find that we are likely to be enemies."

"No, not enemies," she cried, in a hasty manner; and I saw a look of disappointment pass over her sweet face. "I can never be the enemy of a brave man, one willing to risk his life for a child's."

"I know it," I cried, with a low bow and a smile of gladness. "I was well aware that Miss Goldthwaite was too noble to scorn so humble an individual as myself."

"I do believe that you are laughing at me," she said, with a frown, and a pout of her pretty lips.

"Heaven forbid," I remarked. "I have too much respect for you for that. In a few days we must separate; so let us have peace until then."

"Separate?" she repeated. "What do you mean?"

"Why, we leave you at Queenstown, and take a run through Ireland. The Fenians are at work in the Emerald Island, and we are anxious to catch a glimpse of them."

I saw her face change at once, as though she had experienced her first disappointment.

"O, dear! I supposed that you were going direct to Paris with us."

"No; we shall join you there in the course of a few weeks, and then commence our serious work."

"You don't intend to connect yourself with those horrid Fenians, do you?" the lady asked.

"No; but we want to see what they are doing, and Ireland at the same time."

She did not say that she was sorry; but her face expressed what her lips failed to utter: so the rest of our stay at the table was passed in silence, and when we arose, we went on deck, and there I was joined by my son and his nurse; but there was little occasion for the services of the latter, as all the ladies united in taking charge of him, and in petting him and Rover to their hearts' content.

Just as the gentlemen had walked forward to smoke their cigars away from the ladies, the earl came to us, and said that his wife was quite anxious to see Fred and myself, and to thank us in person for what we had done; and although we wanted no thanks, still his lordship was importunate, and we followed him to the lower cabin, where we found little Alice playing with her doll, making believe that it had tumbled overboard, and that she had jumped after it; and as the child's efforts to swim were rather comical, we could not help laughing at the picture.

The countess arose to receive us, and welcomed us by extending her hand, which I may as well state was small, white, and delicate, but entirely destitute of rings, affording a strong contrast to some of the lady passengers whose fingers were covered with diamonds, as though the latter added to their importance and position.

"I wish that I had words to thank you, gentlemen, for what you have done. You can imagine my gratitude, and I trust will feel it."

We said that we did not want any thanks for what we had done, and were so earnest in our statements, that the lady made us be seated, and then entered into an animated conversation respecting our own country, Australia, and England. She told us how she had travelled through the United States in company with her husband, and smiled in a good-natured manner at the eagerness with which our republicans had striven to get them to accept of invitations to dinners and parties, and confessed that she had thought the Americans were too democratic to care for rank or titles.

I took good care to convince her that while some of

my countrymen were just snobbish enough to toady to foreigners of rank, in imitation of Englishmen, there were others who would rather see a good man than a great one. In fact, I did the best I could with a bad case; but I don't think that the earl or his countess were thoroughly convinced by what they heard; yet they had Fred's and my example to back our assertion; for although we were far from despising rank, yet we would not for a moment let the two representatives of British aristocracy suppose that we perilled our lives for the purpose of saving their child simply because the little girl was above the common stock, through the fortune of birth.

"I see that you, gentlemen, are sturdy democrats," the countess said, with a pleasant smile, after we had explained to her our positions; "but, democrats as you are, you will not refuse to visit Buckland Hall while you are in England?"

"Isn't that in Lancaster?" I asked.

"Yes."

"Then it must be near Sir William Byefield's estate," I continued.

"My estate adjoins Sir William's," the earl replied.

"Are you intimate with him?" I asked.

"He is one of my best friends," was the reply, "although for the past few years I have seen but little of him, for we have been on the wing, and so has he. The last I heard of him he was in Australia in pursuit of a daughter; and just as he found her, some bold countryman of yours gained her affections, and married her. It was an awful disappointment to Sir William, and yet I hear that he soon became reconciled to the match, and even had his son-in-law at his house. It is said that the American was a bold, dashing fellow, just the sort of man to captivate a young girl, for he had wealth, and all the independence of a true-hearted Yankee."

I could not help blushing at these words; and the lady, with true womanly perception, saw that something was wrong.

"Perhaps Mr. Jack is acquainted with the person you are speaking of," she said.

"Is such the case?" asked the earl.

"I have the honor to be the son-in-law of Sir William Byefield," I said, in a low tone, and a thought of the lost wife, whose remains were reposing in Forest Hills Cemetery, far away from her illustrious ancestors.

"Is it possible that you are the gentleman whose deeds in Australia are so well known?" cried the earl. "Now I am no longer astonished at what you have this day done; and I am sure that we shall be honored with your presence at Buckland Hall, for, of course, you will spend some time with Sir William."

"Several days, and perhaps a few weeks. I shall leave my child and nurse with his grandparents, while I travel over the continent."

"You will go through with us direct to Lancaster?" asked the lady.

"No; we land at Queenstown, and take a look at Ireland before we visit England."

"Then let us take charge of your son, and conduct him to his grandparents. He will be an excellent companion for Alice; she will amuse him."

"I fear that the trouble will be too much."

The earl and the countess protested that they would be delighted to take charge of the boy; so I consented, knowing that my movements while in Ireland would be rapid and uncertain.

"I would not advise you to land in Ireland at the present time," his lordship said, after Fred had asked a few questions respecting Dublin and its hotels. "I fear that it is in too disturbed a state for safe and comfortable travelling. The Fenians are active at the present time, and giving government much trouble."

"We shall not be likely to see much of them," I remarked, "for we do not propose to meddle with them."

"I am glad of that; and if I can be of any assistance to you while in Ireland, let me know."

We thanked him, and told him that we only proposed to look at the country, and mingle but little with the people for the want of time. We knew that if we partook of Irish hospitality we should not be able to act as free agents; so we would not accept of letters of introduction to the earl's friends, although we little thought how soon we should have to ask his assistance in releasing us from trouble.

We passed a pleasant hour in company with the earl and his wife, and then I sent for my son, and he and little Alice soon struck up friendly relations, and went to playing with all the zeal of childhood.

Fred and I then went on deck, and smoked our cigars in company with his lordship, for the earl seemed to have taken such a fancy to us that he rather sought our company in preference to any on board, and, as he assumed no airs of superiority, we were rather glad to have him as a companion. I introduced him to Mr. and Miss Goldthwaite; and for the remainder of the passage, he and his wife paid them marked attention, to the great envy of all the other passengers, male and female, who wanted to be on terms of equality with a live lord and a real countess, yet did not know how to succeed in accomplishing such a desirable result.

But time passed rapidly. We had a pleasant passage, and but few of those on board were sick. Miss Josie escaped the usual infliction; and she and I flirted, quarrelled, became reconciled, read poetry together, talked nonsense, and acted as young people generally do when each is desirous of creating a favorable impression, and yet is uncertain whether to advance or recede, whether to become serious or laugh at all that had passed. I must confess that I was rather pleased with Miss Josie. I liked her better than any one I had ever seen on so short an acquaintance, and I hoped that she was a little partial to me; but how could I tell from such a laughing, fun-loving girl? Ah me, Miss Josie, you were a natural born coquette, and loved dearly to play with men's hearts; but who could blame you for wielding so pleasant a power? Not I.

"And you will soon join us in Paris?" asked Miss Josie, as I held her hand for a moment before I entered the boat that was to land us at Queenstown. Her face was a little troubled, and her dark eyes looked as though the wind had affected them, or else the smoke had weakened them.

"In a few weeks, at the farthest," was my answer.

"And you will sometimes think of — of — my father?" she asked, in a tremulous tone.

"Yes, and his daughter also;" and I pressed the little hand that I held; but perhaps she did not think that I was serious enough, for she snatched her hand from mine, and turned from me as though she would enter the cabin.

"Josie," I said; and she came towards me again, but her veil was now over her face, and I could not see her eyes.

I took her hand, and she did not resist me.

"God bless you, Josie!" I said, in all seriousness.

"Does that come from your heart?" she asked, in a low tone.

"Yes, from my heart, Josie."

"Then repeat it. O, do repeat it!"

"God bless you, Josie, with all my heart, and all my soul, until we meet again!"

"And by that time I may have half a dozen Frenchmen for lovers," the little jade cried, with a laugh, and broke away from me as though she had accomplished one great object, and that was, to make me sentimental.

"Sold again," whispered Hez, who had seen all that had passed.

I suppressed an oath, took a kind farewell of the earl and his countess, kissed my son and little Alice, shook hands with Mr. Goldthwaite, and the next moment we were going towards the town, while the passengers were cheering us, and Rover was barking as though glad once more to be near land.

Once I turned my head, and saw Miss Josie waving her handkerchief; but I took no notice of her salute, for I was mad, and almost hated the girl for the manner in which she had treated me.

As we landed on the soil of Ireland, a crowd of people met us and eyed us from head to foot, and we repaid their glances with interest. They were a rough, uncropped set, barefooted, bareheaded, and with clothes of many colors, for they were patched up and down, fore and aft; and where patches were not seen, rags fluttered in the wind.

Murden was so affected at the idea of landing on English soil after an absence of so many years, that he stooped down, filled his hands with earth, and raised it to his lips.

"Whoop!" yelled the crowd, in an agony of excitement, when they saw the action of Murden. "*The 'Merican hed sinters is com to relave us from bondage, and lade us to victory or death!*"

A yell, a cheer, and then the vagabonds charged upon us.

CHAPTER VI.

A STRONG ESCORT. — SUSPECTED OF BEING FENIANS. — THE ATTEMPTED RESCUE. — THE FLIGHT AFTER THE FIGHT.

WE looked at the crowd of ragged, dirty fellows who charged towards us with astonishment. What did they mean? Were they determined to rob us of our valises which we carried in our hands, and contained but a change of clothing? No, they did not mean to rob us, it was evident, for when they were within six feet of us, the fellows tumbled down on their knees, and held out their hands towards us, some of them crying, —

"Whoop! Here's the hed sinters from 'Meriky. O, how we has longed and waited for ye!"

"What in the devil do they mean?" cried Murden, who was cleaning his hands of the soil which he had scraped up and kissed, on first landing.

We were unable to answer the interrogation to his satisfaction, for the thought had not entered our heads that the Irishmen mistook us for American head centres or emissaries, anxious to peril our lives for the sake of giving freedom to Ireland.

"I'm the boy to be trusted, if yer honors has any share of silver or goold," one of the ragamuffins cried. "Jist give me a show of goold, and I'll fight till Ireland is covered with blood. Whoop! we'll be free, and the harp shall play over the lion."

"We have no gold or silver for you," cried Murden, "and we don't know what you mean by blood and freedom for Ireland."

"Thin what in the devil is the use of yer comin' here with empty pockets?" asked one of the wildest looking of the gang. "We want money, for it's starvin' we is; and a man can't fight on an empty belly. Give us money, and put arms in our hands, and thin we'll show you what we can do for ourselves."

Just at this moment some custom-house officials approached us, and the instant they were seen, the ragged fellows scattered in all directions, and left us alone.

The custom-house officers did not make a thorough examination of our valises, for the reason that Murden summoned all of his English impudence, and soon made himself known.

"We want a hotel and something to eat," the Australian said. "Can we find what we desire here, or must we starve until we reach Dublin?"

"The Irish Harp is open, and good cheer is found there. Any of the boys will show you the way, and carry your luggage. It is a Fenian resort, but you won't care for that, I suppose," one of the custom-house officials replied, in a careless tone; but at the same time he gave us a look that showed some little suspicion on his part.

"Let me carry one of your valises," cried the smallest of the officers; and, in spite of our protestations to the contrary, the firm, determined little fellow seized Murden's carpet-bag and my own private property, while another man, in a sort of uniform, took possession of Fred's valise, and a third would have relieved Hopeful, but that genius resisted most manfully.

"No, you don't," the son of New Hampshire said, in a most determined tone. "I've heard tell of yew fellers and yer tricks, and I guess I'll jist hold on to this plunder of mine, ef yer has no objections."

"I think you are Americans," one of the officers said, with a smile that did not look just right, it was so full of malice. "There can be no doubt on that point."

"Of course there can't be," Hez replied. "Do yer think we is regular Britishers like yerselves? No, sir; we is true-hearted Americans; and we can make the lion of yer country roar when we lets loose our eagle burd."

We would have stopped Hez in his tirade, but found it impossible to do so, for fear of giving him offence, which he was likely to take on slight grounds if opposed.

The Englishmen listened in profound silence while Hez was speaking, but they glanced at each other in a most expressive manner; and one of them, the smallest fellow, even had the impudence to wink at his companions.

"I think, gentlemen," said the little fellow, in a firm and decided tone, "that the best thing we can do is to show you to the inn ourselves."

"O, we couldn't think of giving you so much trouble," Fred said, and then whispered in my ear, "These fellows mean more than appears on the surface. All this honor is not intended for mere compliment."

I thought as much, and, while Fred was speaking, glanced at the rabble that had first met us on landing. They were standing off at a distance, watching our movements with much interest, apparently, and whispering among themselves. The dozen or twenty had increased to a hundred, and in the hands of some of them I saw regular Irish shillalahs; and once in a while the sticks were whirled over uncombed heads, and a shrill whoop was uttered, that expressed suppressed rage or great joy

I saw the little custom-house officer make a sign, and half a dozen coast-guard men came towards us from the landing. They did not appear to be in a hurry, or to care for the remarks which were thrown at them by the Irish lads who were clustered together. They looked like men who could be resolute if occasion required it, and never recede an inch in the face of a foe.

"These gentlemen will go to the Harp for the present," said the small custom-house officer. "Take their luggage, and look to it sharp. Now, then, we will show you the way, gentlemen."

We protested that we did not need an escort, but the officials were firm; so we marched along in silence, Hez with his head thrown back in perfect contempt for Great Britain and her officials.

"You have seen something of military life — haven't you?" asked one of the officials, as we moved along, speaking to Hez.

"I guess I have," was the ready reply. "During the late war, I jest commanded the best company of home guards ever raised in Hillsborough County, New Hampshire. Lord bless you, they could eat more gingerbread and drink more cider than any hundred men in the county. My wife used to be real proud of me when she seed me at the head of my men. She said I never looked so well, even if I was a little green —"

"Ah, then you had green uniforms — did you?" asked the little man, in an eager tone.

"Wall," said Hez, after a moment's reflection, "I don't know but some would call them green, but I never harped —"

"Green uniforms and a harp'" said the little man; and he looked satisfied, as he glanced at his companions. "I think we are on the right track, gentlemen. Be careful and see that our friends do not escape our polite attentions."

The coast-guard men seemed to vie with each other in their vigilance, for they completely enclosed us and moved along, regardless of the rabble that followed at a little distance.

"What in the devil does all this mean?" demanded Fred, who began to get a little angry at such uncalled-for demonstrations. "We want no such notice as this."

"Of course not; but perhaps it is a custom of the country to always welcome Americans in this manner."

One of the custom-house officers overheard me, and replied, with a quiet grin, —

"Yes, sir, we allers welcome distinguished American visitors in this manner, and pay much honor to returned Australians when they see fit to visit us."

He pointed to Murden, who was just at that moment making comparisons between the mountains of Australia and Ireland — a remark that seemed to attract much attention on the part of those who were close to him.

The little man drew out a paper and looked at it, and then scanned our persons with a critical eye.

"Yes," he said, with an exultant smile, "we are all right. It is just as they appear. The description is perfect."

Just at this moment, one of the gossoons who was following us threw a stone that struck the little man — whose name was Parish — full on the back, and sent him to the ground as quick as though knocked over by a Minie ball.

But he was on his feet in an instant, a little wild, perhaps, but turned on the foe with a look that was full of danger to his assailants.

"Who did that?" he asked; and as he spoke, a pair of pistols were produced from under his jacket, and pointed at our heads, and then at the heads of the parties who were following us.

"I would recommend you," said Fred, in a gentle tone, "not to point your weapons at us, unless you mean murder. If you do, bang away, and so end our existence at once; but don't make believe shoot, unless you are in earnest."

"I will shoot the dog who threw that stone," Mr. Parish cried, in no wise appeased. "Can any one tell me who did it?"

"One of the gossoons," a companion replied. "I don't know whether it was Tim O'Brien or Mike Luskin."

The little man made a rush for the gossoons; but the latter, somewhat astonished at the audacity of the man who threw the stone, commenced retreating in quick order, and for a few rods were pursued by the custom-house official, while the rest of his companions did not move, for fear we should move also.

Of course the gossoons were too quick for the custom-house officer. They scattered in every direction, and when at a safe distance, uttered the most outrageous yells of defiance and cheers of ridicule; and some of them, more insolent than others, called for whoops of welcome for the "'Merican hed sinters" who had come to liberate Ireland.

"Jack," said Fred, lighting a cigar in a cool and deliberate manner, "do you know what those vagabonds take us for?"

"Yes; targets for stones. But, luckily, Englishmen are getting the largest share, as usual, and they are quite welcome to all they receive."

Fred allowed a grim smile to pass over his face, as he replied, —

"The fools think we are American head centres, and therefore Fenians of the first respectability; and I tell you it is no trifling matter to be thus suspected. We have got to prove our respectability."

Murden turned on the coast-guard like a lion at bay, for he had overheard Fred's remarks.

"Damnation! do I look like a Fenian?" he roared, in a voice that would have frightened a bushranger into an immediate surrender. "Do you know me? I'm a cabinet officer of the province of Victoria, Australia, and will complain to the crown of the outrage. You see if I don't."

By the time Murden had thus freed his mind, which had no effect on the listeners, the little man had returned to his command.

"Forward," he cried, "or we'll have a rescue before we reach the jail. Run, one of you, to the barracks, and ask the commanding officer to send us a file of soldiers as quick as possible. We have captured four prizes, and must not let them escape. Two hundred pounds for each head centre. Remember it, boys, and hold on to them."

"We will," was the cry; but at this instant the Irishmen who had followed us, and dispersed half a dozen times, now returned in greater numbers than ever, in front, in rear, and on all sides; and, confound them, they were armed with old muskets, pistols and stones, clubs and scythes.

Our escort began to manifest symptoms of alarm, for they were inferior in numbers and in point of activity; and I saw some anxious glances towards the quarter from whence the troops were expected.

"Speak to them, gentlemen," said Mr. Parish, "and tell them that a rescue is useless, and will only cost them their lives and your lives. We shall fight to the last."

"Speak to them yourself, then," Fred remarked. "We are not on terms of intimacy with the rabble of Queenstown."

The little man uttered a curse, and once more glanced in the direction of the quarter where the soldiers were stationed. The red-coats did not make their appearance, and the gossoons seemed to be aware that they were expected, and that the custom-house officers and coast-guard men were disappointed in not having such an accession to their strength as would put all thoughts of rescue out of the question.

"Down with the palers, boys!" was the cry from the rabble, who hemmed us in on all sides, and whose numbers increased every moment.

"Damn them," our polite friend muttered, "they mean mischief, if men ever did. If we were better armed, some of them should lose the number of their mess."

"Gentlemen," I said, "let us escape from your pleasant company, and report ourselves at the hotel half an hour hence. You can fight it out on this line all day, if you please, but I am sure you can spare us from the conflict that is about to take place."

"You remain with us," was the reply of the little man. "We have captured the prizes, and now we shall hold on to them."

"When we have protested that we are not Fenians?" Fred asked.

"Your protests are not believed," was the unsatisfactory reply; and just at this moment I heard a whizzing in the air, and on looking up I saw a shower of stones coming towards us, propelled by no gentle arms.

The Fenians were good marksmen. I don't think that I ever saw stone-throwers take better aim than they did; for although several grazed my head and the heads of my friends, yet not one of us was hit or injured, while our kind escort were tumbled over, and some of them quite severely hurt. Four went down in the dust; the little man was of the number, but he was on his feet in an instant, the blood streaming down his face from a cut on his forehead.

"Forward!" Mr. Parish said, and wiped the lump on his head, from which the blood was streaming. It was a black and blue lump, and of the size of an egg. He was a game little Englishman, even if he did have us in charge as suspected head centres of the Fenian persuasion.

"Forward!" cried the little fellow. "Don't let the prisoners escape, for your lives!"

"Damn my bloody eyes if my life ain't worth more than these head centres," whispered one of the custom-house officers, or police; and just as the Irish uttered a shrill yell for vengeance, and charged towards us, the fellow darted from the escort and ran like a deer for the town, and I think succeeded in breaking through the circle that surrounded us. I did not have time to follow the man's flight, for I had to look after myself and friends, to escape being killed; for the Irish came down on us like an avalanche.

A dozen or fifteen shots were fired at the Fenians, but the latter did not even snap one of their rusty pistols at us, perhaps for fear of injuring our party, who were supposed to be head centres, and loaded down with money for the cause of Ireland. I saw some of the Irish fall, but the others pressed on with such frightful yells as reminded me of a bushranger rush in Australia.

But the charge was not met with the police-like firmness that I had seen when Murden, Fred, and I stood shoulder to shoulder, and beat back the waves that would have swamped us.

I heard blows struck, and I saw men fall on all sides. The police fought well, and I'll give them the credit of it; but they were overwhelmed by numbers, although the result might have been different had the police been free and clear of prisoners.

During the *mêlée* we stepped aside, or, rather, were forced out of the ring by our friends, such as they were, and compelled to see heads broken, and grievous wounds inflicted, by the various weapons with which the Fenians were armed.

"Come wid me, and run for it as though the devil was arter yer," some one whispered in our ears; and, turning, I saw an old gray-headed fellow close to me, a sickle in one hand, and a bludgeon in the other.

He was a fierce-looking genius, with black eyes, and a nose that was like a coal of fire, it was so red; animated, probably, by whiskey which never paid duties to the government.

"Why should we run?" I asked. "The quarrel and fight does not concern us."

"Ah, now, to the devil wid yer fair words," was the fierce rejoinder of the red-nosed man. "Come wid me, or ye'll find that the hemp is all growed that will be put around your necks. To be sure, we has lots more of head sinters, but divlish few that has money; so while the bastes hang the former, we must take care of the latter. And will ye come now, and have done wid it, and no more palaver?"

"Why should we go with you?" asked Fred. "We have no desire to run away."

"Ah, is that the kind ye are?" he demanded, a grim smile passing over his rugged face, and even rendering his nose more brilliant than ever; and while he was asking the question, I saw a certain respectful admiration in those fierce-looking eyes, so small and yet so cunning.

"Is ye on it?" demanded the old fellow. "Thin go in and bate the palers afore the sogers come up, for they will be here in less than no time. Go in and slash 'em." And the old fellow thrust into Fred's hand a sickle, and in mine a shillalah, or heavy bludgeon, loaded with lead at one end, and capable of splitting a skull with a moderate tap on the head.

The old fellow evidently expected to see us pitch in with a vim and relish; but in this he was disappointed, for we handed the weapons back to him, and made him take care of them.

"Ah, the devil! and it's not on the fight that ye are?" demanded the old fellow, with a look of indignation, and a nose that resembled a red light in a dark night.

"No, we have nothing to fight for," Fred replied.

"Bah! thin give us the money, and I'll take care of it for the cause, and the devil may care for you if he likes. Ye's great hed sinters, if ye shirk a glorious little fight like this, which any Fenian would be delighted to share. Whoop!" And the aged Irishman made a dash at the struggling crowd, and disappeared in its midst for a moment, and but for a moment; for he reappeared as suddenly as he disappeared, and came staggering towards us disarmed, and with a cut on his nose that nearly severed that useful member, and from which the blood streamed in torrents, and covered beard and breast.

"Ah, it's as illigant a little scrimmage as I ever saw in my life; and to think that I can't have another hand in it is enough to make a man's soul sad for a lifetime." And the Fenian endeavored to stanch his blood, and at the same time looked most wishfully at the raging fight, which was still going on without his presence.

"Ah!" cried the old Irishman, a look of pride on his blood-stained face; "ye niver had anythin' like this. No country but Ireland is capable of the likes."

"Let us leave this gay and festive scene," Fred said. "I never like to look at a fight unless I can take a hand; and in this we must remain neutral. Come, let us strike for the Irish Harp Inn, and not for the Irish Harp and its flag."

"I'd like one crack at 'em," Murden muttered; but he overcame his inclination, and followed Fred.

We had taken but a dozen or twenty steps, when some one cried out that the "sogers were comin';" and, sure enough, we saw a number of red-coats marching towards us on the double quick, their guns glittering in the sun, and a crowd of ragged gossoons running on each flank, cheering and yelling like mad, as though delighted at the prospect before them.

We stopped, uncertain what to do. To advance was to involve us in the crowd of soldiers and rabble, and to remain was to place us in a false position; and while we were hesitating, a dozen or twenty of the gossoons who had been fighting the police threw themselves upon us, pinned our arms, seized our legs, and so ran with us up a narrow street, in spite of all our exertions to escape, or to free ourselves from their embraces.

Up the narrow street we went, sometimes touching the ground, and scraping the skin from our bodies by the contact, until we reached a little lane that contained a dozen houses or more, and in one of them we were hurried, and the door shut and barred after us; and not until then were we permitted by the Fenians to stand on our feet.

CHAPTER VII.

A SECRET UNDERGROUND RETREAT. — WHISKEY STILLS AND FENIANISM. — THE ATTACK AND DEFENCE. — A BLOW FOR LIBERTY.

For a moment or two after the Fenians had entered the building and set us on our feet, our indignation was too great to permit us to use our tongues with effect, much as we desired to. As for Murden, who had seen life of all kinds in Australia, from a hardenened bushranger to a broken-hearted, unjustly-convicted convict, he was so thoroughly enraged that he would have struck several of those who surrounded us, if I had not held his hands, and whispered the danger we were in if we provoked the Irishmen by sudden violence, for they were armed and we were not; all of our weapons being with our clothes, in valises and carpet-bags.

"Now," said the Fenian, who appeared to command the others, a stout fellow with shoulders like Hercules, and a savage, determined face, "by my soul, but we has yer here, and safe, for the present, from the palers and redcoats; but what in the devil's name is we to do with yer now is more than I can tell."

"Then I can," was my respose. "Let us out of this, and we will go to the inn, where we can eat our dinners in peace."

"No," said the stout ruffian, with a laugh. "Hed sinters, with drafts and lots of goold, ain't so plentiful in this part of the world as all that. We has sworn to protect yer, and we will, and afore the palers and the sogers get yer, we'll die fust, and yer shall die wid us."

"Which we decline to do," returned Fred. "We have no desire to interfere in the affairs of this country, and once for all, let me assure you that we are not Fenians never were, and never expect to be."

"That's right," answered the large man, with a cunning laugh, "kape sayin' so; but the boys what is round yer knows better, and can keep a sacret as well as the next one. Trust to us, and we'll see that ye is put at the head of the armies that will kill the red-coats like flies; and give us all our rights agin, and Old Ireland will then be indade the gim of the sea. Never fear us, yer honors, for we is the boys to be trusted."

"With untold gold," one of the gossoons muttered.

"Faith, I'd like to be told where some of it is," replied another, with a laugh; but just at this moment we heard a commotion in the alley, and some one put his head in a window, where panes of glass once were, and shouted, —

"The red-coated divils is comin' this way, as fierce as black rats, and no blarney about 'em."

For a moment, the Irish who had us in charge, whispered together, as though debating some project of importance. We hoped they would conclude to let us escape in the best way we could, and take themselves off; but such was not their intention, for the burly ruffian approached us, and said, —

"Gintlemen, we is intrusted with your safety by Ireland's hed sinter, and take care of you we will at the risk of our lives. Come wid us, and lose no time."

"We shall do no such thing," I replied. "Let us alone, and go to the devil if you want to. Once for all we tell you that we are not Fenians."

There was a murmur of dissatisfaction, and then the scamps made a rush for us, and once more pinned our arms and legs. If we had had our revolvers on our persons, we should have used them regardless of consequences; but, alas! our weapons were on board the steamship, with the rest of the luggage, so we were powerless to defend ourselves against so many hardened customers.

But Rover had no idea of seeing us ill-treated; and although he had kept remarkably quiet, in obedience to commands, now he made a rush at the Fenians, and seized one of them by the neck and bore him to the floor.

"Call off the dog," the Fenians cried, "or we'll soon finish him!" and one of the fellows raised his club, but Rover saw the meditated blow, and leaving the prostrate man, sprang at the gossoon, and made his teeth meet in his arm, and then gave the limb such a shake that the club was dropped as though the hand that held it was paralyzed.

"Call off the dog, or, by the God that made us, we'll smash his head, even if he does belong to 'Merican hed sinters!" was the general cry, and as quick as I could, I broke away from the men who held me, and rushed to the rescue of the animal.

"The one who touches him dies!" I shouted, and knocked down a wild man, who had just aimed a blow at Rover's head. Others I pushed aside until I stood over the faithful animal as a shield and guard.

For a moment I thought I was lost, and so did my companions, for I saw all three of them make frantic efforts to escape from those who held them, and come to my assistance. But they were unable to clear themselves, and it was lucky for us that such was the case, for we should have had an awful fight and suffered great injuries, if not even death at the Irishmen's hands.

But my firmness saved us; for the Fenians were awed at my self-assumed importance, and so kept their hands off of me, and thus I saved my own life, and that of Rover, which I valued so highly. The fellow whom I had knocked down, got up, rubbed his eyes, and looked mad; but not a word did he say, nor did any of his companions assume his quarrel.

The sound of tramping feet now grew louder, mingled with the yells of the mob who accompanied the military, and were most anxious to witness a fight of some kind or other, just for a novelty.

"Come wid us!" cried the burly ruffian, who seemed to lead the party. "No harm shall come to yer while I is able to protect yer. Come, be alive, men, or the sogers will be on us."

As he spoke, he touched a spring on the side of the wall, and a portion of it swung back and revealed a flight of steps, damp and decayed, which led to a cellar. A strong smell of spirits steamed up through the narrow opening, and some of the Fenians snuffed at it most eagerly.

"Down wid yer!" cried the big man. "We has no time to lose. Lift 'em up, Pat. So — softly, man. Don't yank 'em, for remember they is hed sinters, and come to help us with goold and men."

I can't say that this advice was strictly followed, for we were hustled and lifted through the opening, dog and all; and then carried down the steps, dark and slippery, until we were dropped on the ground; then, by the aid of a lamp, we saw that we were surrounded by kegs and kettles, grain and tubs; and we had no hesitation in arriving at the conclusion that we were in some deep cellar, where whiskey was manufactured and sold without the aid of government taxes. It was evidently a place known to but few, and we had been brought there in the hope that we should be concealed until it was safe for us to seek other quarters.

"Here ye is," said the stout ruffian, motioning us to be seated on some sacks of grain. "Yer nice and snug here, and divil a paler in Queenstown knows this place, or will be likely to know it, unless yer splits on us, and if ye does that, it's a long way ye must be from me to keep my hands from yer throats, now I tell yer, whether ye is hed sinters or plain common Fenians like the rest of us."

"Let us out of this, and you need not fear our uttering a word respecting the still," Fred said, as soon as the murmurs of the Irish had subsided, for they showed by their faces how terrible would be the fate of any one who should dare to betray their secret rendezvous.

"Whist, and don't bother us wid that kind of blarney," the big ruffian replied. "Here ye is, and here ye must stay, till we hears from Hed Sinter Stevens, who has given us our orders, and faith, we will mind 'em at all hazards."

"Even if he should tell you to kill us," Murden said, in a tone that showed how much dissatisfied he was.

"If Hed Sinter Stevens should say that the safety of the Irish Republic demanded yer lives, we would take 'em, and never give the matter a thought, would we, boys?"

"No!" was the universal cry; and we saw that the men were in earnest, if ever men were in their lives.

The chief rascal saw that his conversation was not instructive or entertaining, for he soon changed the subject to one more agreeable.

"Pat," he cried, "bring the gintleman a noggin of whiskey, and thin stir round and see if ye can't find 'em somethin' to eat, for it's hungry they are."

A wild, long-haired fellow, naked to the waist, crept from behind some kettles, where a fire was burning, and heavy steam escaping, and after a long stare at us filled a mug with whiskey, just distilled, and warm, and handed it to us.

"Drink," said the leader, "and see if ye can taste the smoke of Old Ireland's whiskey. There's not a single drunk in a whole keg of it."

We did not refuse the offer, for we needed a little stimulant after our exertions. We found the whiskey soft and oily, and with a strong, smoky taste, that was far from disagreeable, although to really like new Irish whiskey, an apprenticeship must be served in the drinking line, that but few men can endure unless their stomachs are copper-lined.

By the way of keeping us company, all those present, some dozen men, helped themselves to spirits, and tossed off each a half pint, and appeared to like the same, for they would have repeated the dose had not the chief interfered, and put a stop to their helping themselves.

The scene was not calculated to make one feel at peace with all the world, for the cellar was damp, and black with smoke, and the two candles, stuck in the necks of bottles, gave but little light, or just sufficient to make those who surrounded us appear hideous and wild, dirty and savage in the extreme, almost equal to what we had witnessed in Australia.

"If I only had a dozen of my police force here," whispered Murden, "I would soon make short work of these fellows."

"Hush!" returned Fred, who knew that the word police would stir all the bad passions of the rough men who surrounded us; but the caution was too late, for the burly ruffian who sat near us heard the ominous word "police," and it acted on him like a spur.

"Who talks of police in this place?" he demanded, and put one hand on a huge knife which he carried in his belt. "The man who spakes of políce in this sacred retreat is a traitor, and deserves death. Have we a traitor amongst us? Spake, and let us know."

A howl of rage from the men who surrounded us, and all turned their flashing eyes and dark faces towards us, so that we could read murder without the least trouble.

"Put up your knife!" cried Fred, in a tone that was so calm and indifferent, that even the Fenians who surrounded us were awed into silence. "Don't make fools of yourselves and get into a passion, until you see that there is occasion for it."

"But what did he mane by speakin' police here?" demanded the chief of the ruffians.

"Couldn't you hear?" Fred said, in a tone of contempt. "Didn't he say that we were safe from the police in this retreat? Put up your knives and clubs, and let us have another drink of whiskey, for the last was the best that I ever tasted. Ah! if we had such in America, I'd never leave her to fight any one's battles."

The men uttered grunts expressive of pleasure, for Fred had touched them on a weak point. Their national drink was too dear to their hearts not to delight in hearing it praised. Their faces relaxed their savage expressions, and good-nature once more beamed on them.

"Pat," roared the chief, "more of the spirit that gives the buys heart, and courage, and strength to their arms. We'll make a night of it, for the poteen is plenty, and our minds is willin'. Fill up the measures, and we'll drink to the Harp, and confusion to all bloody Britons."

We but put our lips to the spirit, for we wanted to keep sober, at the same time we made great pretension of drinking; but most of the whiskey was spilled on the ground, and the Fenians were none the wiser for what we did.

"Hist," cried the burly ruffian, "I has a toast to propose. Here it is, buys. May 'Merica never want a friend as long as Old Ireland has one to furnish!"

A yell was the response; but it died away suddenly, for over our heads we could hear the reports of musketry, and the tramp of many feet, the shouts and imprecations of enraged men, and all the evidences of a free fight.

"By the holy St. Patrick! but they is at it," cried the chief, as he sprang to his feet, and dashed down the can from which he had been drinking.

For a moment we listened in silence to the strife that was going on, and then the Fenians who had us in charge could no longer remain quiet. Their pugnacious dispositions were too excited to hear the sounds of battle and not join in it.

"Shall we stay here and let our friends have all the fun?" asked one man; and he flourished his shillalah in the air, and uttered a wild yell.

"But who will take care of the hed sinters? They must remain here till Stevens is heard from, and on no account can they mingle in the fight."

Fresh yells and more firing quickened the action of the Fenians. A terrible struggle was going on in the street, and in the rooms overhead, and our friends were anxious to join in the mêlée as soon as possible.

"Here, Pat," cried the chief, "do you look to these gintlemen, while we goes up and has a hand in the fight. I'll hold yer responsible for their safe keepin', and see that not a hair of their heads is hurted, or that they does not foller us. Now, buys, come on and hit the red-coats and palers hard."

The men darted into darkness and disappeared from sight. They had some secret passage which led to the outer world, and to find that passage would be our endeavor as soon as the proper time arrived.

Pat, the guardian angel of the place, lighted his pipe, and sat down on a keg of poteen, looking at us most attentively; and at last he said, —

"Ah, and what the divil sent ye here now? Couldn't ye find enough rows in yer own country, that ye must come here for' em? Bedad, when yer heads has bin broken as often as mine, it's little ye'll care for sich fun. Ah, whin I was young, sich things was agreeable; but time takes the fight out of us, and at last he knocks us down without a blow."

The old fellow helped himself to more whiskey, and passed the noggin to us. We made believe drink, but were too much excited at the row overhead to pay our respects to the liquor.

"Won't the police be likely to find our retreat?" Murden asked of Pat.

"Divil a fear of that. The place has been used for the distillin' of pure poteen for twenty years, and no one has dared to inform of it. Faith, it's little a man's life would be worth who should spake the word that led the palers to this place. Big Mike would make short work of him, unless the mane scamp was shiltered in the midst of the queen's officers; and even then, some Fenian might strike him down."

"Big Mike is the chief of the Fenians in these parts, is he?" Fred asked.

"Yes, he is; and a man what makes himself respected, now, I tell yer."

"And he owns the still, does he?" Murden said.

"And what is that to yer?" the fellow asked, with a cunning grin. "It's too much knowledge ye is arter to suit me."

Still the row continued overhead; and once in a while we could hear the reports of pistols and muskets, as though those in the house were firing on people outside, and attempting to hold them at bay.

"Keep the fellow in check for a while," whispered Murden. "I'll return in a few minutes."

The ex-commissioner of police of Australia was as light-footed and subtile as an Indian. He could walk across a creaking floor and make no more noise than a mouse, or he could pass over a Victoria prairie, and even puzzle a native to track his course; and that is saying much in commendation of his light step, for an Australian native is as keen-scented on a trail as a bloodhound, and can trace a man over a desert of sand, even where it shifts with every gust of wind.

Murden dropped behind the bags of grain and disappeared in the darkness, followed by Rover; the rest of us apparently not noticing the absence of the commissioner, for we kept the Irishman's attention so employed that he did not miss our companion.

"More poteen, Pat," cried Fred. "Come, man, don't be mean with the drink. If we had lemons, sugar, and hot water, an elegant bowl of punch we would have, and no mistake."

"What! would ye drink punch when yer friends is havin' a scrimmage overhead, and some of 'em is sufferin' with broken pates?"

The Irishman uttered a growl of disgust at the idea; but still he did not refuse to fill the noggin with whiskey and to pass it to us; and then for the first time he discovered the absence of Murden.

"Where is he?" demanded the keeper of the still, in a fierce tone. "One of yer has gone, and I must know where he is. Tell me, or no whiskey does yer get from me."

"Gone? Why he has gone to sleep, I suppose," returned Fred, in a careless tone. "Give us the whiskey, and don't bother us with idle questions."

"Tell me where the other one is, and ye shall have all ye wants. Don't play any of yer tricks on me, or by St. Patrick ye will repint it, now I tell yer."

The fellow had drank enough to be ugly; but we did not care for his anger, if we could only effect our escape from the place before the Fenians returned.

Pat seized a candle and took a survey of the sacks on which we sat, and the first object on which his bloodshot eyes rested, were the forms of Murden and Rover; the former apparently fast asleep, and the latter winking and blinking as innocent as a baby, although he did show his teeth when Pat held a candle too near his nose; and it would have required but a word to have sent the hound flying at his throat.

"You see that we told you the truth," cried Fred, as soon as we saw that Murden had returned, and was counterfeiting sleep. "Now you feel satisfied — don't you?"

"Yes; but if he sleeps there long, it's little will be left of him by mornin'."

"Why?" asked Hopeful, whose curiosity was excited.

"Rats," was the reply. "Big ones is here, and they eats men when they sleeps arter too much drink. Pat Maguire lost his nose a few nights since, arter he'd taken a quart of whiskey; and many's the time the four-legged divils has dragged me all round the cellar, and banged my head on the ground."

Pat, after uttering this monstrous lie, turned away to look after one of his stills; and then we had a moment to confer with Murden.

"I've searched in every part of the place, and can see no outlet," he whispered. "There is a secret door, but I could not find it. To do so requires more time. What shall we do?"

"Bind the Irishman, and compel him to reveal the outlet," Fred replied.

"What do you all say to that?" demanded Murden.

"We all agree," was the reply.

"Then stand by and give me aid in case I need it,"

Murden said; and just at that moment Pat came near us with another noggin of poteen in his hand, with which he intended to serve our party.

Murden slipped from the sacks, stole around to the rear of the Irishman, and before the latter suspected a trick his arms were pinioned to his sides, and he was struggling like a maniac, and uttering a few shrill yells, probably as signals that his prisoners had risen in revolt.

The scuffle was of short duration. Hopeful caught the fellow by the legs, and in an instant he was jerked to the ground, and his mouth stopped by a cloth, while his arms were secured by ropes, which were found near at hand.

While we were thus employed, Pat glared at us like a fiend; but we cared nothing for his glances, and, leaving him on the ground, took candles, and started off to search the premises, and find an outlet so that we could escape.

CHAPTER VIII.

AN ATTEMPT TO ESCAPE.—ROVER AND THE FENIAN'S LEG.—A GAME THAT WAS BLOCKED.—STORMING THE CELLAR.—A FAMILIAR VOICE.

WE had no time to lose if we would escape before the soldiers carried the premises by storm, or before the Fenians returned to see that our safety was provided for, according to their estimation of safety, not ours; for we felt quite anxious to keep clear of the peelers, soldiers, and their enemies, the Fenians, who would be certain to do us some injury the instant they discovered that we had no connection with the order.

The row overhead still continued, so we knew that our late companions were too much engaged to return just at present, and as Pat was securely bound and gagged, there was no danger of his giving an alarm, and thus attracting attention to our movements.

Hopeful and Murden, armed with pieces of iron which they found near at hand, started off in one direction, while Fred and I, quite as well provided with weapons of defence, took another, our paths being lighted with tallow dips, which we found in a box out of the reach of rats.

"The gang went in this direction," Fred said, as we pushed past the stills, some of them in full blast. "There must be an opening out here somewhere, and I hope that we shall find it."

But we did not discover the secret passage, although we looked very sharp for it. The sides of the cellar were black and grim with smoke, and in some places soot and mould were two and three inches thick, showing that it had been undisturbed for years.

There was no use in looking in such places, so we hurried along in another direction; but no trap-door or ladder met our eyes, hard as we looked, and while we were thus employed, we met Hopeful and Murden, who had been as unsuccessful as ourselves.

"No luck," said Murden, although we had not asked him the result of his labors. "The scamps have had the address to conceal the place by which they left the cellar, and it will require more time and better light than we possess to find it."

"What's to be done?" asked Fred.

"We must return to Pat, and *induce* him to show us the door," Murden said.

The manner in which he spoke showed that he meant something.

"Do you mean Australian style of inducement?" Fred asked, in a low tone.

"Yes, if all other means fail. We can't stand on trifles just at this time. Our lives and liberty depend on expedition."

"That's so," muttered Hez; and back we started to

wards the Irishman, whom we found lying on his back, with several large rats on his head and near his person, holding a consultation as to the expediency of nipping the Irishman, and seeing whether his flesh would taste better than the grain, of which they were a little tired.

The vermin retreated when they saw us; but they went off in a slow manner, as though they were half inclined to show fight, and would if we were too independent. At any rate, they exhibited some teeth that were long, sharp, and white, showing their weapons for attack and defence.

"Faith," said Pat, as we removed the gag from his mouth, "don't lave me in this manner agin, for if ye does the bloody rats will make a meal of me, and no mistake."

"We won't, on one condition," said Murden, with one of his commissioner scowls and stern looks, such as used to wilt the stoutest bushranger in Australia.

"Name it," Pat cried.

"Show us where the secret passage is, so that we can get out and join those overhead," Murden continued.

"Niver!" was the firm reply. "You might give me untoold goold, and I'll kape the secret. I've bin here twenty years, and no man knows what I knows about the place; but I tells no one: now mind that, if ye plase."

"We can waste no time with you," Murden said. "Give us the information, and we will reward you. Refuse, and you must suffer. Choose quickly."

"I niver will turn informer, like a thafe," was the reply.

Murden snatched up a small tunnel, a tin one, such as had been used to fill bottles with poteen.

"Bring me a gallon of water," the commissioner said; and then we knew the punishment that awaited the Irishman, for we had seen the same torture applied in Australia, and always with success, as far as making the victim yield his will to the one who wanted certain secrets, and had the power to apply punishment.

The water was brought and placed by the Irishman's side. Pat looked at the tunnel, at the gallon measure of water, and then at our party, but he did not speak a word, for the reason that he could not, his mouth being once more securely gagged, and his limbs tied with ropes which he could not break.

"For the last time, I ask you to show the door which leads to the open air," Murden said.

Pat scowled at us and shook his head, in token of his refusal to comply with our request. The row overhead was decreasing, and each moment we feared that the Fenians would return and demand reparation for our conduct towards the man whom they had left in charge of us. We had no time to lose.

Murden made a motion, and out of the Irishman's mouth came the gag. As soon as he found his throat clear, he uttered one shrill yell; but this was just what we expected, and hardly had the scream died away, when the tunnel was forced into the man's mouth, and in such a manner that he could not expel it if he tried ever so hard.

"Pour!" said Murden, in a tone of voice that showed he had not forgotten his policeman's decision.

Hopeful raised the gallon measure, and emptied some of it in the tunnel. Pat kicked and squirmed with astonishment, and what he could not swallow oozed from the sides of his mouth.

Murden made a sign, and pouring the water was suspended.

"Will you show us the secret door?" was demanded.

"A look that said "no" was the answer, but it was not so defiant as the first one.

"Pour!" was the command; and once more the water commenced flowing down the tunnel.

A small stream was emptied from the gallon measure, and passed into the throat of the wretch, powerless to resist it.

One, two, three minutes passed, and still the man endured the torture without a sign to show that he submitted. He struggled; but the water continued to flow, and at the end of five minutes Pat had had enough, and signified so by a nod, which we could not fail to understand.

The tunnel was removed from his mouth at once. Pat uttered a half-choked sigh of relief, but made no attempt to raise an alarm. His spirits appeared to be a little too much subdued for all that; but, as soon as he could find words, he said, in a protesting tone, —

"Ah, the divil, and did ye want to drown my insides wid yer vile water, when so much good whiskey was near, that ye could have used jist as well. Had it been poteen, I'd have stuck out till I'd bust."

"You will show us the secret entrance?" Murden asked.

"Ah, now, it was the sacret outlet ye wanted a while ago," cried Pat, in a blarneying tone.

"It means the same thing," Murden said.

"No, sir, I axes yer pardon; it don't mane the same thing, and it can't mane the same thing, for the reason that —"

Murden once more took up the tunnel, and motioned to Hez to take charge of the water; but no sooner did Pat notice the signs than he withdrew all equivocation.

"Gently, gintlemin," he said; "we may differ a little on minor pints, yet still be agreed on the principal thing. Let me have a chance to breathe afore ye ask me many questions."

"Not a moment," was the stern reply. "Show us how we can make our escape from this place, and we'll reward you. Refuse, and punishment awaits you."

"And sich punishment!" Pat exclaimed, in a doleful tone, as though he was thinking how he should continue to puzzle us, and thus gain time. "Only to think of pourin' water into a man's stomach, when whiskey is within reach of all! Bloody zounds, but it's formin' cakes of ice in my insides it is, and a hot punch alone will thaw it."

All the time that Pat was speaking, he was slowly leading us along, past bins of potatoes, kegs of spirits, empty barrels, and sacks of grain. We suspected him of some trick, yet kept such a good watch upon his movements, that we certainly supposed him incapable of doing us the least injury, yet the result showed that Pat was more crafty than we had given him credit for.

"You see," said the Irishman, "how snug a man can be here. Now divil a red-coat knows that in this same place there is gunpowder enough to blow a regiment to Ballywack and back agin."

"Gunpowder! D—n, you don't mean to tell me that there's gunpowder in this blasted cellar, where fires is burnin' all the time — do you?" demanded Hez.

"I does that," was the response. "See here," and Pat pointed to a keg that stood at his feet. "In this keg is cartridges, and I wish every one of 'em was in a paler's body."

"Keep the light from the keg, or we'll all go to the devil together," Murden said; and just as he spoke, Pat stepped towards us, a sudden movement that we did not notice, and then, with one blow of his fist, he struck the lamp which Hopeful held, and dashed it upon the keg which was said to contain gunpowder.

We gave several jumps, and tumbled over barrels and sacks, expecting an explosion that would blow us into eternity in a moment. We were in darkness, and wished for light, but not such kind as gunpowder produced.

Confused as we were by tumbling and groping in the dark, we all recovered our feet; and, as we did so, a current of fresh air entered the cellar, as though a door or window had been opened, and then we were startled by Pat's well-known brogue.

"Ah, boys, what do yer think of it now? Is a Irishman up to Yankee hed sinters' tricks, or is he only fit to be filled with coold water by the aid of tin tunnel, begad? Whoop, don't ye wish that ye had me near the keg of gunpowder, and the light in yer hand? Do ye think I'd fly away to glory? Hist, I can hear yer teeth chat terin', even here, and so I'll wish yer a good day, till the boys returns to settle wid yer."

"One moment, Pat," cried Fred.

"Well, be quick about it, thin, for I'm in a hurry. I'm afeard that the explosion will take place;" and then the fellow laughed as if to mock us in our misfortunes. We could not see him, for we were in pitch darkness; but we could hear the slippery scamp, and would have felt better if we could have laid hands on him and punished him for his treachery.

"Pat," said Fred, "let us be friends."

"Yes, and fill a friend's belly with coold water. Ugh, is that the way to treat Ireland's friends?"

"But listen to me for a moment, Pat. We will give you ten gold sovereigns if you will let us out."

"Not for tin hundred, arter pourin' water in my belly with a tin tunnel. I go to tell the boys of it; and won't they feel wild when they know that I've had to drink water, and that is somethin' that they all despise, and they despise the man what dales in it. Good by, and take mighty good care of the gunpowder."

Here he stopped for a moment, as though to take breath; but he little thought that an enemy was stealing on him in the dark.

"Jasus!" suddenly shouted Pat, and that exclamation satisfied me that Rover had done his work in a faithful manner; for while Fred and Pat were discussing terms, and when I saw that there was no danger of an explosion, I had laid my hand on Rover's head, and whispered a few words in his ear, which the hound understood as readily as if he was human.

His scent was true, and his instinct wonderful. He had crept along in the dark; and just as Pat was bidding us farewell, Rover had seized the Irishman's leg, and held it as if in a vice.

"What is the matter?" asked Fred, as Pat commenced shouting his surprise, and struggled to escape from the strong teeth of the dog.

"Matter enough. Call off the dog, or to the divil I pitch him."

"If you offer to strike the animal, he will tear you in pieces!" I shouted, fearful that my favorite would suffer harm.

"He's doin' it now, the baste," was the reply. "He's tearin' at me leg like a bull bedbug. O murder! how he bites if I offer to stir."

While Pat was uttering his lamentations, I had reached for the fallen candle and found it, and hastened to the fire under the stills and relighted it. Then I lost no time in returning to my companions, who were so completely in the dark that they could not move until I joined them.

"Mind the powder, honeys," cried Pat, as soon as he saw me approach with the candle. "It's but one touch, and we go to the divil together."

We approached Rover's prisoner, and saw that the fellow was securely pinioned by the leg. He was on his hands and knees, and had endeavored to crawl through a small hole, not more than two feet square, close to the ground, which was the reason we had missed finding it, for neither of us supposed that it was necessary to get on all fours to make an exit from such a place.

We took hold of Pat's feet, and jerked him into the cellar, and as we did so the secret panel shut of itself; but we noted the place, and had no fear but that we could find it again at any time, even if Pat was disposed to play us another trick.

"What do you think of Yankees now?" I asked, as we made Rover relinquish his hold of the man's leg.

"Think is it?" demanded Pat, as he rubbed the place where the dog's teeth had been planted. "Faith, I think that the brute is the smartest of the lot. He cotched me whin the rest of yer couldn't."

"And what do you mean by cheating us in the manner in which you did?" Fred asked.

"And what do you mane, by pourin' water down me throat, when me preference is for whiskey?" Pat demanded, in an injured tone. "You have ruined me constitution, and I'll never recover from it. It's ice I'll be turned to."

"We have no time to fool with this fellow," Murden said, in a tone of impatience. "We must escape, and not spend a moment in talking with him. The Fenians are liable to come back at any moment."

"Ye may well say that," responded Pat, in a complacent tone. "And if they do come, look out for yerselves, for they'll prove perfect divils, when they know that I has had water poured down me belly. They has no respect for men what does that, now I tells yer."

"We must secure and gag him," Murden said. "It won't do to leave the fellow at liberty."

"Especially wid the gunpowder," Pat cried, with a grin on his face, which proved most conclusively in my mind, that the Irishman had blarneyed us.

Fred went to the barrel, that had been pointed out as containing cartridges. He stooped down, and then raised the barrel and placed it on its head. As he did so, the end fell in, and revealed pikes and spears, and a few bayonets, rusty and old-fashioned.

"There is no gunpowder here," Fred said in an indignant tone.

Pat grinned, and scratched his head.

"It's one of me mistakes," he said. "The coold water confused me, and warped me judgment. Sure yer ought to be satisfied that it's iron instead of powder, for if it had been powder, sure yer all would have been to glory afore this."

While Pat was speaking, Murden had produced some cords, and commenced tying the fellow's hands behind his back, although the Irishman uttered the most indignant remonstrances at such treatment. But little heed was paid to Pat's words, and as soon as his arms and hands were secured, we laid him on his back, and were just about to stuff some rags in his mouth, when we heard renewed outcries overhead, a heavy tramping of feet, several discharges of muskets and pistols, and then the secret panel, by which we had entered the cellar, was dashed open, letting in a flood of light, and down the slippery, damp stairs came half a dozen policemen, with wondering looks upon their faces, pistols in their hands, and glances that seemed to express a fear that some trap had been entered, which would cost the party dearly.

Following the police came half a dozen soldiers with muskets in their hands, and after the soldiers an officer sword in hand.

We saw that escape was impossible, so considered the next best course was to submit, and explain matters, as well as we were able, to those in authority, and thus effect our release as soon as possible; but to prevent all mistakes, which could not well be rectified afterwards, we extinguished our light, and were thus left in darkness; but at the same time could see the movements of the police and soldiers, owing to the door at the head of the stairs being left open.

If the soldiers had seen us when they first entered the cellar, it is quite probable that they would have given us a volley, for they were excited over their contest with the Fenians, and cared but little whom they fired at, as long as they drew blood. We knew this from our Australian experience, for when a man's blood is hot, he will do that which will make him feel sorry, as soon as reason resumes its sway.

We blew out our light, therefore, and seated ourselves on sacks of grain, and awaited the result of the soldiers' entrance with much composure, knowing that the fellows would soon beat up our quarters, and make us prisoners.

Fred, who was as cool as the night he whipped the bully of Ballarat, during our days of inexperience in Victoria, took pity on Pat, who was lying at his feet, and removed the gag from his mouth; but while he was thus employed, the Irishman nipped his fingers out of revenge for the treatment which he had received, and this caused Fred to utter an exclamation that attracted the attention of the invaders.

"Halt!" cried the officer in command; "some of the d—d rebels are in the cellar, and in ambush. Shoot the first one who shows his head."

The red-coats came into line, like well-drilled men ready to receive a charge of cavalry; but the police were too wary for such needless show, and the instant they suspected an ambush and a surprise, they scattered like bushrangers, and dropped behind arches and kegs, until only their noses could be seen, as they were poked out in search of the whereabouts of an enemy, — a movement simple but wise, and one that commanded the greatest respect on the part of Murden, who could not forget that he had been a police commissioner, and had had dealings with cruel men, cunning as foxes, and deadly foes of the mounted "traps," so he gave vent to his admiration by shouting, —

"Well done, my lads. You have been drilled in a good school."

"Who speaks?" cried the officer who had charge of the party. "Advance and surrender yourselves, or the worse for you."

"It's the four hed sinters," yelled Pat, who found his voice, as soon as the gag was removed. "Come and take 'em, for a divil a fear ye need have of 'em."

Fred, who remembered his bitten fingers, — for they still smarted, — gave the Irishman a punch with his foot; but still the noise continued.

"Advance and surrender, if you would have quarter," cried the officer, in a stern tone. "Come out of your hiding-places, and lay down your arms, or my men will not show you mercy."

"Don't fear 'em," Pat yelled. "Come on and take 'em, and don't let 'em escape. They is without guns or pistols, and have trated me in the most scurvy manner. Filled me body wid water, in fact, when lots of fine whiskey was round."

"Strike a light, one of you police officers," commanded the lieutenant, who had charge of the party. "Don't skulk behind barrels, but come and let us find the fellow who is yelling so lustily about head centres."

One of the police speedily produced a lantern, and threw the light in our direction, so that all of us were revealed to the gaze of the exploring party.

"Move a hand or foot, and you are dead men," the lieutenant said, in a tone that showed he was in earnest, and how much he distrusted us.

"How can we advance and surrender without moving hand or foot?" asked Murden, with a laugh that did not show much fear.

"D———n! whose voice is that?" asked the lieutenant, starting towards us, far in advance of his soldiers, as though the tones of Murden's voice had awakened recollections of earlier days.

CHAPTER IX.

A STRANGE MEETING. — AN OLD ACQUAINTANCE. — PAT AND HIS ACCUSATIONS. — IN THE STREET. — THE BARRACKS. — THE DESPATCH.

THE lieutenant was much surprised at Murden's voice, and the latter seemed far from astonished that such was the case. He appeared to act like a man who knew that affairs would come out all right, without much trouble on his part, and so sat still and smoked a cigar with an air of real enjoyment that was quite provoking to us who were in a state of some uncertainty as to whether we should get our brains beaten out, or have several bullets lodged in our bodies by the infuriated peelers and soldiers.

The police, by the aid of the dark lanterns, discovered our position, and hastened towards us as soon as they saw that we were not disposed to fight. They came on, pistols in hand, and with handcuffs all ready to slip upon our wrists.

"Hold on one moment, my pretty little dears," said Murden, when the peelers would have placed the steel upon our hands. "Don't be so fierce. No one wants to escape or resist. If we had desired to leave this gay and pleasant place, we could have done so some time since — long before you appeared upon the scene."

"Don't belave him," yelled Pat, whose limbs were now free; for we had cut the ropes that bound him. "They tried to lave, but I prevented 'em, and now claim the reward for the discovery of four hed sinters."

"Yes, that is all very well; but how does it happen that we find you here, Pat?" one of the peelers said — a sergeant, who seemed to know the Irishman's face.

"Faith, how should I come here, but to sarch for the hed sinters? I seed 'em enter the cellar, and so I follows, to keep an eye on 'em, so that I could rin and tell your honors the fust chance I had. O, I'm a true blue son of Ireland, and loyal to the backbone."

"D—n such loyalty as yours," was the response. "I know your face too well to believe your stories. You can't ring in here for a reward, now I tell you. If these men are head centres, you won't stand much of a chance at the money that is offered for them."

"We hope not, for the scamp did not have the least hand in taking us," Murden said. "All the reward that is received for us must go to the brave police; for they have shown as much pluck as my own fellows would have done had they been here."

"You hear," cried the police sergeant to his companions. "He has confessed that he has brave accomplices. Recollect his words."

"We will," was the response.

"And swear to them, I suppose," Murden said.

"Yes, that we will," was the unanimous response.

"How like the fellows I used to command!" Murden muttered, as he nodded his head with signs of approval.

"Come," said the sergeant, shaking the handcuffs. "We have no time to lose. You must go with us, and submit to be ironed."

"That's right. Don't let 'em escape yer hands, for they is slippery spalpeens as ever ye did see; and the dog — to the devil wid him — knows as much as any of 'em. Faith, I think he is half human. At any rate he has a mighty fine taste for beef, and tinder at that, for he took most a pound lump out of the calf of me leg when I tried to prevent the hed sinters from escaping."

"What a splendid liar this fellow is!" Murden said. "How he would have honored our Australian corps! He would have sworn a bushranger off his feet in no time, if we-had requested him to do so."

In the mean time, while we were thus talking with the police, and endeavoring to devise some means to prevent our hands from being manacled, the soldiers had kept in the background, the lieutenant in charge having seated himself on a keg, and appeared to listen to our conversation with much pleasure and interest. One thing, however, had struck me with surprise; and that was the fact that Rover was making friends with the officer; and I saw the dog lay his paws on the lieutenant's shoulder, and lick his face, which the animal never did to any one unless on good terms with him.

"Come," cried the peelers, who began to grow impatient at our delay and amazing coolness; "just let us slip on these ornaments, and we promise you that they won't hurt in the least."

"We decline the ornaments," Murden said. "We will go with you as quiet as lambs; but as we have committed no crime, we must protest against being handcuffed."

"As far as your crime is concerned," said the sergeant, "others must judge of that besides me and my mates. We only has to do our duty; and if we is a little rough, you know, you must blame yerselves, and not us, 'cos we would be careful if you would let us."

The sergeant made a sign, when his men prepared to

throw themselves upon us, much to Pat's delight; but just as we expected the onset, the lieutenant started to his feet, pushed Rover aside, and came towards us.

"Hold on there for one moment," the officer cried, in a calm but authoritative tone. "Don't put irons on these gentlemen. I'll be responsible for their good conduct."

"Hang me if it ain't Maurice!" cried the ex-commissioner of police, as he sprang to his feet, and rushed towards the lieutenant; but the peelers, who thought they saw a Fenian trick in the movement, seized Murden by the collar of his coat, and held him fast.

"Release that gentleman, this instant!" thundered the lieutenant. "How dare you lay hands on a person whom I have vouched for?"

The peelers removed their hands from Murden's person in an instant, and manifested all that abject humiliation which is so characteristic of a British civilian when brought in contact with an officer of the army who bears the queen's commission.

"We was only fearful they would escape us, sir," the sergeant of the police force said. "You know there is a reward offered for 'em, and we is entitled to it, sir. Here is four head centres, and we've took 'em just as they landed, and afore they could do any damage."

"Nonsense, man; you don't know what you are talking about. You are on the wrong scent entirely. These gentlemen are no more head centres, or connected with Fenianism, than you are."

"True for you, Maurice," cried Murden; and then the lieutenant and the ex-commissioner shook hands like old friends, and as though they were really glad to see each other.

In the mean time I had been thinking where I had heard the lieutenant's voice before, but could not make out. It was familiar, and I taxed my mind to recall the time and circumstances of hearing it, but could not; so I was somewhat surprised to see Hopeful rush towards the officer, and exclaim,—

"Cuss me if it ain't Maurice;" and then Hez hugged the officer, and the latter, in spite of his red coat, sash, and sword, hugged Hez in return.

"Maurice, old fellow, who would have thought of seeing you here?" Fred said; and then he rushed towards the lieutenant, and another hugging match was the result of the meeting, until I almost suspected that the soldier was a young girl disguised as a man, and that my companions had found it out before I did, which was something wonderful, for I generally had my eyes open when a pretty face was near me. But the lieutenant's face was not handsome for a woman, for it was dark, and had a black, heavy beard, and a mustache that was long and silky, and decidedly warlike.

"Well, Mr. Jack, ain't you glad to see me?" asked the lieutenant, as he turned towards me, with extended hand.

"If I could only recall where I have seen you," I said. "Your voice sounds familiar, and your face is one that I have not forgotten. Let me see; was it in —"

"Australia, old fellow? Yes, it was in Australia where we met, and where we parted. Now do you remember me?"

I rather think I did. We had been together too many times on the plains and in the bush of Victoria, not to recall to mind some of his dashing exploits when he served as second in command in Murden's flying troop, hunting after escaped convicts and desperate robbers; and the only reason why I had not recognized the gallant fellow in the cellar in Queenstown was because I did not have the least idea that he would part from his adopted country. If any one had told me that Maurice was in Ireland, taking care of suspected Fenians, I should have laughed at the idea, as one too absurd to be mentioned.

In a moment the lieutenant had convincing proof, by the warm pressure of his hands, that he still retained a hold of my affections.

"Tell me," I said, "if you have time, and can converse

with your prisoners, how it happens that you are here, and holding a commission in the British army."

"Prisoners be hanged; you are no more prisoners than I am. As for holding a commission in the army, I am indebted to our mutual friend Murden, who aided me with his influence. Six months ago my regiment was ordered to Ireland, and my company to Queenstown. Here I am, just after a sharp fight with the rabble in the streets; and by accident I discovered this secret still, and four old friends at the same time. What more could man desire, to render him happy and contented with the world?"

"And ain't the four hed sinters to be taken and tried and condemned? and ain't I to have some of the money for the information?" asked Pat, who was amazed at the turn which affairs had taken.

"You shall have your reward — never fear," Lieutenant Maurice replied.

"Ah, captain, I knew ye wouldn't chate a hard-working man like me out of me own," Pat said, with a whine that contrasted in a striking manner with the assurance which the man had assumed a few minutes before.

"Sergeant," cried Maurice, turning to the police, "this man comes in your line. He has been running a secret still; so you know what to do with him. I turn him over to you."

"Yes, I'll take charge of him," was the response; and the next moment Pat's hands were secured by a pair of steel bracelets, much to his surprise. He uttered the loudest kind of protests, but no one paid the least attention to them.

"And these gentlemen — what is to be done with them?" asked the sergeant, pointing to us.

"These gentlemen are my friends, and must be treated as such. Why, man, you don't suspect they are Fenians — do you?" Maurice asked.

"I don't know, sir, but I s'pose it's all right, sir, if you say so; though I heard one of the gentlemen say that he'd just come from Australia, and that, sir, you'll acknowledge, looks a little suspicious — now don't it, sir? — when so many ticket-of-leave men is round, makin' disturbances."

Maurice laughed most heartily.

"Why, man alive," he said, "this gentleman," pointing to Murden, "was at one time a commissioner of police in Australia, and was recently a cabinet officer, and stood high in the estimation of the governor."

"Glad to hear it, sir, I'm sure;" and all the police touched their caps, in token of their respect for one who had risen to so high a position from the force.

"Might we hear the gentleman's name?" the sergeant said. "Perhaps it is known to us; for all great men are recollected by the police."

"Murden," was the reply.

"Well, I'm sure I never expected this honor," cried the sergeant; and off went his cap, and he ducked his head to our friend, "We have all heard of the celebrated Mr. Murden, the commissioner who had command of the mounted police. Indeed, sir, we have your portrait, cut from an illustrated paper, pasted on our walls at the station-house; and I must confess that the likeness is remarkable. Quite wonderful, sir."

"And these gentlemen," said Maurice, pointing to Fred, Hopeful, and myself, "were his constant companions and aids in all dangerous enterprises."

"Ah, we have heard of 'em, sir," the sergeant remarked, with a bow and a chuckle, as he rubbed his hands. "We read The Gold Hunters, and The Bushrangers, when they were published in England, and don't forget all that we reads. Never expected to meet such distinguished gentlemen in such a place as this, I am sure."

Of course we acknowledged the compliment, and then Pat, who saw that he could hope for no aid at the hands of the police of Queenstown, burst out with, —

"Ah, now, is it possible that men what I took for hed sinters is nothin' but snakin' peelers, come all the way from Australia to suck poteen and pour water down me throat? O, blood and zounds! when I think of the manner in which I have been chated by these impostors, it seems as though the water which is in me would turn to ice, and fraze me bowels and what compassion I had in 'em. Ah, cap'n, if ye knew how much of the whiskey they had drunk, ye would ax the queen to pay for it. They'd ruin the best still in Ireland, if they had free run of it."

Of course no one paid the slightest attention to Pat's words, for the simple reason that he was not believed. We were too sober to corroborate his assertion, and the fellow, finding that we were not molested on his statement, was about to attempt another, when Maurice interfered.

"We have heard enough of your blarney," he said. "You can do my friends no harm, and yourself no good. Keep your mouth shut, and you will fare better than if it is opened too much."

"And don't you want a witness?" asked the fellow. "I can testify as to who run the still, and on other matters that will make the queen's friends stare. O, I know a hape, I do."

Maurice turned from the fellow, disgusted at his treachery, and then the police, who delighted to meet with just such customers, took charge of Pat, and we heard no more of him for some time.

"Come," said the lieutenant, "let us move from this place. We have no further business here."

"Can we get through the streets?" Fred asked.

"My men will make a way for you," the officer said, with all the pride of a Briton with unlimited power at his back. "My soldiers are not in the habit of being frightened by mere numbers, any more than their commander is. Come; I'll leave a few men to take charge of the still; if I do not, it will disappear in a wonderful manner, as soon as our backs are turned. We must retain possession of the prize, although every Irishman in the neighborhood will swear vengeance against me for doing my duty."

"Perhaps we had better leave the cellar without your

company," Murden suggested. "You may escape some annoyance if it is thought that we are not under arrest."

"It is better for you if it is supposed that I have you in charge," the lieutenant said, in a significant manner. "Once have it understood that we are on friendly terms, and all the oaths ever uttered in Ireland could not convince some of the half savages that all of you have not turned informers; and an informer is something that is hated beyond all expression. Death is not too good for all who blab of the doings of the Fenians."

We knew that as well as he, and so concluded to go with him in the seeming capacity of prisoners, knowing that we might escape being knocked over by stones or stray shots while on our way to the jail or hotel.

When we reached the upper surface of the ground, we found the soldiers drawn up in line in front of the house. There were about one hundred of them — stout, tough, well-disciplined fellows, who seemed to care but little for the crowd of excited men who were in front and rear of them, apparently all ready for an attack, yet without weapons to compete with the rifles with which the soldiers were armed.

As soon as we appeared in sight, the mob uttered such a series of discordant howls that it seemed as though some of them had gone mad with rage and indignation.

"There they are!" was the general cry. "Look at the brave hed sinters, and see 'em prisoners in the hands of the tyrants. Down wid the sogers, and up wid the Fenians! Long life to the 'Mericans what come over here to lend us a helpin' hand!"

While the crowd were cheering and yelling, some of them made a rush as if to break through the line; but the soldiers brought their rifles to the charge, and the Irishmen saw before them a long line of bayonets which meant business; so when the Fenians were almost impaled, they would stop, utter fierce curses and cries for vengeance, and then retreat out of reach of those who held such deadly weapons.

"Don't attempt to get through such an excited crowd," Murden said to Maurice. "I fear that trouble will ensue. Send for reënforcements if you have them, and if not, wait until the crowd disperses."

"And let the fellows think that they have frightened British soldiers, and so give them courage to make bolder demonstrations? No, that is not my style of doing business. I'll not yield them an inch as long as I'm in command of a company." And he was as good as his word; for the next moment he was addressing the crowd, and for a wonder they listened to him in silence, and did not even throw a stone at him, showing that some respect was still entertained for a commissioned officer.

"My friends," Maurice said, "I want to give you a word of advice, and I hope you will take it. I have but the most friendly feelings for you, and therefore don't want to hurt you if I can help it. But you must understand me, and I mean what I say when I tell you that I intend to take these gentlemen to the barracks, and when they are there they will dine with me, and help empty a bowl of real Irish punch, made from the best whiskey that can be found in Queenstown. Now, my good friends, don't get in my way, for if you do, some of you will get hurt."

Some of the listeners cheered at his words, and others maintained a stern silence. At any rate, Maurice's speech had done no harm, and we had no expectation of trouble when we fell into line and marched towards the barracks with a soldier on each side of us, and a surging crowd in front and rear.

To be sure we heard hard words and some loud threats, and many of the Fenians urged each other to rush in and secure the head centres from the power of the English tyrants; but the firmness of the soldiers and the dread of their rifles prevented any concentrated attack on our column, and we reached the barrack quarters with no other damage than such as results from stones and sticks, and one or two dead cats, when aimed at a man's head with all the force of a strong arm.

As we marched into the soldiers' quarters, the gates were closed, and the Fenians were left in the streets, to shout until they were tired of such fun, and then disperse until some new excitement claimed their attention. I must confess that I was glad to feel that I was in a place of comparative safety, for I was sick of hearing hoarse shouts, and seeing stones fly through the air.

"Now," cried Maurice, as the soldiers were dismissed, and the guards doubled, "we will have some dinner, and I hope that you will enjoy it. We have finished our fun for the day. All danger is past, and we can have a long evening to talk of Australia and old times."

We had no objection to such a course, and were just about to enter the mess-room for the purpose of being introduced to the lieutenant's brother officers, when an orderly placed a telegraphic despatch in Maurice's hand.

Our friend read the despatch, and a look of vexation passed over his face.

"The devil!" he said, and stamped his foot with impatience.

"What is it, Maurice?" asked Murden.

"Somebody has telegraphed to the lieutenant-governor that four noted head centres have been arrested, just as they landed from the steamer, and I am ordered to forward them to Dublin, under a strong escort, without the least delay. Was there ever anything more unfortunate?"

"Why not telegraph that we are not Fenians, but friends of known loyalty to government?"

"I will; but it won't make a particle of difference, as you will see. Government is so suspicious, that no one's word is relied on unless a lord is ready to vouch for character. But cuss me if you start for Dublin until to-morrow morning, even if the governor does want your presence. I'll first try what an explanation will do;" and off went the despatch, while we washed and got ready for dinner. We made some little change in our toilets, having, to our surprise, found all the baggage which we had brought ashore safely housed in the barracks, where it had been placed by the police after their struggle with the Fenians on the shore.

We all sat down to dinner, half a dozen officers and our party, and had just commenced on the soup, when a telegraphic despatch from the lieutenant-governor was brought in and read aloud by Maurice.

CHAPTER X.

ORDERED TO DUBLIN.—THE WARNING.—THE MYSTERIOUS VOICE.—OFF FOR DUBLIN.—DRUNKEN SOLDIERS. —THE FENIANS AGAIN.

"JUST listen to this, boys," Maurice said, as he held the despatch in his hand, "and hear what his excellency says about our prisoners."

His brother officers were all attention in a moment. There were several of them, and they had made us feel at home as soon as Maurice had explained to them who we were, and that we had no connection with Fenianism, which they seemed to detest with all their hearts.

"The governor," continued Maurice, "seems to run away with the idea that we have been deceived in the estimation of our friends, for he telegraphs to me to send on the prisoners without the least delay, and under a strong escort, so that escape shall be impossible. He says he is certain that we secured the right men, and that we must not let them play a Yankee trick on us by believing what they say."

"The lieutenant-governor is not complimentary to our sagacity," Maurice remarked, as he folded up the despatch; "but then he is a suspicious man and hates the Fenians, as the devil is supposed to hate holy water."

"Maurice," Murden said, "you know your duty, and we

know your feelings. Don't endanger your position for one moment by keeping us with you. Once in Dublin, we can explain to his excellency that we are innocent of all designs upon his kingdom."

"Hang me if you shall leave until you have dined, and finished a bowl of punch," the lieutenant remarked, in a sulky tone, and one that showed he was in earnest; so, after he had given a few orders for our departure, we once more renewed our attention to the dinner, and had a lively time.

When cigars were passed around, I had occasion to step to the door of the mess-room for a moment, just to get a breath of fresh air; and while I was looking at the barrack-yard, I felt some one touch me on the arm.

Turning, I saw one of the servants who had waited upon the table. He laid a finger on his lips, and then slipped a piece of paper into my hand, and the next moment was gone.

With my back to the mess-room I unfolded the paper, and found the following, written in pencil:—

"Head Centres: Don't despair of a rescue. There are more Fenians in Ireland than were killed or wounded to-day, and they will shed their blood to prove to the head centres of America, that patriotism is still in bloom in Ireland. Keep your eyes open and trust to the brotherhood. Destroy this as soon as read, and be assured that careful eyes are watching your movements. You have already deceived the soldiers, and made them think that you have no sympathy with Fenianism. Still wear the mask, and all will be well in time."

The note was not signed or directed to either of us. I turned to find the man who had handed me the paper. He was not in sight. I glanced around the mess-room. No one was looking at me, or taking the slightest notice of my movement.. A few yards from where I stood, half a dozen soldiers were lounging, and discussing the events of the day; but they did not look towards me, or seem to be aware of my presence; but for all that, I was just as certain that some one was watching me as I was that I had eaten a hearty dinner, and therefore no longer felt hungry.

Slowly I tore the paper into the most minute fragments, and then scattered some of the pieces in the yard, while full one half of them I put in my pockets, to be thrown away in another direction.

Then the thought came uppermost as to what I should do in the present emergency. Had I better reveal all to Maurice, and so let him be well prepared for coming events, or had I better remain quiet and consider the note as so much bombast? It was evident that the Fenians still considered us as head centres, and had relied on my honor not to expose the correspondence. Under the circumstance I resolved not to, but to let events take their own course. We had been arrested as Fenians, when we had not a Fenian idea; and now we could not turn against the rebellious subjects of the queen, and betray them just at a time when they thought we were in danger, and needed aid.

With a firm resolve to keep the matter of the note a secret, I returned to the table, and once more joined in conversation, and continued it until near dark, when Maurice declared that he could delay no longer, but must forward us to Dublin by the seven o'clock train, and then resolved to accompany us, and see if he could not explain matters to the satisfaction of the lieutenant-governor, who was known to be a fair-minded sort of man, though a timid one, and terribly afraid that the Fenians would send him to London in a great hurry, some fine morning.

My companions received Maurice's announcement with a shout of delight; but I thought of the note which I had received, and did not respond with that enthusiasm which I should have done under other circumstances. However, no one noticed my silence.

"Yes," said Maurice, "I can run up to Dublin to-night, and come back in the morning. A few words from me, personally, will set his excellency all right, I know; and if I can't, why, we must remind him that a member of the Australian cabinet is before him."

"An ex-member," hinted Murden, in a gentle tone, as though he still wished that he was in office.

"Well, just as you please, although I know that the people of Victoria will not allow your valuable services to be dispensed with for any length of time. When you return an office will be open to you."

"Thank you, Maurice; but I fear you are too partial to be a good judge of my merits;" and then we all laughed, for we recollected some shrewd movements of Murden's when holding the office of commissioner, and dealing with obstinate bushrangers who refused to impart valuable information.

In a few minutes after we left the table we were ready to start for Dublin. The train was to leave at seven o'clock, and a special car had been ordered by Maurice for our accommodation and those who accompanied us, some half a dozen soldiers, with muskets, so as to keep up an appearance of force, in case any one should be rash enough to interfere with our movements.

Just as we were about to start for Cork, where we were to take the cars, a stout, plain-dressed man entered the mess-room. Maurice seemed glad to see him, and proceeded to ask him questions.

"What is the news in town?" the lieutenant demanded. "How do the people feel after the taste of our quality?"

"Sullen," was the answer. "They feel more like killing Englishmen than ever. The Fenians are active in town, and mean mischief some time or other. Better ask for more men, and keep them on the alert, or a surprise may be effected in some part of the town, or at Cork. If the fellows had arms they would not wait many hours for deliberation."

"I know it, Brady; but the fact of it is, they haven't the arms; so we can well afford to treat their threats with contempt," replied Maurice, with that confidence which always distinguished him in Victoria.

"But they can sting, sir, they can sting, and they will, the first opportunity," Mr. Brady replied. "I know their feelings, for I have been in their midst. They do not talk as loud as they might, and as I could wish, but still I know enough to be sure that they mean mischief."

I remembered the paper which had been thrust into my hand, and wondered what Mr. Brady, who was an experienced English detective, stationed at Queenstown, would think if he had read it. It was evident that the detective expected trouble, but did not know when or where it would strike.

"The people," said Mr. Brady, taking the glass of wine that was offered him by the lieutenant, "are firmly persuaded that you have secured the persons of four head centres from the United States."

"You know better than that, Brady?" Maurice said.

"Well, yes, sir, I should think I did. I learned all about 'em from the boat's crew that brought them ashore. They gave me full particulars; and I'm just as well satisfied, sir, that these gentlemen have nothing to do with Fenianism as I am satisfied that I have finished my wine, sir."

"Help yourself to some more. Of course you intimated that these gentlemen were not head centres."

"Of course, sir; but when an idea enters an Irishman's head, it is hard work to eradicate it, sir."

"Yes, I know; but what conclusion does that lead you to?"

"This, sir. The leaders of the Fenians have an idea that the gentlemen who landed from the steamer to-day have brought enough gold and bills of exchange to pay off the national debt and give every Fenian leader a large fortune with which to commence life and the new republic at the same time."

"The d—d fools."

"True for you, sir; but still the fellows believe it, and nothing can convince them that they are mistaken; consequently they will fight hard for the possession of the men who have so much money to throw away on so many worthless objects. It is the gold they want, and the gold they will have, if it is to be obtained; so let me advise you, sir, to take a strong escort with these gentlemen to the cars, or else let them go without a guard, so as not to excite suspicion on the part of those who are on the watch."

"I'll take your advice, Brady, for I think it is good. I'll send the soldiers to the cars singly, and let my friends go in the same manner. In the mean time, let it be given out that the four gentlemen will remain here for the present as prisoners, but that they will be discharged in the course of time, as no proof of their connection with the Fenians can be found."

"Yes, sir, I will cause such a report to be circulated, and hope that it will do some good, although I have my doubts." Mr. Brady moved towards the door, but a sudden thought entered his mind, causing him to return.

"I heard a faint rumor, sir," he said, "that the Fenians would attempt a rescue somewhere between Cork and Dublin; but I could not trace the rumor to any responsible source; so do not think that there is much truth in it. Still it is best to be prepared for anything, sir, for there is no knowing what the fellows may be up to. They are in earnest, and mean business; so a few broken heads won't amount to much in their ranks."

The detective then left us to do some more of his dangerous work. The conversation which he had carried on with Maurice had not been overheard by a single person in the room except our party and the lieutenant; and, although some of the servants had been engaged in clearing the table, they had not heard a word that was uttered, for the reason that all conversation was carried on in a whisper.

"I wish," said Fred, in a low tone, "that we were once more safe on board the steamer. I would agree not to trouble Ireland for a long time."

"So would I," was my response, as I thought of Miss Goldthwaite and her black eyes and coquettish ways, pleasant, yet at the same time rather heart-rending.

"I fear that we shall meet with trouble on the route," Fred continued, still speaking in a whisper.

"Have you had a warning?" I asked, as I thought of my own.

"Yes, and I am thinking if I shall mention the matter to Maurice, or keep quiet, as I have been requested to."

"As a friend, we should warn him. He goes with us on our account, and you know how we would feel if any disaster should happen to him."

"True; and so, in spite of the warning to keep secret, I will tell the lieutenant all that I have heard and read."

"Better not, if ye plase," some one whispered, close at our elbows, in Irish brogue, but in a strange tone of voice — one that we had not heard during the day.

Both of us turned to look for the man who had spoken, in tones that appeared threatening, even if they were uttered in a whisper.

To our surprise, no one was near us. There were several servants in the room, but they were at work clearing the table, so could not have been near us when we were consulting together and whispering.

"It seems to me that we are surrounded by spies," muttered Fred, in a tone of vexation that showed how much he was annoyed at the idea of being surprised at anything. "I wish that the devil had them and their Fenianism at the same time, if we have got to mix up in it."

"Speak to Maurice about it," I said. "Perhaps he can understand the business better than ourselves."

"Don't you do it," was whispered close to us — so close that it seemed as though we could feel the warm breath of the owner of the voice on our cheeks.

A quick turn and a look in all directions, and once more we found ourselves at fault. The waiters were not even near us, and the one who was nearest was engaged in packing the plates in the mess-chest, with his back towards us, and so could not have been heard had he chosen to whisper a warning in our ears.

"Maurice," said Fred, "can you rely on the men who are to accompany us as an escort?"

He spoke in so low a tone that even Murden, who was smoking a cigar and standing near, could not hear the conversation.

"O, yes; they have been with me for two years in the same company, and are considered Fenian proof. Why do you ask?"

"Because I believe that you and the barracks are surrounded by spies."

"O, I guess not," was the careless reply. "The Fenians take good care to keep out of the reach of soldiers and barrack-yards."

"But what would you say if we should report that we have had warnings of an attempt at rescue this very night?" demanded Fred.

"I should say, my dear boys, that some one has been making a desperate attempt to humbug you — that is all."

"And you disbelieve all warnings which purport to come from our would-be friends?"

"No, not all, for I know the Irish character, and how desperate it is at times. But at the present moment I do not think there is danger, for we taught the Fenians a lesson this day that they will remember for some time to come. My boys did not spare them when they were told to use their muskets or their bayonets; so I have the most convincing proof of their fidelity."

"And you don't suppose for a moment that the soldiers would turn on us if a crisis should arise?"

"No, I will not harbor such a thought for a moment; and I'll tell you the reason why. All those who were suspected of Fenianism, or who were Catholics, or, in fact, were Irishmen, were weeded from my company before it was stationed here; so I have only Englishmen to deal with and command."

The explanation was satisfactory, but still we did not

feel quite as much confidence as the lieutenant, knowing that human nature is weak, and that all soldiers have a large amount of it stowed away under their knapsacks and beneath their cross-belts.

We gave up the argument, and then received directions how to proceed to find the cars. We did not desire to take cabs, or a jaunting car, for the simple reason that they would have attracted too much attention from the people, had they been seen leaving the barrack-gate, while we supposed that we could walk through the streets, and thus escape all notoriety.

We started. Fred and I led the way, and after us, a few rods in the rear, came Murden and Hopeful, while following them was Maurice, in citizen's clothes, and with watchful eyes for our safety. On the other side of the street, under the charge of a corporal, were six soldiers, who marched as though they were off duty, and had nothing particular to do.

A few indignant natives of Queenstown groaned at the soldiers, but, as a general thing, no notice was taken of them or us, until we were half a mile from the barracks, when some blundering fellow, who appeared to be two thirds drunk, stumbled against us, and would have fallen to the ground and rolled into the gutter, if Fred had not caught him in his arms, and helped him to regain his feet.

"Now then, old fellow," said Fred, in a kind tone, as he steadied the inebriate, "are you sure that you are all right if I let go of you?"

"Am I sure that I am all right?" repeated the man; and then, while he was swaying back and forth, I noticed that he looked at us in a manner that did not resemble the dull glance of a drunkard.

"Well," repeated Fred; "are you sure that you are all right if I let you go?"

"Yes," said the man, in a tone that seemed to me to be significant; "now I'm sure I'm all right."

"Then go home." And as Fred gave this advice, he released him; but, instead of obeying, the fellow drew back and made several passes with his hands and arms — signs after the freemason pattern; but we could not interpret them quite as readily as we could the masonic passes, for the reason that we had never been initiated in the mysteries of the Fenian brotherhood.

"What in the devil do you mean?" demanded Fred, who saw that the man waited for some responses.

"And what do you mane?" the man responded, "by not givin' me the grand hailin' sign in return for what I've showed yer? Faith, ye can trust me if ye are hed sinters. Devil a fear of me, now I tell yer."

"Go to thunder," responded Fred and I, simultaneously.

"Faith, let me have a clutch at the goold that ye brought over wid yer from 'Meriky, and I'll go enywhere, and fight all the red-coats in Ireland. Don't fear to trust me, I tell yer, for I'm one of 'em."

Just at this moment the fellow caught sight of Maurice, and seemed to know him, for his drunken look returned to his face, and soon found its way to his legs, and off he went, staggering like any other inebriate; and I must confess that we met several more before we reached the cars.

We found that the last car had been reserved for us, while the one before it was used by the soldiers. There were but few passengers that evening, I recollect, and those were slouchy sort of men, with hats drawn over their eyes, as though they did not care to be known to their most intimate friends. They took first-class passage, and were in the compartments just in front of the soldiers.

"Hadn't you better have those fellows in with us?" asked Murden, as the soldiers took their places in the compartment.

"There is no room," was the reply. "The compartment will only accommodate six persons, and here we have the six," replied Maurice, with a laugh.

"No, only five," said Murden.

"Then you don't count Rover anything; and yet the old dog is equal to half a dozen men." And Murden pulled his ears, and the hound returned the caress by placing his paws on the ex-commissioner's shoulders, and licking his face, as a proper tribute of respect for being noticed.

We entered the car with certain misgivings that we should not have a pleasant journey; and perhaps Maurice felt so, for he went to his men and spoke to them in a low tone, and then joined us, and all of our party commenced smoking as if for a wager.

An hour passed, and then we heard the soldiers in the next compartment singing. In a quarter of an hour more they were howling, and from howling they commenced quarrelling.

"Your men have been paying too much attention to whiskey," Murden said. "I fear they would be useless in an attack to-night."

The lieutenant seemed to feel mortified; for, while he did not answer, he made several attempts to open the door of the carriage, so that he could walk along the side and communicate with his men. But the door was locked, and the guard was not to be seen.

Then Maurice called to his men; but they did not hear him, or if they did, took no notice of his voice or commands.

"D—n the fellows, they are getting drunk as fast as possible," muttered the indignant lieutenant.

"They can't get much drunker," Murden said, in reply; and just at that moment the train commenced to slacken its speed, and the car almost stopped, although I could not hear the brakes, or see the guard at work.

"We are now near—"

Maurice had proceeded so far, when the car stopped with a sudden jerk, as though some obstruction had been placed on the track.

"What in the devil is the meaning of this?" asked the lieutenant; and then the answer was returned in the shape of a shout, and, on looking out, we saw that we were once more in the hands of the Fenians; for the car had been separated from the train, and the latter had gone on and left us.

CHAPTER XI.

SURROUNDED BY FENIANS. — THE SEARCH FOR GOLD. — A DISAPPOINTMENT. — MAURICE IN DANGER. — FRED TO THE RESCUE. — A SIGNAL.

The Fenians made no attempt to disguise themselves, and did not seem to care a pin for the soldiers, who were shouting and singing in the next compartment, and did not appear to be aware that the car had stopped, or that their natural enemies were surrounding them.

I looked out of the window, and could have sworn that I saw men who entered the cars at Cork. I knew them by their slouched hats and gray coats, confined around their waists by belts and ropes. Half a dozen of the fellows had torches in their hands, and as the night was dark, and the place where the car stopped dreary enough, a mass of bog and waste, the scene looked rather wild and none too pleasant, somewhat reminding me of the night when our carts were stopped by bushrangers on the banks of the River Murray, in Victoria, and when we escaped from the hands of the robbers through mere pluck and impudence.

Perhaps we were surprised; but if we were, we determined not to let the Fenians, or whoever they were, discover it, but to take matters as we found them, and make the best of it.

But if such was our secret determination, Maurice, like a bluff English soldier, had come to another conclusion, and showed fight like the brave man that he was; and as soon as the people who surrounded the car uttered a yell of satisfaction at the result of their strategy, Maurice grew hot with indignation, and of course wanted to fight at once; but while he was in the act of drawing his revolver Murden stopped him.

"Don't yo do it, old fellow," the ex-commissioner said,

in a low tone. "The fellows outnumber us four to one. They have all the advantage; so we had better submit, and see what they propose to do."

"And I hear such advice from you — do I?" asked Maurice, a little bitterly; "you who never shrank from odds in Australia, at least while I was under your command, and made no more of charging two to one than I should of dispersing the Fenians who surround us."

"Ah, Maurice," replied the careful ex-commissioner, "don't you know that I carried a moral influence with me, as well as brave men each side of me, when I undertook a rash act in the bush of Victoria?"

"And I, too, have brave men with me. In the next compartment are seven soldiers armed with rifles, who will fight to the death."

"So they would, Maurice, if they were reasonable beings, but just at the present time they ain't. Hark! do you hear that drunken roar? Since we left Cork your men have been tampered with, and now they don't know their commanding officer from a Fenian. Don't call upon your men, for if you do you will be disappointed and mortified. I'll warrant you that they have not a charge of ball and powder in their boxes, and that their rifles are unloaded. Some one has been smart enough to look out for that."

While the conversation was going on, in a low tone, the Fenians seemed undecided how to act, or what course they should pursue. To be sure they cheered and waved their torches, and some of them flourished muskets and pistols, but they did not offer violence to us or the soldiers. Once in a while some one would cry out for three cheers for the 'Merican hed sinters; but I noticed that the distinguished gentlemen from the United States did not create that excitement which one would naturally expect.

"Three cheers for the hed sinters' goold!" was the cry of some practical Fenian, who knew the substantial from the weak — the real from the ideal — who wanted the substance, and not the shadow.

At this there was a loud laugh, and some one shouted, —

"Ah, Barney, it's the goold ye care for more than liberty for Ireland."

"Faith," replied the sage, "give me goold, and it's little I care for things that I can't buy wid it. Plenty of goold is liberty, and the lack of it is slavery and toil."

"True for you, Barney," was the cry; and then some one, who appeared to be a man of authority, sprang into their midst, and began to make his presence felt.

"What in the devil's name do ye mane by standing here idle when there's work to be done, and no time to lose about it, to be sure? Don't ye know that the palers will be down on ye in a special train as soon as they suspect foul play? Open the doors and let the gintlemen out, and let's see what we've got."

I recollected the man as soon as I had caught sight of his form by the aid of the torches. It was Big Mike, the man whom we had met for the first time in the cellar where the whiskey still was concealed, and the one whom Pat said owned the place and machinery.

Big Mike seized a torch as he spoke, and sprang to the side of the car, and got upon the platform that ran fore and aft so that the guard could collect the tickets from the passengers. The window was down, and into it he thrust the smoking torch, so that he could see our faces.

"Well, gintlemen, we has met again, ye see, and once more I'll do the honors for ye, if ye has no objections. You see that the Fenians of Ireland can do some work even if they is surrounded by tyrants;" and then his eyes fell upon Maurice, and he leered at our friend as if he did not mean him any good will.

"Ah, lieutenant, it's little ye thought that ye would see me in command of more men than there's sojers in Queenstown or Cork — now did ye?"

"Mike," said Maurice, "you had better let us alone, and go your way before you give much trouble. If I call upon my men to fire, it will be the worse for you."

"Bah, lieutenant! yer men is all drunk and asleep. O

we took good care to look arter 'em as soon as we left Cork. They took to the whiskey like laches, and loved it better than their mothers' milk. But I has no time to waste in blarney, lieutenant. You has some friends of mine, and I want 'em."

"They have no desire to go with you, Mike; so let us alone," Maurice replied.

"What!" cried Big Mike, with a laugh, "do you 'spose that four hed sinters from 'Merica don't want to see their own dear friends afore they take sarvice wid the queen? Ah, lieutenant, ye has done me and mine damage enough for one day, in killin' one of me friends, in takin' another, and seizin' the best secret still in the south of Ireland. Don't offend me by sayin' that these gintlemen don't want to lave yer company and go wid us; for ye know that Ireland isn't free just yet, and we need all the strength that we can get."

"Look you, Mike," Fred said; "we tell you, once for all, that we are not head centres of the Fenian organization, and we never had anything to do with it, never intended to; so let us alone."

"Faith," returned Mike, with another grin that was far from pleasant to look at, "I don't blame yer for talkin' the way ye do as long as a queen's officer is near yer; but I don't think ye need fear him just now;" and the fellow winked one of his fierce-looking eyes, as though he meant mischief of some kind, and I really began to think that our friend was in danger of his life, as I knew that, if the Irish passions of hate were once stirred, blood or some act of cruelty alone would allay them.

If the Fenians meant to ill-use Maurice, what could we do to save him, provided we had the power? These thoughts flashed across my mind while Big Mike stood at the window, grinning at us; and I know that Fred thought of the same thing, for he told me so afterwards. As far as defence was concerned, we were powerless. All of our arms were on board of the steamer, and the most that we had in our pockets were small penknives. Even if we had been armed with pistols, we should have fared rather hard, for the reason that while we could not have killed but a few, had they extinguished their torches, they would have had good marks at us, locked up as we were in the car. All of these considerations induced us to keep quiet, and see if a stout denial would not get us through.

"Who has an axe?" asked Big Mike, after he had expressed his opinion of our frankness, although he thought it evasion. "Ye must come out of this; and it's unfortunate that the guard has taken the key wid him. I can't ax sich honorable gintlemen as hed sinters from 'Merica to crawl out of the winder; so I'll smash the door, and very quick, too, I'll do it. Who has an axe?"

One was put in his hands. The burly fellow threw his torch to the ground, and then hacked away at the door of the car with the axe. Half a dozen blows accomplished his object. The door was torn from its hinges and thrown to the ground, and then a wild waving of torches ensued as we were requested to walk out of the compartment and meet our friends who had assembled to do us so much honor.

"Look to the dog," cried Murden, as we left the car in accordance with the invitation of the wild Fenians.

The warning came none too soon, for Rover had somehow got it into his head that the men who were shouting and waving torches were enemies, and must be looked after, and he had settled it in his own mind that he was just the one to do it. I need hardly say that he would have fared quite badly in the crowd had he made an attack on them; but still he would have made his mark before the Irishmen despatched him, or did him much harm.

Seeing that the dog was excited, I stepped back and held him by his collar, while my companions passed out.

"Rover," I said, speaking to the animal just as though he was a human being and blessed with reasoning powers, " we are in a bad fix; but fighting won't help us just now; so be a good dog, and don't show your teeth until I tell

you to. When I'm ready we can go in and do our best;
but not until then. Do you understand?" and I patted
his massive head and made him look me in the face.

He uttered a subdued howl, as though he thought I
was putting him to a severe test; but I could see that he
promised compliance by the way in which he wagged his
tail and tried to lick my face.

"There's one more," cried Big Mike, as he counted my
friends after they had alighted.

"Here's the other," I cried, as I sprang from the car,
followed by the dog.

The Fenians gathered around us so that we could not
escape had we been so disposed; and the wild-looking
peasants stared at us and examined us from head to foot,
as though we were made of different material from themselves.

"Now out with the bags and boxes," Big Mike said, in
a tone that showed how much he was pressed for time.

Two or three of the wild peasants sprang into the car,
and seemed to be looking for our luggage.

"Out with it!" roared Mike.

"Faith, there's none here," was the cry.

Mike uttered a howl of rage, and jumped into the compartment which we had just left. In an instant he reappeared, and I saw anger and disappointment on his rough
face.

"Where's yer luggage?" he yelled.

"In the van with the rest of the stuff," Maurice answered.

Big Mike uttered such a hearty curse that I thought
the air was filled with brimstone.

"Didn't I tell ye to look after it afore all things?" he
roared. "Didn't I say that it was the luggage as much as
the hed sinters that we wanted? What in the devil's
name is the good of a hed sinter, even if he does come
from 'Meriky, unless he has goold to back him, and pay us
who is sufferin' and doin' the work?"

A murmur of applause from those who were near

enough to listen, as though they sympathized with a man who had expected much for some hard work, and yet had been cheated out of pay in some manner that was not quite comprehensible.

"Is this yer doin's?" cried Mike, as he sprang from the car, and came towards us. "Did ye put the luggage away on purpose?"

Maurice was about to make a reply that would have further enraged the ruffian, but I pressed his arm and kept him quiet.

"Look here!" said Fred, in a tone that he could assume when an excess of dignity was required; "how dare you talk to us in this manner? Who do you take us to be, one of your workmen, or gentlemen who are visiting Ireland for pleasure? Be assured that Stevens shall hear of your conduct as soon as we can communicate with him."

"I care more for the goold than I do for James Stevens or all the hed sinters in Ireland," Mike said, in a dogged tone. "I've lost my still, and I must have money enough from some one to pay for it."

"And you would let the cause of Ireland suffer, would you, just because you can't make more money in selling whiskey? This is not the kind of Fenianism that we expect to meet with in Ireland. In New York, Irishmen give up all for the sake of the cause, and you grumble because you have missed our luggage. It would do you no good if it was here, for not a penny should you handle."

"And how could you help yourselves?" Mike asked, in a sneering tone.

"By appealing to these brave fellows to stand by us," said Fred, and turned to the crowd of wild-looking wretches who surrounded us, as though confident that they would assist us in case we required help.

"D———n," muttered Murden. "Fred is doing all that he can to make us Fenians. What does he mean?"

"Hush!" I replied. "He sees a way for us to escape, and is trying his best to work out a path that leads to safety. Let him alone, and see how he comes out."

The "brave fellows" began to think that they were of some account, for they commenced murmuring that Big Mike was not going to take the bread out of their mouths; and that the hed sinters from 'Meriky were not to be treated with disrespect, for they had come to free Ireland, and the boys would stand by them.

Mike heard the cries and knew what they meant. He smothered his rage as best he could, and then adopted a different style of proceeding.

"Well, boys, don't look at me as if I was a thief, 'coz I ain't that, and no man in the crowd can say so, and spake the truth. If I wanted the goold, it was so I could take charge of it for ye, and share wid ye; for to whom does it belong but to those who run all the risks? and show me a lot of boys what has done more for Ireland and the cause than those who is now near me."

"True for you, Mike," was the approving reply; and then we saw that for the moment Mike had a portion of the Fenians with him.

But he had had a warning, and so concluded to let us alone for a while, and turn his attention to the soldiers, who were sleeping in the compartment.

Ever since we had left the car, Maurice had endeavored to get near his men and hold some communication with them; but the Fenians had prevented this, not by actual force, but had surrounded us in such a manner that we could not leave the circle, strive as hard as we might. If we crowded one way, they would crowd in another, and manage, by waving their torches, to either singe our heads or make us relinquish our purpose.

There was no occasion to smash open the door of the compartment in which the soldiers were confined. Some one had managed to open it while the cars were in motion, for the purpose of supplying the men with liquor; and when the crowd waved their torches and laughed at the position of the soldiers, we saw that they had swallowed some drug with their whiskey, for they were lying in all directions, heads and feet together, utterly regardless of their trust.

"The slapin' beauties," shouted one man, as the door of the compartment was opened, and the position of the soldiers was seen.

"The seven slapers, more like," cried another; and then there was a laugh, in which all joined.

"Faith, if I had my way, they would slape the slape that knows no wakin'," muttered a brutal-looking fellow, close to Maurice's elbow, and with a glare at the officer that meant murder if it meant anything at all.

In an instant, Maurice had the ruffian by the throat, and was shaking him with the strength of a giant.

"Dog," cried the rash officer, in a tone that meant mischief, "how dare you threaten a queen's officer, or her men?"

In an instant there was an intense excitement, for the Fenians crowded around us to see what was going on, and to take a part in the contest in case there was a free fight.

The burly ruffian was so much surprised that for a moment he allowed himself to be shaken; but recollecting that his companions would laugh at him if the thing continued, and that he would lose all prestige as a bully if whipped by one man, he managed to tear himself from Maurice's grasp, and to retreat several feet, as if for the purpose of recovering his scattered senses, and then renew the fight. But, instead of rushing on the officer with some display of the manly art of self-defence, the scamp drew a knife from his bosom and bounded towards our friend.

It was a critical period for Maurice and his life. He was never so near death and yet so easily avoided it; for in one instant he would have been impaled, had not Fred's presence of mind saved him.

As the bully rushed on the lieutenant, a long, murderous weapon upraised to give it more force when it struck the victim's body, Fred rapidly took his measures to save a friend's life. Out went one of his feet — an old trick of his in Australia; and as the ruffian blundered on, he stumbled over the foot and fell headlong to the ground, burying the weapon in the earth, and bruising his nose at the same time, and in such a manner that blood spirted out in all directions.

An Irishman is as fond of a joke as any people in the world; so I was not surprised to hear the crowd roar when the ruffian missed his aim and brought misfortune on himself.

"Whoop, but Paddy is fond of the airth, for don't you see that he is kissin' it with his mouth and smeller," cried the wit of the party; and then there was another laugh, which did not add to Paddy's good temper, for he sprang to his feet with a roar, his face stained with blood, and his eyes resembling those of a demon more than a man's.

With a shout and a horrible imprecation, Paddy once more rushed to the charge, for he had not yet been punished enough to keep him quiet.

But this time Fred determined to use a different member than his foot. He saw that it was time for action, and not for sport; and as the ruffian came on with his hands up, a knife in one of them, and the other like a wild beast's claw, my friend let him have a blow between his eyes that would have staggered an ox, had it received it on the nose.

Paddy dropped like a man shot dead with a bullet through his heart, and he did not move for a moment after he touched the ground.

I do not know what would have been the consequences of the blow, in that wild crowd, if we had not, just as Paddy struck the earth, heard the shrill whistle of a locomotive, showing that the car had been missed, and that the train was backing up to find it. The signal was the sign for a commotion among the Fenians, and they showed that they intended to do something without delay.

CHAPTER XII.

A LONG TRAMP. — A CAVE IN THE MOUNTAINS. — A PROPOSITION. — THE REFUSAL.

As soon as Big Mike heard the whistle of the approaching train, he passed out the rifles of the sleeping soldiers, and then followed them, and gave his orders in a hurried manner, as if aware that time was becoming valuable.

"Look to the gintlemen," he said, "and mind that they is taken care of at all risks. The rest of yer scatter, and devil a soul of you know what was done this night. If there is a man what lisps a whisper, he will be found and dealt with, even if he should be guarded by the whole of the queen's men. Go, now, and don't waste yer time in stoppin' here to see what others is doin'."

Some of the gossoons did not seem disposed to move as fast as Big Mike would like; so he adopted the novel process of running at them, and striking to the right and left, hitting some severe blows before the fellows could get out of his way. But the violent means seemed to result in dispersing the crowd quicker than the mild methods, for I noticed that some of the Fenians took to their heels and ran, disappearing in the darkness as though quite familiar with that section of the country.

For a moment we had great hopes of escaping from our dear friends during the confusion; but we soon found that the men who surrounded us were determined that we should be looked after, for they gave us no chance to get out of their way. We were the head centres of attraction, and could not escape notice.

The sound of the whistle grew louder and louder. The engine could not have been more than two miles from us when Big Mike returned from his task of driving off the hangers-on of his army.

"Now then," he said, "look alive. Gintlemen, we must

hurry you a little, to get rid of our friends who are in the train. Come on wid 'em to the old place."

There was no help for it but to obey. We tramped along in the darkness, over some very indifferent roads, through bogs, where the water was up to our ankles, not meeting a soul, and all the time preserving the utmost silence, not a loud word being spoken while we were on the march.

But we did some grumbling, and that wretched Hez, who was not fond of romance unless a pretty girl was concerned, uttered more than one emphatic oath when he found that his feet were getting wet, and that Ireland's bogs were working into his boots. More than once the Fenians cautioned Hopeful to be quiet, and this was especially the case when we left fields and struck public highways.

We saw several huts on the roadside, but they were apparently deserted, or else the owners were in our ranks, for not a light was seen in one of them, nor did a single person appear to be loitering near them.

There were no signs of pursuit; so we could not understand why the Fenians should wish to hurry us along as they did; and when I spoke to Big Mike about it, he only laughed and said that he "s'posed the boys wanted their supper, and that they couldn't get it till they reached the place where they were to stop."

"And is it far from here?" I asked.

"Faith," replied the leader, with a grin, "I don't know what ye call far. Let us understand that, and thin I'll tell ye."

I saw that no satisfaction was to be obtained from Mike, so trudged on, although most heartily wishing that I had a small force of mounted men at my disposal, so that I could scatter our guards, and thus escape to civilization.

Murden had the same thoughts, for he whispered to me, —

"If I had a score of my mounted police, — such fellows

as I led when we beat up Darnley's quarters, — there would not be a Fenian in sight in ten minutes."

Suddenly our escort made a flank movement. They left the highway once more, and took to the fields, passed over a mountain that was slippery with recent rains, and, after descending, found ourselves in a valley that was dark and difficult of navigation.

Here, for the first time, a halt took place, and a consultation ensued between Mike and several of his men. The result of it was, two of the Fenians were sent forward to see if the coast was clear, while we were invited to take seats on fallen trees, or such stones as were handy.

"How long have we got to wait here?" asked Maurice, who had sulked all the way from the cars, on account of the trick which had been played on him.

"I must request you to kape silent, lieutenant," Mike said. "You are too good a military man not to know that sometimes even a whisper is apt to betray one."

Maurice did not deign to reply, for the reason that argument was useless. We were in the fellow's power, and he could do as he pleased with us.

The Fenians, apparently as tired as we were, seemed to listen for some signal, and at last it came, in the shape of three shrill whistles.

"The coast is clear," cried Mike, starting up. "Come on, boys. We'll soon find a fire, and plenty of real Irish whiskey."

Once more we were in motion, staggering over stones and stumps, until Mike suddenly halted, uttered a shrill whistle like the call of some night bird, and then a light was exhibited in the side of the mountain, and we saw a narrow entrance to what appeared to be a cave.

"Now, gintlemen, we have reached a place of rest. Enter and be welcome. I don't think the queen's troops will find ye here — do you, lieutenant?"

Maurice was too indignant to reply. Mike led the way and we followed him; and when we had entered, we found that we were in a cave, some twenty feet high, and thirty or forty feet square, a portion of it cut from rock and clay years and years before, for the roof and sides were black with smoke and dirt.

In one corner of the cave was a roaring peat fire, the smoke from which disappeared in some mysterious manner overhead. There was an outlet, no doubt, for the cave was well ventilated and free from smoke.

Seated in one corner of the fireplace, smoking a pipe with an air of extreme relish, was an old woman, who was so hideous that she was enough to frighten a stout-hearted man into fits, had she but smiled on him in a friendly way, and had she looked cross at any one with weak nerves, he would have been a lunatic for life.

She was the only female present, and ugly enough for all the women of Ireland. Her occupation appeared to be superintending the boiling of a pot of potatoes, about a bushel of the esculents being over the fire in a huge copper kettle that looked as though it had seen better days when engaged in distilling whiskey.

The old woman merely glanced up as we entered, took a survey of us, and grunted her disapprobation, or approval, I could not tell which, at the number of visitors, and then applied her mind to the care of her pipe, the potatoes, and the fire.

"Well, mother, is the prates most done?" asked Mike; and I noticed that he, big as he was, was rather conciliatory in his manner of addressing the presiding genius of the establishment, as he continued:—

"The boys and the gintlemen what we have brought home with us are as hungry as watch-dogs, and a dish of prates and whiskey won't be bad for 'em this night."

The old woman growled out some answer which we could not hear, and then Mike replied,—

"It's true for you, mother, the boys do like their whiskey; but you know it is mate for 'em arter a long tramp. But don't you be hard on 'em, mother, dear, 'cos you knows you like a sup yerself as well as any person in the county of Cork."

The woman did not pretend to deny the insinuation, and we, thinking that the fire would feel grateful to our wet feet, went towards it; but a fierce growl from the old hag warned us that we were encroaching on her domains, and so we retreated with the exception of Fred, who, instead of being alarmed, went boldly up to the spitfire, and laid one hand on her bare, dirty, bony shoulder.

We looked on, lost in astonishment at his great audacity. We expected to see him scratched or soused with hot water, or else pelted with steaming potatoes; but, to our surprise, nothing of the kind occurred. The old woman submitted to it as though she had found a new pleasure and rather liked it.

The Fenians remarked the liberties which Fred was taking with unutterable astonishment, and even Big Mike was open-mouthed on the subject; and their astonishment was still further increased when they saw the old woman kick a block of turf towards our friend, and intimate by signs that he might seat himself on it near the fire — an invitation which I will do Fred the justice to say he was prompt to accept.

A murmur ran through the crowd as they saw these marks of favoritism, which caused the old woman to turn on the grumblers like an angry cat, determined to scratch all whom she disliked.

"Ye don't like it, ye miserable gossoons that ye are; and ye think that all of ye is entitled to the same favors — don't ye? Wall, now, I don't believe it. This boy looks like me own Bill, what you all recollect. There wasn't a man of ye that could stand afore or by the side of him. Ye know it now — don't ye?"

"Yes," whispered Mike, in so low a tone that the old woman did not hear him, "there wasn't a man in Ould Ireland what could bate him at staling a shape. Faith, he allers took the fat ones and left the poor ones, and he could tell one from the other on the darkest night."

"And where is he at the present time?" I asked.

"Over the water," was the response, and a motion of

the thumb in the direction of Australia, as near as he could indicate. "He took one shape too many, and was caught at it; and the judge said that his health required a jarney that would kape him out of Ireland for five years. The ould woman mourns for him, and well she might; for, had he been lucky, and the law had spared him, he would have made a great ornament to the Fenian organization. Faith, there was few things he would not have dared had he but set his mind on the subject. O, we lost a good man when Teddy left the country, because he could not help himself."

I did not care what means Fred resorted to for the purpose of ingratiating himself in the good graces of the old hag, for I knew that he had a purpose in all that he did; but what that purpose was no one could divine until he chose to show it.

As soon as Fred was seated, the old hag took her pipe from her mouth and offered it to Fred, but he did not accept it, although he did not refuse in such a manner as to offend her sensitiveness, provided she had any. He merely smiled, and pulled from his pocket his own choice meerschaum, and showed her that he was prepared for a smoke without using her great comforter.

"Wonders will never cease," whispered Mike. "He is the fust man she ever did the like to that I know of;" and all those around him corroborated the assertion.

In a few minutes, seats were found for us. They were empty kegs, which looked as though they had at one time contained whiskey, and I strongly suspected they would, at no distant day, be again filled with spirits; for although no one had hinted to me, yet I knew that we must be near one of those secret stills which are so common in the mountains of Ireland, and which serve, and have served for years, as the secret depository of arms for the disaffected class.

The pot of potatoes was taken from the fire and set in the middle of the cave for the Fenians to help themselves if they were hungry; but Fred fared a little better; for the old woman, still showing friendship for the man she had taken a liking to, whipped a half dozen of the steaming potatoes from the pot on to a plate that had once been whole, but was now cracked and broken, and black with age and dirt.

Fred received the plate and its contents with a smile and a bow, as polite as if the first lady in the land had handed them to him, and, even if he was not hungry, manifested a keenness of appetite that caused the old woman to grin an approval of his course.

The Fenians fell upon the potatoes like wild beasts, and some of them must have burned their throats, the way they masticated the hot esculents, for I heard more than one half-suppressed howl of anguish at the torture which such gluttony entailed.

But the potatoes soon disappeared, although I had, by some management, secured enough to give Rover a comfortable supper, for he ate the vegetable because there was nothing else for him to take hold of. He was a wonderful dog in the eating line, and would take just what he could get, provided he could not obtain delicacies like sirloin steak cooked to a turn, and spring chickens neatly broiled.

As soon as the potatoes were cleared away, Mike made a sign, and from some secret recess, which I was not permitted to explore, a keg of whiskey was introduced. The boys hailed its appearance with a shout, and seemed determined to make a night of it.

"Now, gintlemen," said Mike, speaking to our party, "I s'pose you is tired, and would like a little rest while the buys is drinkin' success to the cause. Jist lay down there in the corner, on the sacks and the straw, and it's an illegant bed you will find it. The buys may keep ye awake by their noise, but it's better to pay no attention to 'em, if you can help it."

"And how long do you mean to keep us here?" I asked.

"Who can tell?" was the reply. "Ye is too important to us to lave us so soon. It's few friends Ireland has, and them she must take care of, ye know;" and the fellow winked at us in a knowing manner, and then pointed to the straw and potato sacks.

"If you do not believe us," I continued, "send for Mr. Stevens, and he will assure you that we know nothing of the Fenians or their movements."

"We would be mighty grane to do that," was the reply, with a knowing laugh. "We don't intend to kill the goose that lays the golden eggs. Mr. Stavans and the rest of the hed sinters of Ireland can wait till we is through wid ye."

I saw that the fellow had motives of his own for keeping us, and would not suffer us to depart until he was willing; so we made the best of our way to the straw, and lay down and rested; but the Fenians made such a confounded noise, quarrelling and fighting over their whiskey, that we could not sleep until near midnight. Then we began to doze; but Fred and I were awakened by Big Mike, who laid his hand on us, and, as soon as he saw us open our eyes, put his fingers to his lips in token of silence.

"Get up and come to the fire," he whispered. "I must spake wid ye for a moment."

We looked around the cave, and saw that the whiskey had done its work, for the Fenians were laid out in all directions, dead drunk; and even Big Mike, who could swallow whiskey like water, looked a little flushed and flurried, and his voice was husky — an evidence of thick tongue which the man made no attempts to conceal.

"Now, thin, to business," said our host, and threw on the fire a few pieces of turf, so that the flames would light up our faces.

"I didn't know that we had any business," responded Fred, with a sleepy yawn.

"Well, then, it's time ye did know it; and it's a fine opportunity ye have to talk it over wid me, for I'm yer friend at present, and by yer actions shall I continue to be yer friend."

"What do you mean?" demanded Fred.

"Jist this and no more. You see the buys what is scattered on the floor — don't yer?"

"Yes."

"Well, them buys is rather short for money, for divil a stroke of work has they done for months. They is true Fenians, and want to free their country of the tyrant, afore they returns to the spade and the shovel."

"And what is that to us?"

"Much. You has come from a rich land, one that we loves, and we wants ye to jist distribute some of yer favors wid us afore ye comes to the big ones what will take all, and never let us see a penny."

"But we tell you, once for all, that we are not head centres, and are not Fenians."

"Faith," chuckled Mike, "I'm willin' to believe yer, and I've thought so all along; but it don't make much difference, any how, as long as we is acquainted. You has money, and we wants it. My men wants it, or they must starve."

"Then let them starve," cried Fred, in his passionate, impulsive manner; "for no money do they get from us."

"Let us have a little rason on this pint," replied Mike, although his brow darkened as he spoke, as though he was controlling his passions for some definite object. "Don't fly in the face of Providence, now, I beg of you. You is wid us, and all we want is that ye should stop wid us for a while, or until we can feel that we has been paid for our trouble."

"You have been to all the trouble without consulting our wishes, and we don't see that we are called upon to pay you a penny for interfering with our movements." And Fred expressed his opinion in so emphatic a manner that Big Mike could not fail to understand him.

Big Mike's face looked dark and lowering as he heard these words, but still he managed to ask, —

"Do you tell me that ye ain't got no bills that can be turned into gold at the banks in Dublin?"

"All of our bills of exchange are on board the steamer.

We brought on shore only enough money to pay our expenses in Ireland."

"And is it the truth ye is tellin' me?"

"Certainly. Do you dare to suppose that we would tell an untruth?"

The Fenian uttered a curse, a roar of disappointment.

"To think that we should be after all this trouble for nothin'! But it's the worse for ye," he added, as a fierce look entered his eyes. "The buys will be furious when they understand that they will make nothing by this night's work. They was so sure that they had four hed sinters in their hands, that I don't know what they will do. It's little power I shall have to protect ye."

"We can protect ourselves if we had weapons," answered Fred, a little proudly.

"Yes, I s'pose so; but ye see ye hasn't the weepins, and so it's no use to talk in that manner."

"But if you are so friendly, you could get them for us," I remarked.

"And so turn agin my own buys, hey? No, I'll not do it."

"Not even if we had some gold to pay you for your trouble?"

"Produce the gold, and then I'll talk wid ye," was the response; and I saw a cunning look of expectation light up the man's face, and I had no doubt in my own mind that we could buy our escape if we had money enough on hand to do so.

"We have but few sovereigns with us, Mike," I said, "but I'll tell you what we'll do. Let us out of this cave, and guide us to some place where we can take the cars for Dublin, and then you shall have ten pounds in gold. How does that suit you?"

"It don't suit me. The buys will be more mad than ten pounds, now I tell yer."

"Well, what do you want?" Fred asked.

"One hundred pounds, in gold, and devil a penny less."

"We will see you —"

Fred was about to utter an oath, but he checked himself.
"You won't do it?" Mike asked.

"No, sir."

"Thin you'll stay here some days, or else the buys may get mad like, and take the power out of my hands, and if they do, it will be bad for yer. Don't blame me, though, for I'd stood yer friend at all times, provided ye made it an object. But we won't talk any more: I'm sleepy; so go back to yer straw while I take a nap."

The giant took a long drink of whiskey, and threw himself upon the ground before the fire, and in a few minutes was snoring; and then, by the dim fire-flame, I saw the old woman who acted as cook crawl from a heap of sacks, cautiously approach the snoring Fenian, and stand over him as if to be certain that he was asleep. When she was assured that he was not pretending, she crept towards us, and laying one of her claws on Fred's arm, motioned for him to keep silent.

CHAPTER XIII.

A PLAN FOR AN ESCAPE. — SENTINELS AND WHISKEY. — SECURING MUSKETS. — A STRUGGLE. — A SENTINEL ON THE WATCH.

The movements of the old woman were so singular that Fred and I were a little startled, for we did not know but that she meant to either rob or murder us. But as soon as she laid her claw on Fred's arm, and put her other claw on her lips, I suspected that she had some scheme in her mind that related to our welfare.

Rover had his ideas on that point, however, and did not manifest that cordiality to the woman's advances which one would have supposed. He knew his master's taste, I imagine, and did not understand how we could tolerate, near us, so hideous a female. Had a pretty girl come towards us, the dog would not have growled or shown his teeth.

In the mean time Hopeful was snoring and dreaming of the pleasures of Paris, and Murden was concocting, in his sleep, plans by which Australia could be made a great nation, provided he had a seat in the cabinet, and an unlimited amount of the people's money to expend on internal improvements, and sheep-raising.

As for the queen's officer, Maurice, he was so disgusted with the world and the Fenians, that he was dreaming of the time when the latter would be extinct, and he would have command of a regiment. Perhaps the whiskey which he had drank might have inspired his ambition and disgust at the same time.

"Hist," said the old woman, in real melodramatic style, as she laid a hand on Fred's arm. "Don't ye spake, darlin', or make noise enough to wake the big blackguard what is sleepin' by the fire. Do ye listen to me now?"

"Yes, what is it?"

"Do ye mind that I'm yer friend, now?"

"Yes, I know that you are," returned Fred.

"Will, then pay attention to me, or by the holy St. Patrick, ye never was in more danger than ye is at the present time. Do ye mind that, now?"

"Explain to us what you mean, mother."

At the word mother, the old woman uttered a whine that was loud enough to awaken a dozen ordinary men. But the Fenians were sound sleepers, and under the influence of whiskey at the same time, so that considerable noise was required to start them.

"For Heaven's sake don't utter such a shout as that again," begged Fred. "Say what you have to in a low tone, and we will listen."

"But ye look so much like him when they sent him across the water; and he, the noble buy, only took one shape jist because he was hungry. O, hoh!"

She commenced rocking her body back and forth, which

was a signal that some tall howling might be expected unless she was checked before her grief got the start of her discretion.

"D———n," muttered Fred, and took hold of her arm and shook her until her gums rattled in her head, as they grated against each other.

This treatment, severe as it was, had the desired effect, for the old lady ceased her moaning, and spoke up rather sharp to her particular friend:—

"Let go me arm," she said. "What do ye mane by makin' yer fingers mate in the flesh in that manner? It will be all black and blue in the mornin', and a sight to see."

I thought of the smoke and dirt on her arm, and wondered how a bruise could be discovered through the coating that the flesh had received in the months that she had lived in the cave. As far as her face and hands were concerned, they did not look as though they had seen water for many weeks.

The old lady seemed hurt in her feelings as well as in her flesh, at Fred's treatment, for she sat on the straw rubbing her arm and muttering at the same time, and it needed a few kind words on Fred's part to bring her up to her former mark of kindness.

"Don't take offence, mother," my friend said. "You know how much I like you, and how kind you have been to me. Come, be a good soul, and let me know what you want of us."

After a moment's more grumbling the old woman thought that she had made fuss enough; so she turned once more to Fred.

"My dear boy," she said, "I heard all that you told that big brute, and I blaves yer. Ye must lave this place as soon as ye can, for it ain't safe for yer to be here. They is bad men all round yer, and they'll take yer money and yer blood and think nothin' of it. Kape the dog still, or he'll wake some of 'em, although they has taken enough whiskey to make 'em slape for a wake."

I checked Rover, and the old woman, after taking breath, continued, —

"It's little I cared for all what come here, afore I seed you. But 'cos you look like one what I loved I'll help yer, and so spite Big Mike. Now listen to me, and pay attention to what I has to say. Unless ye give the devils goold, they'll kape ye here and starve ye for a wake. I've seed 'em do it, so I know. They allers make a raise somehow."

"Then we might as well leave while they are asleep," Fred said. "What is to prevent us from going at this moment?"

"The Fenians what is outside on the watch would stop yer, and bring yer back. They has men stationed all along to give warnin' in case the sojers or the palers come near. Now, do yer think ye could get past 'em, if I took care of the gossoon what is at the mouth of the cave?"

"Yes," answered Fred, without the least hesitation. "We need but directions to the nearest town, and then we can take care of ourselves."

"Well, listen to me. Do ye mind, now, that ye must kape a lookout all the time for Fenians, for they will start up in all directions, and ax who ye is, and all that. When ye lave this place, jist turn to the right, and go up the gorge till ye come to a big cross, and there ye will find a path that will take ye over the mountains, and to the town of Athone. There's sojers there, and they will take care of ye if ye axes 'em to do so. Do ye mind, now?"

"Yes; we will recollect all that you have told us. Is there anything more?"

"Only this. If ye should meet the Fenians on the watch, and they should ax ye who ye is, jist answer 'em. 'For Erin,' and they will let ye pass. But if they shouldn't, say 'The Fanians is alive,' and may be they'll let ye pass If they don't, ye must be men and get past 'em at any rate. Now make blave sleep, while I 'tend to the gossoons who is outside."

She left us and went to the entrance of the cave, and in a short time returned with two fellows whom we had seen in the cellar in Queenstown. They were armed with muskets and pistols, and appeared to be wide awake as to their duties; for they first looked us all over to see that we were asleep; and finding that our eyes were closed, and that we did not move, they turned their attention to Big Mike, but he was snoring most devotedly; so they were assured that he slept. The others they did not appear to care for.

"Be quick, old woman, for we must go back to our posts," one of the men whispered. "Let us have the whiskey, and no delay about it."

"Faith, there's no hurry," she answered him. "You can stay here till mornin', and who'll be the wiser for it? Here, drink; and there's more where it come from."

She handed them a noggin that must have contained a quart of whiskey, and they attacked it like men determined to vanquish it, or die in the attempt.

First one took a long swig, and then the other; and then the first one did not appear satisfied, so he finished what whiskey there was left in the noggin, and then looked at the old woman in a reproachful sort of manner, as though she was alone to blame for the rapid disappearance of the liquor.

"Ye will take jist another sip — won't ye?" asked the woman.

The fellows hesitated, looked at each other, at the fire, at their guns, and then concluded that they would just wet their lips, and no more.

The woman had accomplished her object, and I saw a grin steal over her face, and even crackle the dirt that was enamelled on her cheeks. She had induced them to so far forget their duty that they were anxious for a second pull at the liquor, and while waiting for her to draw it, sat down on the floor of the cave, with strong manifestations of singing or quarrelling.

"Here is more of the same kind," the woman said, and handed them the whiskey; and before the noggin was emptied, she pointed to the entrance of the cave, and made motions for us to take our departure while she attended to the two sentinels.

In a quiet way we managed to awaken Murden and Hopeful, and to explain to them what we were about. They were too well accustomed to bush life to manifest the least surprise at our information, and, without a word, they prepared to follow our lead.

"I can't go without those guns," whispered Fred. "They will be of more use to us than the Fenians;" and, without waiting for a reply, he crawled along on his hands and knees to the spot where the weapons were lying.

We watched his course with considerable anxiety; for if his movements were discovered, an alarm would be given, and we should suffer by a closer imprisonment. Once, just as Fred laid a hand on the stock of a gun, one of the Fenians turned his head and looked straight at Fred, and we certainly thought that he was discovered; but, luckily, the light from the fire was rather dim, and the whiskey had so affected the fellow's eyes, that he was uncertain whether he saw a live man or a shadow.

For a moment he stared at Fred, but the latter did not move, or appear to breathe; so the Fenian supposed that he must be mistaken, and accordingly once more turned his attention to the whiskey, which he loved more than he did his disagreeable duties.

As soon as the fellow's eyes were turned towards the old woman and the spirit, Fred renewed his labors. Quietly and cautiously he moved the gun until he was enabled to hand it to us without noise or attracting attention. Then he fished for the other one; but here he met with some little difficulty, for the owner of the musket had placed his foot on the barrel, and did not seem disposed to move it in a hurry.

This set Fred studying out a plan to make the fellow move his foot and free the musket, and he soon hit on one, although it was a dangerous experiment, and such as but few men would have adopted. Taking a pin from some portion of his dress, he inserted it in the calf of the Feni an's leg, and in an instant up went the heavy foot, and down went a heavy hand to the spot where the pin had entered; but unfortunately the stupid replaced his foot once more on the gun as firm as ever.

We all wanted to laugh at the scene, and should have done so had our position been less precarious. As it was, we smothered our inclination, and once more watched the play which was going on.

Fred was not in the least disheartened at his failure. He was too firm a piece of humanity to be baffled at one defeat, so renewed the attack as soon as he thought it safe to do so.

"Holy St. Patrick!" cried the Irishman, in a tone of great indignation, as he raised his foot and put one hand on the place where the pin-point had entered.

He rubbed his leg, covered with the tight, thick stocking of the country, and then muttered, in a half-drunken tone, —

"Ah, but the flays is hungry to-night, the way they bite one! It's a monster I has on me leg, and he's suckin' the lifeblood out of me. Whoop, but he's a bill like a nadle, now, I tell yer!"

We were compelled to stuff some portion of our clothing in our mouths to keep from laughing; and that wretched Hez did giggle a little, making just noise enough to attract attention.

"What's that?" asked one of the Fenians, as the suppressed giggles struck on his ear.

He turned his head to look towards us; but the old woman came to our rescue in an instant.

"Sure," she said, "a slapin' man can snore, can't he, widout frightening yer out of yer wits? Don't ye hear 'em, or do ye care more for the whiskey that I holds in my hand?" And the old lady put it under the nose of the suspicious man, who snuffed the liquor, and no longer thought of sleeping men and their noises.

He put the noggin to his mouth, and drank like a person who was thirsty; and while his companion was regarding his proceedings with some little show of anxiety, for fear that the noggin would be emptied before it left his mouth, Fred removed the second musket from its place, and passed it over to us, and then motioned that we must be ready to leave the cave at once.

Quietly we arose to our feet, and stole to the door, waving the old woman an adieu, as a token of our friendship and gratitude for her aid. She uttered a low-toned howl as she saw Fred disappear; but the Fenians supposed that it was only an encouragement to drink, so did not turn their faces towards us, as we feared they would do.

In another moment we were in the open air, and found that it was starlight, cool and still. We remembered the directions which the old woman had given us, and were about to find our way through the gorge, when some one laid a heavy hand on Fred's shoulder, and a strange voice said,—

"Don't ye be in sich a hurry, gintlemen. I wants a word wid ye."

We stopped and looked at the fellow, and saw that he was one of the party who had taken us from the train, so knew that his intentions were far from being pacific.

"What do you want?" Fred asked, in a short, curt manner.

"Nothin', unless yer honors has a handful of goold that yer honors would like to bestow on a desarving buy."

"We have no gold to give away," was the reply, and then Fred made a motion to move on; but the Fenian held to his coat, and did not relish the idea of being thus shaken off.

"Sure yer honors has a few pieces that yer honors does not want," the man whined.

"Not a single piece but that we know how to employ."

"Ye had better;" and the Fenian spoke in a threatening tone.

"We can't waste our time with the fellow," muttered Murden. "Come on."

"Look at me for a moment," the Fenian said. "I know

ye is lavin' the cave while Big Mike is slapin', and I'm not the buy to say a word agin it if I is paid a little somethin' fair for my trouble. Come, say ten sovereigns, and I shut my eyes. Divil a cent less."

He laid one hand on Fred's collar, a little rough, perhaps, for the purpose of enforcing attention; but the next moment the fellow was on his back, laid there by a blow from the nervous arm of my friend, who had a fist as hard as iron.

"Quick!" cried Fred, as the fellow struck the ground. "We must gag and bind him, so that he can't give an alarm. Who has a spare handkerchief?"

"I have," responded Hopeful, "but it ain't none too clean. My cold—"

"Never mind your cold. Give me the handkerchief. It must go into his mouth, to keep his tongue from waggin'. Now, then, a cord. Who has one?"

"Here is what you want," replied Murden. "I always carry such things about me. An Australian habit, you know. Let me bind him. I can do it better than you, having had experience. O Lord! when I think of the cusses I've slipped the irons on in Victoria, it almost makes me wish that I was back there, and once more on the police force. Ah, you needn't kick, for it's no use."

The last remark was addressed to our prisoner, who began to manifest symptoms of rebellion when he felt the cords cutting his legs, as they were drawn together too tight for comfort.

All of this work had been done without the least noise or confusion; and although we were not more than twenty feet from the cave, yet those in it had not heard the struggle.

"There," cried Murden, as he arose from his task, "now I think we can move on. The fellow will be found in the morning, and released."

"Good by, Pat," said Fred. "The next time you want gold, you had better apply to somebody else besides American head centres. Give our regards to Big Mike." And with these words we once more resumed our march through the ravine, stumbling over stones and into holes the moment we left the path, which was far from being distinct, even by the aid of starlight.

We did not meet any one until we were a mile from the cave, and when we were looking the hardest for the cross which the old woman had told us was to be used as a guide-board in shaping our course for the little hamlet of Athone.

All at once, when we least expected it, some one stood in our path, musket in hand.

"Halt there!" the stranger said, in a tone that meant something. "Tell me who ye is, or I'll fire."

"Why don't you ask for the password, you stupid?" Murden replied, and advanced towards the sentinel.

"Well, thin, give it to me, and be quick about it, for by the Cove of Cork, me musket is burnin' to go off."

"Let it burn, but save your powder, for you know that we are all for Erin."

"And what else has ye to say for yerselves?" the sentinel asked, in a tone that was not quite as fierce.

"Only this; that the Fenians are alive."

"And by the powers ye may well say that, when four hed sinters come all the way from 'Merica with lots of goold, to help us poor fellers in the cause. Do ye know where they is now?"

"O, they are in the cave," Fred answered, for he saw that the sentinel did not recognize us.

"And atin' and drinkin', I s'pose?" the Fenian asked, in a doleful tone, which showed how much he would have liked a hand in that line.

"Yes, the whiskey is flowing free, and as for the eating, it is most beautiful. Meat and steaming hot potatoes."

"And me here, and dying for something to drink and ate; and I s'pose when mornin' comes, there won't be a drop or a morsel left for the gossoons what has been on duty all night. Faith, this ain't the kind of treatment I expected, at all at all, when I jined the Fenians."

"O you will find enough left for a dozen men," Fred

said. "If you don't, we will see that you have your share of the good things that we bring to the cave in the morning."

The sentinel was about to express his thanks in choice brogue, when his attention was attracted by a light on the side of the mountain, in the direction we had just left, and apparently somewhere near the cave.

Once, twice, three times the light flashed up and disappeared. It was meant as a signal, that was evident; and the sentinel so understood it, for he muttered to himself some words that we did not understand, and then spoke.

"Did ye see it?" he asked.

"What?"

"The fire signal."

"Yes, we saw it."

"And do ye read it like meself?"

"How do you read it?" Murden replied, in his usual non-committal style.

"Why, it says, just as plain as words, that the prisoners have escaped, and that we sentinels must be on the lookout for 'em."

"You have read the signals right," Murden replied. "We are glad to see that you are so attentive to duty, and will speak to Big Mike of your faithfulness. We are in search of the fellows who escaped, and hope to cut them off in case they get over the mountains; so you see we can't stop long to talk with you."

"Yes; but —"

The fellow had a suspicion that we were not just right, but he did not know how to express himself; so, while he was making up his mind, we walked off as fast as possible, but had not got more than twenty paces from him when he came running after us, and shouted, —

"Look ahere! who in the devil's name is ye, anyhow?"

"Answer the signal, and don't bother us with any more questions," replied Murden, a little roughly, and with some assumption of authority; and on we went, as fast as our legs could carry us, and in a few minutes had the satisfaction of seeing that the sentinel had attended to Murden's hints, and had kindled his signal fire to warn all the rest of the Fenians in the valley or gorge, that the prisoners had escaped from the cave, and must be recaptured as soon as possible.

"On we go," whispered Murden; "and may the Lord keep the sentinels out of our course!"

"Amen," we replied, and pressed on as fast as possible; and in a few minutes the stone cross which the old woman had told us of came in sight, but under its shadow stood a man with a musket in his hand.

We had met another Fenian sentinel, who was wide awake, and had seen us on the run. He had been warned by the signals that the prisoners had escaped, and were to be recaptured. We halted, and resolved to temporize before proceeding to violence.

CHAPTER XIV.

CAPTURING AN OUTPOST. — ON THE MOUNTAINS. — THE HUT IN THE VALLEY. — THE STILL AND ITS OWNER. — A SURPRISE.

For a moment we stood regarding the sentinel, and he looked at us in silence, as much surprised as we were at the unexpected meeting. Then Murden stepped forward, and assumed that commanding tone which was so natural to him.

"Who are you that is on duty here?" he asked.

"Faith," was the answer, "that's more'n I know meself. Sometimes they calls me Pat McKenny, and at other times a Fenian thafe of the world."

"And which are you best known by?"

"Faith, if there was a shape near me and I was hungry,

I think they might call me a thafe and welcome, as long as I had some of the mate."

"And yet you are a good Fenian, I trust?" Murden continued.

"You can well belave that; and it reminds me that the signal says I'm to look sharp for escaped prisoners. God save all here; I hope you are not some of 'em."

"No; we are on the lookout for the men. Be sure and not let them escape you."

"Faith, then," answered the man, with a chuckle, "I'd better hold on to you till some one can tell me that ye is all right. So jist squat on the ground till I'm told that ye is friends."

The fellow was not so stupid as we had supposed. He had suspicions that we were not all right, and was determined to keep us until such time as some one should prove that we were of the proper stamp.

"But, Pat," said Murden, "you know —"

"I know that ye must squat down on the ground," replied Pat. "Ye may talk all that ye want to, but don't do it standin' thar if ye plase. It is inconvanient to all of us."

"You blockhead, do you mean to say that you want us to remain here until some one comes from the cave?"

"Them's me very words," was the reply.

At this moment Fred dropped to the ground, and, snake-like, worked his way out of sight. I suspected that he had gone on some important errand, and that he required time to accomplish it; so when Murden failed to find words to express his indignation at the Fenian's folly, I helped him to a few choice epithets, and so the conversation continued until I saw Fred's form rise up in the background; and then came a grand explosion of rage, as Fred's stout arms pinned Pat's to his side.

The musket which the Fenian carried dropped to the ground, and was quietly picked up by Murden; and then the owner of it uttered some doleful comments at the manner in which he had been entrapped and disarmed.

"I don't call it fair," he said. "It wau't mating a man tace to face, as all true-hearted sons of Erin will do. Well, now that I'm down, what do ye mane to do wid me?"

"Will you let us pass, and say no more about it?" Murden asked.

"Faith, ye has me permission to do as ye plase. I'm powerless now to detain yer. Go 'long wid yer; I don't say that ye has spoken to me."

"And you will promise not to inform any one of the direction in which we go?"

"Yes; I'll promise anything that ye want. Now, does that satisfy ye?"

We informed him that it did, so released him, and once more hastily proceeded on our way; but we were not more than ten yards from the fellow when we heard the report of a musket, and an ounce ball whizzed past our heads, sent after us by our late captive, who thus reminded us that promises in Ireland were not always to be relied on.

We all stopped; and the impulse of the moment was to return and take vengeance on the fellow; but we recollected that he had only done his duty, and that we should waste time if we sought to find him in the dark.

Besides, in answer to the Fenian's musket came another report up the glen, and in the direction we were pursuing. It showed that the sentinels were awake and on the lookout for our party, and that if we would escape the net that surrounded us, we had but little time to lose.

"Forward!" cried Murden. "The Fenians are on our track, and we must shake them off."

We found the path that led over the mountain to Athone, and up this we pressed for a few rods, and then halted under the shadow of some trees for the purpose of consulting in low tones on the next movements, so as to avoid outlaying Fenians.

"We shall be certain to stumble on one or more sentinels," Fred said, after we had listened to see if we could hear any one in pursuit, "if we follow this path. Now, the question is, can we hope to find the hamlet of Athone, if we leave it and pick our way over the mountain?"

"We must try it," answered Murden. "There is no other course left for us. We may as well risk our lives one way as another. Come on. Time is precious to us."

Murden, who was a good mountaineer, led the way, and we followed him in single file. We turned to the left, from the narrow path, and scrambled over rocks and ground that did not present a good foothold; and more than once we came near rolling down precipices that were a hundred feet deep.

When we met such obstructions to our course, we would turn aside and follow the edge of the precipice, until we came to a place where we could descend, and by this method we were enabled to cross the mountain and reach its base just as daylight began to show itself. Then, tired, hungry and thirsty, we sat down and rested, and lighted our pipes.

"Well, of all the horrible tramps that man ever endured, I believe we have had the worst to-night," cried Maurice, whose life in the army had not tended to keep his muscles in good order.

"You don't call this much of a walk — do you?" asked Hopeful. "Ah, you should see some of the mountains that I've tramped over in New Hampshire. This is merely a mole-hill, compared to them ere."

"Did you ever walk over them in the dark?" asked Maurice.

"No, not exactly; but then you know they are so high that a feller what goes up one, has daylight during the whole twenty-four hours, so there's no 'casion for him to walk in the dark."

"What a whopper of a mountain!" Maurice replied; and then we all took a sip from Fred's pocket-flask, and resumed our journey.

For an hour we toiled on, in hopes of once more striking the path which was to lead us to Athone; but although we looked from the top of the highest mountain, yet not a sign of a road did we discover, or anything in the shape of a village, except a mud hut at the foot of the hill on which we stood.

The sun was just rising when we made this discovery. At any other time we might have paused to admire the brilliant scene, but we were too tired, hungry and dirty to stop for sentiment.

"We must make for the hut, and see if we can't procure a guide," the lieutenant said.

"And breakfast," muttered Hopeful.

"Don't be too sure of that, my friend," Maurice said. "If you are very hungry, don't anticipate too much, for the reaction will be terrible. If you obtain a potato and a drink of water, you will be fortunate."

"Well, let us hope for better things," Fred said; and down the hill we plunged, and in the course of an hour or more, we reached the hut.

The only sign of life that we could discover, as we approached the hut, was some smoke making its escape from one of the windows, for the want of a chimney; and a gaunt pig that was rooting and eating grass-roots, for the want of a better breakfast.

"We shall find some one at home, thank Heaven," Maurice said; "and if we don't, the Lord have mercy on that pig."

"Amen," cried four hungry men; and they cast savage glances at the wild-looking porcine.

We quietly approached the hut. The pig was so astonished at our appearance that he curled his tail in fright, and ran to the shelter of a small bog, grunting disaffection all the way. Perhaps his instinct told him that we were desperate men, and capable of desperate deeds in the eating line, if our appetites were once aroused.

The flight of the pig startled some chickens from a bog-hole, where they were scratching for a living. This was so encouraging that we were disposed to give three cheers, and would have done so, had we not been too tired. However, we marked the flight of the biddies, and resolved that some of them should die, if money could purchase their death.

We approached the door of the hut. It was off its hinges, and stood against the mud wall, so we had no trouble in looking in; and there we saw a man and woman seated over a kettle of steaming potatoes, and eating them in the most primitive manner, without the aid of knives and forks, or even plates, and I think that they did not stop to scrape the skins off.

"God save all here," cried Murden, entering the hut, and so astonishing the couple that they managed to kick over the kettle between them; and I think the old woman, who was dirty and smoke-dried, received a little of the hot water, in which were the potatoes, on her foot, for she uttered a howl and a blessing at the same time, and then sat down on the ground, and rubbed the member with considerable energy.

In the mean time the master of the hut had stood staring at us, so lost in astonishment that he could not find words to reply to our salutation; and it was not until we had again spoken to him, that he managed to stammer out some kind of a welcome.

"God save all here," repeated Murden.

"The same to you," was the Irishman's reply; at the same time he did not look as though he meant what he said, and I saw astonishment and distrust in his eyes.

"And what is the cause of this visit, yer honors?" asked the proprietor of the hut. "Biddy, don't be sated there a rubbin' yer foot, when it will do yer no good. Git up and find some sates for their honors."

The wife, as we supposed she was, here arose, and found four or five stools, on which we were glad to seat ourselves and rest; and then we looked at the smoking potatoes, and wished we had something better.

"Pat," said Murden, with one of his most engaging smiles, "how far is it to Athone?"

"And who told yer my name was Pat, to be sure?"

"O, we guessed it," was the reply.

"Faith, then, couldn't yer jist as easily guess yer way to Athone?" And here the impudent fellow laughed at his own wit, and that wretched Hopeful joined him, as a sort of encouragement.

"Come, come, Pat, or whatever your name is," replied Murden, "don't let us fool each other. We have lost our way, are hungry, and would like to reach Athone as soon as possible."

"And ye look hungry," was the consoling remark. "Faith, if ye has been in the mountains all night long, I don't blame ye for being empty. But it's little I has here. A poor man like meself don't have a house overflowing with all the comforts of the land."

"And why do you live here all by yourself?" asked Maurice. "It must be hard work obtaining food at such a distance from town."

The owner of the hut gave the lieutenant a sharp glance, as if to take his measure, and then replied,—

"Faith, it's as well to starve here as in the cities and towns. I has me pratie-patch, and me little piece of bog for turf, and what more can I want?"

"Then what do you do for whiskey? If you could manage to let us have a drop, we should know how to pay for it," Maurice hinted.

"Whiskey," cried the Irishman, in astonishment. "Devil a drop of whiskey has I seen or tasted since I was in Athone, two weeks since."

This was a severe blow to Murden and Maurice, and in fact all of us, for we felt the need of stimulants after all our fatigue.

"Athone is ten miles from here, you say," Fred remarked. "In which direction?"

The Irishman stepped to the door of the hut and pointed in a direction directly opposite to that in which we supposed Athone to lie.

"Ye can reach it in two hours' time if ye walk fast enough," our host said. "'Tis but a trifle. Ye cross two mountains and a valley, and thar ye is. Ye know McLaughlin's house — don't ye?"

No, we did not know anything about McLaughlin's house. We had never heard of it.

"Well, then, ye know McGuire's whate-field, near the pratie-patch?"

No, we did not know anything about McGuire's fields. The Irishman cast a look of contempt at us, as though we were most too ignorant for notice.

"Faith," he said, "I don't think ye know much about Ireland, at any rate. I thought most any one knew McGuire's land. Where did ye come from, now? Answer me that, will ye?"

"Never you mind where we come from," was the answer. "Just get us something to eat. Kill two or three of your chickens and put them on the fire. We will pay you for them."

The Irishman looked as though he doubted that assertion.

"Show us the color of yer money," he said; and when each of us exhibited several sovereigns, the man's face no longer wore a doubtful expression. He spoke to his wife in Irish, and the old lady brightened up from her fog of dirt, and even made an attempt to smile; but of course it was a lamentable failure. There was no breaking through that crust of smoke and grease, which had been years in accumulating.

But the sight of money soon made the Irishman and his wife stir around, and prepare us some breakfast. First they induced several of the chickens to enter the hut, by a display of cold potatoes; and when the biddies were captured, our hostess wrung their necks with great composure, and threw them into a pot of hot water. When they were taken from the water they were entirely nude of feathers, and needed but dressing to prepare them for the coals of the turf.

While breakfast was being prepared, we left the hut to avoid the smoke; but our host kept us company, and watched our movements as carefully as if he had been employed to play the part of a spy.

"Do you ever see any Fenians in these parts?" I asked the Irishman, as we started towards the place where he cut his turf.

"Divil a Fanian," was the reply. "Sure what should they come in this direction for? There's no one here but me and the old woman, and we know nothin' about the Fanians, and care less."

"I don't think you'll find it pleasant walkin' this way, at all at all," our host said, when he found that we were strolling towards a hill-side, with no particular object in view. "The bog is wet jist out thar, and is dangerous to walk on."

Now, where we were at the time the ground was hard and dry, so we saw no occasion for the warning. I looked up and saw that Fred was revolving some subject in his mind, so I spoke to him in French, and said, —

"Our host seems quite anxious to keep us close to the hut. What do you suppose is his reason?"

"I have been thinking of the matter," answered Fred, speaking in French, to the evident distress of the Irishman, who could not understand a word that was said, consequently felt that we were talking of him.

"And what is the result of your thoughts?" I asked.

"Well, to tell you the truth, I believe that there is a whiskey still close to us, and that this fellow is the proprietor of it. If he was inclined, he could give us a drink without much trouble."

"By Jove, I think the same. Let us push on and make search for the treasure;" and giving a hint to our companions of our object, we strolled along, in spite of the Irishman's objections, and soon came to the hill-side.

"Ah, now, don't ye hear the old woman callin' ye that the chickens is ready? Come to the house, and don't be wanderin' about in the bit of bog."

"Pat," I said, "we shan't return until we find some

whiskey. We know that there is a lot near, for we smell it in the air."

Pat uttered a howl of grief, and protested by all the saints in the calendar, that there was not a pint of whiskey this side of Athone; but we did not believe him, and after a sharp examination we pulled aside some dried grass, and there we saw the entrance to a cave in the hill-side, and the strong smell that issued therefrom proved that we had hit upon one of the numerous secret stills of Ireland.

"O Pat," I said, "how could you tell us such a shocking lie as to say that you did not know where whiskey was to be found?"

For only a moment was the fellow confused. He scratched his head, and an idea into it at the same time.

"Faith," he said, "it's little I know that this was here. I niver thought it, by the powers. It must have been owned by bad men what lived here years ago."

We entered the cave and found the still in working order, and a fire in the proper place. But when we pointed out these things to the Irishman, he swore that he knew nothing about it, and continued to swear to that effect, although we assured him that we were not gaugers, or in any way connected with the police.

Our assurances, however, did not dispel the suspicions that the man entertained, and in his own mind he looked upon his still as lost to him forever. He had run it for several years, and made a living by it, and no one had suspected him in that dreary, out-of-the-way place, for but few visitors stumbled upon his hut in the course of the year.

"Come, Pat," I said, as we helped ourselves to a measure of the regular mountain dew, "don't look so disconsolate. We will pay for all that we drink, and agree to say nothing about the still. We have nothing to do with the peelers."

"And ye will next tell me that man has nothin' to do with the sojers," Pat said, pointing to Maurice. "Sure, it's many times I've seed him at the head of his red-coats in Queenstown. Ye can't chate me wid him, I know."

We could not deny this; but then we explained that Maurice was not in search of stills at the time, and would hold his tongue regarding this particular one. Pat pretended to be satisfied, but I had some doubt of his sincerity, although I said nothing to my friends.

We returned to the hut in the best of spirits, ready for breakfast. The old woman received us with a savage look of disgust at our inquisitiveness, for she knew that we had found out their secret. If she had had arsenic in the hut, she would have dosed the chickens with it, I have no doubt, and thus ended us and her anxiety at the same time. But as she did not happen to have any poison, we were saved for some other fate, good or bad.

We ate the chickens with as much relish as if they had come from the hands of a French cook, and after disposing of the fowl, attacked the potatoes, and ate of them until hunger was satisfied; and then came the desire for sleep, for we were awful tired with our tramps and exciting adventures during the past twenty-four hours.

"Pat, can you furnish us with some straw, so that we can lie down and rest until afternoon?" I asked.

To my surprise, the Irishman said that he could and would give us all that we wanted; and he took half a dozen armfuls from a stack, and spread it in the hut, and on it we stretched our limbs, and soon went to sleep.

I was awakened by the growling of Rover. I sat up and looked around. All my companions were asleep, and the Irishman and his wife were not in the hut; neither could I hear them outside. I was so sleepy and tired that I only spoke to Rover, and then down went my head, and I was again asleep in less than five minutes, only to be awakened by Rover's licking my face.

I knew that the dog meant something this time; so I got up and walked to the door and looked out, and there I saw a sight that was not calculated to encourage five unarmed men.

CHAPTER XV.

A SURPRISE. — A PROPOSITION. — DEATH OR GOLD. — HEAVY DEMANDS. — THE ROPE AND THE VICTIM. — TERMS ACCEPTED. — AN INTERRUPTION.

THE first thought that flashed across my mind, as I looked out of the door, was, how we could escape from the hut without detection; but a moment's consideration satisfied me that retreat was impossible. The hut was surrounded, and at the head of the column of advancing Fenians was no less a man than Big Mike in person; and — confound him! — he and his companions were armed with muskets, clubs, and scythes fastened to poles.

The Fenians, I supposed, had tracked us from their secret cave to the hut, and for a moment I wondered how they had managed to do so; but just as I was about to turn away and awake my companions, I caught sight of Pat, the owner of the hut, and I had no doubt but that he had been to the Fenians' rendezvous, and then led them to our stopping-place, thinking that we could be captured while fast asleep.

"Up, friends!" I shouted, in a tone loud enough to awaken my companions. "The enemy is upon us!"

The sleepers sprang to their feet, and came to the door to see what was the matter. A glance was enough to satisfy them that once more we were likely to fall into the hands of the Fenians.

"What shall we do?" asked Murden and Maurice in a breath. "Shall we make the best defence that we can? We have two muskets, and can do some little damage with them."

But a glance towards the place where we had left the muskets showed that they were gone. Pat had removed them while we slept, for fear we should damage his friends' consequently we were entirely defenceless, not even having a good-sized knife in our pockets.

"We must submit," said Maurice, in a bitter tone. "There is no use of our standing up and fighting those fellows with naked hands. There is no show, and we may as well surrender."

We agreed that such a course was the best one that could be adopted, and we felt a little humiliated to think that such old Australian bushrangers as ourselves should be caught in such a trap, like a rat, without a chance to retreat. We could only look at each other, and smile a ghastly sort of smile, and wondered where our wits were when we went to sleep.

When the Fenians were within ten or fifteen yards of the hut, they halted for a parley, and then Big Mike hailed us.

"Now, look here, gintlemen," Mike said; "it's no use for yer to offer violence, and kick up a row. We is strong enough to lick the life out of yer, and ye should be sinsible, and know it."

"We do know it, and surrender," Fred said. "It's useless to resist when we have no weapons to defend ourselves."

The Fenians uttered a yell, and charged towards the hut, and the next instant we were in their hands, and Pat was dancing around us like a madman, and asking if we didn't want to poke our noses into some more secret stills, and then go and inform of them, like mean peelers that we were.

"Well," said the Fenian leader, as our hands were tied behind our backs, and he surveyed us with considerable satisfaction; "ye thought ye could play us a Yankee trick —did ye?"

"We left your cave, if that is what you mean," Fred said.

"And ye didn't wait for to take lafe of yer dear friends —did ye?" Mike asked.

"No, we did not."

"So ye thought ye would snake off while I took a nap afore the fire."

"We left the cave while you were asleep, but did not sneak off, as you suggested," was Fred's reply.

"And ye didn't play Yankee tricks on the sintinels — did ye?"

Here there was a howl of indignation from the Fenians who surrounded us, and I thought I recognized in those who made the most noise the men whom we had tricked while on guard.

"Now listen to me," said Big Mike, in an impressive tone. "I wants ye to tell the truth, and to shame the devil if ye can. Who helped ye out of the cave, and give ye the password? Answer that if ye will."

"Whoop! let 'em answer that!" was the general cry, and the Fenians looked some of the rage that they felt.

"We shan't reply to that question," Fred said, in a firm tone.

"Look ye," Mike exclaimed, in a passionate manner; "no man betrayed the Fenians yet, but got paid for it in the long run. Pint out the one what betrayed us, and al. will be well; but if ye don't, by the blood of the saints, one of ye shall die the death of a dog!"

We saw that the man was in earnest, and that the crew who backed him up were in earnest also; but still we hoped that the ruffian would not dare to put his threat into execution.

"We still decline to involve any one in our escape," Fred said.

"Then, by the piper that played afore Moses, one of yes dies like a dog; ye can make up yer mind to that now."

"You dare not lay hands on one of these gentlemen," Maurice said, in a tone of such indignation that all of Big Mike's rage was turned on him.

"I don't dare to, hey?" he thundered. "Who are you, that talks like that to me, the representative of the Fenians in this part of Ireland? We know you, and we knows what you has done wid yer sojers in Queenstown; and let me tell yer that not a word or a look that ye has given the past two months but what I has knowed, and now ye tell me that I don't dare to work my will on ye."

If the Fenian thought that he was likely to frighten Maurice, never was man more mistaken, for the lieutenant was as bold a fellow as could be met with in all Ireland; and while he listened to Mike's speech in all calmness, he was not in the least intimidated by it, and when the Fenian had concluded, he merely replied he supposed there wasn't a man in the whole country better able to die in the cause of duty than himself, and that if it was desirable to put him out of the way, it had better be done at once.

"By the powers, at once it shall be, then. The blood of my people calls for yer life, and don't think that they will fail to take it when I give the word."

The crowd who surrounded us uttered a howl, which showed that they were fully up to the point required for any unlawful deed. In fact, Pat had distributed to them some of his whiskey, and it was telling on them.

"For God's sake, keep quiet, Maurice," I whispered. "The men are insane, and in a short time will have no control over themselves."

"Let the ruffians do their worst," was the answer. "I will not quail if they put a rope around my neck."

Maurice did not speak low, as I intended that he should; so Big Mike heard him, and of course grew more and more enraged.

"He calls us ruffians, buys," Mike yelled. "Will we stand it?"

"No!" was the unanimous cry, and I saw by the flashing eyes that the Fenians were in earnest, if ever men were.

"A rope, a rope!" some of them yelled, and then commenced a search for one.

"You poor fools," the lieutenant said, "of what good is a rope, when not a tree is to be found near us?"

"For Heaven's sake, don't exasperate the men," Murden pleaded. "It will do you no good, and much harm, perhaps."

"D—n them, let them do as they please," was all the reply that the soldier made; and then we saw that he was lost unless something happened in the shape of a miracle to preserve him.

Pat, the owner of the house, as malignant as the worst of them, because he thought that we were detective policemen, on the lookout for just such illicit stills as he carried on, found the rope that was wanted, and put it in Big Mike's hands.

"There is the tool," he said. "Use it wisely. Down with all traters and secret spies, what tells ye one thing and does another."

Mike tossed the rope to some of his men, who were ready for it.

"Use it on the sojer," he said, "and don't be all day about it."

Some of the most drunken rushed upon Maurice, but he let the foremost Fenian have a blow on the face that sent him to the floor with a thug that showed what a hard hitter the soldier was.

"Stand back!" cried Fred, throwing himself between Maurice and the hesitating Fenians. "Let me make a proposition."

The men stopped, as though willing to talk over matters; but Maurice, whose blood was up, told them to come on and do their worst, and that he despised them because he knew they would run if he had half a dozen of his men at his back.

Of course this was rather imprudent, and Maurice would not have thought of such a course had he always remained in the police force, instead of entering the army. In the former position he would have temporized, biding his time; but now that he was a queen's officer, he could not help a little feeling of aristocracy and contempt for the unwashed people.

"Let us hear what the proposition is," Big Mike said,

as soon as Fred had spoken. "Come, we is rasonable — ain't we, buys?"

The boys responded that they were reasonable in all things, and only wanted what was right.

"Then hear me," Fred continued. "Release our friend, and let us depart unmolested, and we will give you, as soon as we can raise the money, one hundred sovereigns."

"Hang him up, buys," was Mike's reply to this liberal proposition.

"Two hundred sovereigns," Fred continued, when he found that his first proposition was rejected.

"Hang him up, buys," was all the reply that Mike ventured to make, although on the scamp's face a smile was seen, as though he knew his power, and determined to use it.

"Don't offer the blackguards a penny more," Maurice said. "You have now offered them more than I'm worth. Let the brutes do their worst. My death will be avenged — never fear."

"We'll run the risk of that. Put the rope around his neck. We'll finish one of the enemies of Ireland, at any rate."

The Fenians threw themselves upon poor Maurice, in spite of his resistance, and commenced binding his arms behind his back. If we had offered to aid him, we should have been cut to pieces with scythes, or else mangled with their muskets, loaded as they were with buck-shot, for the purpose of doing all the damage possible at one discharge.

Of course we were tempted to interfere. We could not bear to see an old and gallant friend like Maurice carried off and hung before our eyes, and we powerless to resist. But we were without arms, and the Fenians outnumbered us five to one, and powerful fellows they were, as ready for a scrimmage as we could desire; so, suppose we had determined to defend Maurice, it would have been useless on our part. We should have lost our lives, and the lieutenant would not have been better off for the sacrifice.

But we showed one thing, and that was our desire to

save the life of our friend, even if it cost us dear; and when the Fenians commenced dragging him from the hut, Fred once more interposed.

"Name your price," he said, "and save his life, for we can't stand here and see him murdered."

"Faith, now you begin to talk rasonable like. The man's life is worth somethin' to yer, after all. Perhaps it's more value to yer than to me or to him. Who knows? Come, tell us what ye'll do."

"Name your price, and let us leave for Athone at once."

"Wall, now, what do yer think he's worth — a fair price, you know? Jist enough to pay us and the buys for our trouble."

"Say five hundred pounds."

"Off wid him," cried Mike, in a burst of pretended indignation. "They is laughin' at us and our soft hearts."

"One thousand pounds," Fred cried.

"Nonsense," Maurice remarked. "I won't save my life at such a sacrifice. They shan't bleed you at that rate. Dogs that you are, take my life, but let my friends keep their money, for they worked hard enough for it."

"Then let them spend it asy," Mike returned. "Faith, there's no better cause than the Fenian cause, and there's no better men than the Fenians. Come, ye are rich 'Mericans, and can afford to pay liberal. Don't be long in thinkin' of the matter; for time is precious to us."

"Name your price and be d—d to you," rejoined Fred, who was getting cross at so much opposition.

"Wall, thin, I'll be liberal and jist, and no mistake. Plant down tin thousand pounds in goold, and the bargain is done."

"Ten thousand devils!" we all yelled, with one accord, astonished at the man's demand, which was a sum beyond our immediate control.

"Never mind me, old friends," the lieutenant said. "My life is not of much value; and as for its being worth ten thousand pounds, I don't believe it. Let them hang me and be d—d. I forbid you to think of money as a means of saving my life."

"Mike," I said to the Fenian leader, "you ain't serious in your demands — I know you ain't. We'll call this a joke, and say no more about it; but you can't think of obtaining such a sum of money. Just imagine how much ten thousand pounds really is."

"I niver was more sarious in my life," was the reply "and as for ten thousand pounds, I know it's a big pile; but then you 'Mericans never travel without a big pile. Come, jist rason a little. Here's five of ye. It's two thousand pounds apace; and that's little enough to pay for friendship — now isn't it?"

"It's more money than we can command."

"Thin it's mighty unfortunate for the soger man. I wish, for his sake, that ye was rich enough to buy his life; but as ye ain't, why, the man must die. I've said so, and I must keep my word, or lose all control of tne buys. It will amuse them, and won't hurt ye a bit."

"You're a brute," I said, in wrath at his coldness and cruelty.

"So would you be if you had lost as much as I have in the last two days. My Queenstown still has been seized by the peelers, and it's all through your means."

"How by our means?" I demanded.

"Why, our folks thought you was the four hed sinters that they was told to look out for, that was comin' from 'Merica with lots of goold and bills of exchange. Will, they was bound to hold on to yer, after they had once took charge of yer. Our folks would have seed yer pulled to pieces and trampled under foot afore they would have gin ye up to the sogers unless I had told 'em to keep quiet, and let ye go."

"Thank you for your kindness; but we don't deserve such attention at your hands."

"I know it; but then, ye see, I soon found out that ye wan't hed sinters."

"How did you find it out?" I asked.

11

"Wall, ye didn't respond to none of my signs. I tried ye wid all of 'em; but devil a bit of notice did ye take of all I did."

"Then why didn't you let us go in peace?"

"Because I wanted to make money out of ye; that's the rason. I thought there was a chance for a few pounds, and I went for it; and here I am, with the game in my own hands; and afore I parts wid ye, I shall have enough goold to pay for my still, and to lave the country, if I want to, when things get too mixed."

"Not a cent do you get from me," I responded; for I thought that the fellow was bluffing, and would not dare to carry out his programme.

"Yes, I shall."

"No, sir; not a penny."

"We'll see, my buy."

"We shall see."

"Now hear me;" and the man's face assumed as much ferocity as it could command. "I shall hang the soger man unless you comes down wid the goold. If you does, all shall go clear. If ye don't, back to the cave ye goes, and I'll take good care that none escapes; for I'll starve ye until ye do come down with the money. Now I mane what I say, and ye can lay it to yer heart that I'm in earnest;" and with these words Big Mike broke away from me, and joined those who were holding Maurice.

"Well," whispered my companions, "what does the fellow say? What does he mean?"

"Death or gold," I replied.

"Had we better combine our fortunes and pay the money?" asked Fred. "It won't ruin us; but still ten thousand pounds in gold is a large sum."

"If the rascals proceed to extremities, we must save our friend, even if we have to pay the money." And this was agreed to without a dissenting voice, Hez being as anxious as the rest of us to contribute his share of the ransom.

Big Mike waved his hand, and a malicious grin stole

over his face as he looked at us, to watch the effect of his signal. We did not respond, for the reason that we wanted to see if the Fenian leader was really in earnest, or only bluffing for the sake of obtaining our money without giving us a chance to see his hand.

The Fenians commenced hustling Maurice out of the hut. We did not say a word or offer to interfere; but when Maurice reached the door, he intimated that he wanted to exchange a word or two with us, and Mike gave him permission, under the impression, probably, that our hearts would relent if we conversed with our friend, and saw that we could save his life at a sacrifice of money.

"Good by, old friends," the lieutenant said, extending one hand as well as he was able for the bands that confined it behind his back. "I would rather have died like a man and a soldier, than been hanged by these ruffians. But my death will be revenged in good time — never fear. I would not have you gratify the fellows so much as to give them gold for my life, not even if I was assured they would act honestly by us, which I don't believe they would do. D—n them, let them do their worst."

"Have you any word that you wish to send to friends?" asked Mike. "Now is the time for yer to do it, for yer will niver, no, niver, see sunlight agin."

"Mr. Murden is acquainted with all the friends that I have," was the doomed man's answer. "When he returns to Melbourne he will tell them how I died, and for what cause. I have but few relatives, and, thank God, no wife or child to weep for me."

"Have ye done?" asked Mike.

"Yes; I have said all that I desire to," was the answer.

"Thin we'll hang yer in the most approved style. Away wid him, buys."

"Hold!" cried Fred, just as the Fenians were urging Maurice towards the ridge-pole of the hut, over which they had thrown a rope.

"We'll pay the money."

The Fenians uttered a cheer, and the cheer was responded to by the blast of a bugle, and looking around we saw a troop of cavalry trotting through the valley and advancing towards us.

CHAPTER XVI.

SURPRISED FENIANS. — THE PURSUIT. — AN ACQUAINTANCE. — FOR DUBLIN. — ANOTHER ARREST.

The blast of the bugle astonished the Fenians as much as anything could astonish them, for they no more looked for cavalry in such a place than they did for a large body of police; and when they found their cheer was responded to by a trumpet call, all present turned to look at the soldiers and see what they were, and what they wanted; so for the moment the lieutenant was forgotten. In fact, the Fenians had dropped the rope that they held, with which they intended to hang our friend, and turned their attention in another direction.

Fred, ever prompt and with presence of mind, ran to Maurice and cut the bands that confined his arms, and the soldier, furious at the treatment which he had received, snatched a musket from the hands of one of the party, who stood near him, and shouted, —

"Down on your knees, you scoundrels, and ask for mercy. Surrender, every one of you, or no quarter will be given."

"Wait till we ax for it," was the reply of Big Mike, who was still bold and defiant. "There's but thirty of 'em, buys, and we numbers forty. Will ye stand by me and drive the dogs back to their town quarters? We can do it if ye will. Remember we loses our gold if we don't."

Half a dozen of the boldest of Mike's followers responded to his appeal, but the largest portion cast anxious glances over their shoulders, to see if the way for retreat was still open. They evidently had no desire to encounter the well-disciplined soldiers of the queen's army, especially when the latter were armed with carbines and pistols, and knew how to use them.

"Cowards that ye are," hissed Mike, "I'll meet 'em and fight 'em single-handed. Ye never had so good a chance to obtain goold, and jist as it is within yer reach ye throws it away."

In the mean time the lieutenant was not idle. He had called on the Fenians to surrender, but they were too confused to pay much attention to what he said, as their eyes were on the advancing cavalry, watching its movements, and preparing to make a run for the mountains as soon as the command for a charge was given.

Suddenly Maurice broke through the circle that surrounded him, and called to the mounted men.

"Charge the cursed rascals," he shouted. "They are Fenians, and should be captured to a man."

Big Mike heard the words, and they enraged him. He was like a wild bull, disappointed and full of wrath. He was likely to lose his prisoners, and the money which he had counted on as certain, and for which he had laid all his little plans so that failure seemed impossible. At our expense he meant to be enriched and retire from active life, and when he saw the whole fabric which he had raised about to be swept away by an unexpected blow, his rage got the better of his discretion.

"Let them charge," hissed Mike. "They'll find your dead body on the ground to begin with;" and he swung his musket over his head, intending to let it fall on Maurice's neck and crush him instantly; and so he would have done, had it not been for Rover. The hound had remained wonderfully quiet, in obedience to a signal; but still he did not exactly seem to understand why he could not take a hand in the row that had been going on, and more than once he had looked at me, as much as to say that he could clean out three or four of the party if permission was but accorded to him. Fearful of his life, however, I had not given him the slightest encouragement to show his strength and courage; but when Mike swung his musket over his head, and I saw no way of saving Maurice's life, for I was some yards from him, except by the aid of the dog, I just pointed to Big Mike and uttered one simple word.

"Go," I said.

With a mighty bound Rover launched himself full at the throat of the Fenian leader, and before the musket could descend upon Maurice's head, the dog had pinned the would-be murderer and bore him to the ground.

"Halloo," cried Maurice, looking around, and for the first time suspecting his danger. "Rover is up to his old tricks, I see. I am indebted to him and his master for my life. Shake the d—d scamp, old boy; he deserves it."

But Rover had been taught different. He merely held the man to the ground, and did not offer to injure him unless he moved, and that Mike was not inclined to do after one or two experiences of Rover's temper.

"Call off the dog," said the Fenian, in a tone that showed he was not confident how the battle would terminate; but no one paid him the least attention, for just at this moment the cavalry got an idea into their heads that something wrong was going on at the hut; so the bugle sounded a charge, and on came the horsemen at a gallop.

"Whoop!" yelled the Fenians, and away they went for the mountains, as fast as their legs could carry them, dropping their guns and scythes in their headlong flight.

Three or four threw down their weapons and took refuge in the hut, as the cavalry came up, and they shouted in unmistakable terms that they surrendered.

"After them, Fitzhugh," shouted Maurice. "They're all Fenians."

The officer looked his astonishment at hearing his name called by one of our party, and then drew up and left his men to continue the pursuit.

"The devil," was the cavalry man's exclamation, as he dismounted and shook hands with Maurice. "Who would

ROVER AND THE FENIAN. — Page 166.

have thought of seeing you here with a party of Fenians?"

"I don't know who would have thought it," was the reply; "but here I am, and deuced glad to see you; for you have saved my life, or, if not that, my friends' pockets."

"How so?"

"Why, the d—d scoundrels had a rope around my neck, and it was—"

"Neck or nothing?"

"No; it was neck or ten thousand pounds."

"Whew!" whistled the cavalry man; "they put your value rather high. I hope they don't place so great an estimate on all of her majesty's officers. If they do, some of us, when captured, will have to go without ransom, I think."

"They will unless they have as kind friends as I have," replied the lieutenant. "These gentlemen, rather than see me hanged, resolved to pay the money out of their own pockets."

"The devil! It is worth while having such friends; and, let me tell you, they are rather scarce. Introduce me."

The introduction was given, and after it was over, the cavalry man saw that his soldiers had made several captures, and were coming towards the hut with their prisoners. Deeming them of little account, the officer renewed his conversation with Maurice.

"I was sent out this morning to look for you and the four head centres who escaped. I was told to patrol the country, and not to return to the barracks until I had picked up some information."

"And what sent you this way? I never was more rejoiced to see you than I am to-day."

"Well, I met a gossoon who said that he had seen a party of men going in this direction; so I followed on, but had little hope of meeting a companion in arms. Very glad I've found you, though, and hope you will do me a good turn some day or other, if I want one, although

I have no fancy for a rope around my neck. It looks too much like your money or your life."

"Count on me," was the response.

"By the way," said the cavalry man, "where are the head centres who were taken from the train with you? The lord lieutenant is awful anxious about them. He has telegraphed in all directions, and has offered some stunning rewards for them. The officer who captures them is certain of promotion without purchase."

"The gentlemen whom his lordship is so anxious to find are here," replied Maurice.

"Thank Heaven for that! I hope they are safe."

"O, yes, they are safe enough, now that you have arrived."

"I don't know about it. Is that one of them on the ground, with the hound guarding him?"

"He is a Fenian, I believe, but not in good *standing* just at this time."

"Because he has a propensity to *lying*, I suppose;" and the cavalry officer laughed at his little joke, as though it was a good one.

"To be candid," Maurice said, "the four gentlemen whom I have just presented to you are the ones whom his lordship is so anxious to capture. They are the terrible head centres, whose landing on our shores was to shake Ireland like an earthquake."

The cavalry officer did not know exactly what to say in reply. He looked at our party, and then at Maurice, for an explanation.

"I see that you are puzzled," the lieutenant said; "but I'll explain matters quite readily. These four gentlemen, as I telegraphed his lordship, are old Australian friends of mine, whom I can trust and have trusted for many years. There is not much Fenianism about them. The whole row is an absurd one — a mistake from beginning to end. The Fenians thought they had caught four head centres. The police and our folks thought they had recaptured them; and so the news travelled all over the country by the aid of telegraphs, and I suppose that at this moment all England is frenzied at the prospect of an outbreak."

"Of course you know your friends, Maurice," the cavalry officer said; "but still his lordship is so suspicious that only a personal interview will satisfy him that all is right. Now, the best thing that you can do is to proceed to Dublin as soon as possible, and lay the whole facts before him. What do you say to my proposal?"

"It is sensible, although I suppose my lord will pick a bone with me for being surprised; but how was I to know that my men would get drunk?"

"To be sure. Soldiers will drink whiskey when they can obtain it."

"And as for the rescue, the best officer in Ireland could not have prevented it, unless he had more information than myself. It was the first case of the kind, but won't be the last if the Fenians continue to increase in strength as they have for the last six months."

"Never mind," said the cavalry officer, in a consoling tone; "we have made a strike in capturing some of the men who stopped the car, and that will go a great ways with his lordship. Here come my men with a dozen prisoners. I will dismount half a dozen of my followers, and you can take their horses and ride to Athone. There leave the animals, and take a jaunting-car to the next station, and before night you can be in Dublin."

"A thousand thanks! I could not ask for more. You will look after the prisoners, and at the same time take care of the secret still, which you will find in yonder hillside. The owner is with the Fenians, and betrayed us to them. For that he deserves no mercy."

Just then up came the soldiers with what prisoners they had captured. There were a dozen of the latter, and very sulky they looked at their position; but there was not a man of them who took his punishment so much at heart as Big Mike, now released from the guardianship of Rover, and allowed to stand erect, but with his hands confined behind his back for fear he might do some little mischief in his desperation and great strength.

"You see, Mike, how the tables have turned," Maurice said, while the soldiers were securing their prisoners.

"Yes, I see," was the sullen reply.

"Now, answer me one question," Maurice continued. "Did you intend to hang me as you threatened to do?"

"On my soul, no," was the answer. "I meant to frighten yer into payin' a ransom, and arter I had the goold, I should have let yer gone."

"Are you speaking the truth, Mike?"

"By the bones of St. Patrick I am, sir. May I never hope to drink whiskey agin if I ain't tellin' yer jist the whole truth, and no more. I should have made yer feel the weight of the rope, and perhaps pulled it a little; but on the honor of an Irish gintleman, I would not have choked yer life out."

"Then, Mike, I'll remember you on your trial, and see that you are not punished too severely," Maurice said.

"Thank ye for nothin'," was the reply. "It don't matter much the year or two that ye could get taken from my sentence. It's little I has to hope from in any court, with its packed juries, in Ireland. I'm a convicted man, sir, afore I'se tried. Well, better luck to the men who comes arter me, and may they live to see Old Ireland free from the rule of the English."

"You haven't much time to spare," said Fitzhugh. "Better mount and be off as soon as possible. I'll send a man to guide you to Athone. It's not more than five miles by a bridle-path."

We took the hint, and mounted the cavalry horses, and then bade farewell to Fitzhugh, and followed the lead of a little ragged gossoon, who, bareheaded and bare-footed, ran before us with the speed of a race-horse, and never tired, up hill or down, over plains or through deep valleys where lurked treacherous bogs; and to be ingulfed in one of them was to be lost, unless assistance was at hand.

Through the bogs the gossoon conducted us until

faltering or missing his way; and after an hour's hard ride, we reached the little hamlet of Athone, where we found something to eat, and were enabled to hire a jaunting-car for the nearest station.

We stabled the cavalry horses as directed, gave our guide a gratuity that made him yell with delight, and by two o'clock we were on our way to the station as fast as two horses, driven by the most reckless driver in all Ireland, could carry us.

Up hill and down we went at a gallop. Each moment I feared that a wheel would come off, or that the car would collapse and tumble to pieces. How it held together was a wonder to me. It was loose in all its joints, and it swayed from side to side, as though determined to go on its beam-ends and never right again. From the top of a mountain to the bottom, on roads that were unworthy of the name, it seemed as though the driver could not urge his horses fast enough. He made no attempt to check them, even when we had to turn a sharp corner; and how the animals kept their feet, with so much pressure behind them, is one of the wonders of Ireland. Had he met a team coming from the opposite direction, nothing could have saved us from total destruction, for a collision would have sent us flying over a precipice two or three hundred feet high.

Two or three times we urged the driver to hold up; but perhaps he misunderstood us, for he only shouted the louder; so we concluded to hold on and remain silent for the rest of our journey, as Maurice informed us that going down hill at such a run was a playful custom of the country, and that drivers always strove to see how near they could kill their passengers and yet keep them alive at the same time.

Thank fortune, at length we arrived at the railroad station. As we drew up with a flourish and a yell, the wild driver turned to us with a face that expressed some satisfaction at the rapidity of our journey.

"Ah, yer honors, what does ye think of that for fast

travellin'? Ain't it worth a little somethin' in drink money? Sure, there ain't a gossoon in all Ireland that can do what I can with hosses."

We were glad to give him a half crown, a portion of which he immediately invested in whiskey; but before he had drank all the money the train arrived, and once more we started on our way to Dublin, which we reached without the least trouble.

"You had better go to the Pride of Dublin," Maurice said, as we entered the depot. "It is the best hotel in the city, and has the best company. I must go to the Castle and report, and as soon as I have explained matters, I'll join you. I may be gone an hour, and perhaps two; it will all depend upon how soon I can get an audience with the lord lieutenant. I'll take a cab and be off at once, while you had better walk to the hotel and save expense. The house is but a short distance from here, and any one will show you the way."

He meant the advice to be good, but it was not, unfortunately. However, the lieutenant entered the cab and was off, and we commenced our search for the Pride of Dublin. We had to inquire of but one person, a bluff, hearty-looking man, with an English face and a cattle-drover aspect. He said he knew where the house was, and would walk along and show it to us, and he did; and while thus engaged, he asked more questions than a Yankee.

If he appeared astonished when informed that we had just arrived at Queenstown from the United States, I can't imagine what his sensations were when Murden happened to allude to Australia, and claim that country as his adopted home.

"All the way from Australia," repeated the man. "Only think what a long distance it is from here, and how anxious you must have been to see Ireland, to come such a journey."

"What is there in that so wonderful?" demanded Murden, in a tone that showed he didn't like the manner of our acquaintance.

"O, nothing, sir. I only thought you must love Ireland, to come to see it after such a long absence. I'm sure I love Ireland, and every Irishman had ought to love her."

"But I ain't an Irishman," snarled Murden.

"Well, sir," with a laugh, "that is no reason why you shouldn't love Ireland;" and then the drover-looking man said no more until we reached the hotel, when he left us, even declining to take a drink for his courtesy, and refusing to come in and smoke a cigar.

We had no trouble in obtaining rooms, and, after a bath, ordered dinner, and were just about to sit down to it, when the person whom we had asked to show us the way to the hotel entered the dining-room, and came towards us.

"Gentlemen," he said, in a low tone, "I don't want to give you trouble, or to cause you the least uneasiness; but let me inform you that I'm a detective, and that I arrest you for being head centres of the Fenian organization."

CHAPTER XVII.

CHAMPAGNE AND WHISKEY PUNCH. — ON OUR WAY TO THE CASTLE. — AN AUDIENCE WITH HIS LORDSHIP.

I THINK that four gentlemen uttered four distinct oaths when the person whom we had taken for an honest English drover informed us that we were under arrest on the charge of being head centres of the Fenian organization. The man was a detective, and thought that he had made a wonderful discovery.

"Now don't let us have any fuss about this thing," the detective said, in a low tone, so that none of the servants or any one in the dining-room could hear him. "I don't want to make trouble, and I'll do my duty in the most pleasant manner."

We looked at the detective, and then at each other,

uncertain whether to laugh or to get into a passion and swear at the man for his officiousness.

"Ah," suddenly cried the detective, "none of that. It won't do, I assure you. I have a dozen men near at hand, to assist me in case I want assistance. Resistance is useless, as you had ought to know; so don't make any fuss about it."

This remark was called out on the ground that Hopeful had, in the most innocent manner, put his right hand into his breast pocket, in search of a handkerchief, his nose requiring a little delicate attention; but the officer supposed that a revolver was being searched for, and so gave us what he supposed a fair warning not to enter into a deadly struggle, for if we did, we should get the worst of it.

"Don't you be afeard," Hopeful said, addressing the officer. "We ain't a-goin' to hurt you, and I is sure we don't want to. I hain't got such a thing as a revolver about me, and neither has my companions."

"It wouldn't make any difference to me," replied the detective, "whether you had a revolver in every pocket of your clothes. I have orders to arrest you, and I shall, even if all the Fenians in the city rise and protest against it."

"Heaven forbid!" cried Fred, with a laugh that made the Englishman open his eyes in astonishment. "We have seen all the Fenians that we desire to see for a month at least."

"Amen!" cried the rest of us in chorus, and with a laugh so cheerful that the detective made a sign to his subordinates, at different tables in the room, to be prepared for an outbreak at once.

"Come, Mr. Officer," said Fred, as soon as he had concluded his laugh, "you don't look like a bad-natured man, and I am sure you will have mercy —"

"I can't promise, unless you will make a full confession," cried the officer, eagerly. "Tell me all you know, and I'll see what can be done."

"We will," responded Fred. "But let me finish my

sentence. In the first place you will have mercy on our stomachs, for we are awful hungry."

The detective nodded. He sympathized with us in our hunger, for was he not an Englishman?

"In the second place," continued Fred, "to prove to you that we want our dinner very much, we invite you to dine with us at this table."

The detective's eyes softened. He loved a good dinner and a bottle of wine. He began to think that we were human, after all.

"And if I comply with your request," the man said, "will you pledge your word as gentlemen that you will not play me a Yankee trick with my food?"

We laughed and promised.

"And will you pledge your word that you will make no effort to escape, or to raise a confounded row and a rescue?"

Just then one of the waiters placed the soup on the table. It smelt so good that it almost made us frantic.

"Yes, yes, we promise," all cried, with one accord. "Sit down and fall to like a man."

Down into a seat dropped the detective, as though he had been shot through the heart, and dinner commenced.

"Waiter, what kind of champagne do you keep on hand?" asked Fred.

"The best in Ireland, sir," was the prompt answer.

"Bring us some, and see that it is well iced."

"Yes, sir;" and with the meat came the champagne.

The wine circulated freely. It touched the heart of the detective, and opened that wonderful organ, and when he heard us give an order for a bowl of whiskey punch, he could no longer contain his enthusiasm.

"Hang me!" he cried, striking his fist on the table, "I don't care whether you are Fenians, or what you are, but you are just the jolliest set of men that I've met with in Ireland, and I say it's a confounded pity that I've got to look arter you and take you to the Castle."

"Must you do so?" we asked. "We don't care about the arrest, of course, but still it is vexatious to be arraigned, and made to explain matters. Besides, our passports are on board the steamer."

The detective winked, as though it was a good joke on our part to say so.

"Of course they are out of your possession," he said, "and perhaps it would be as well if all your papers were beyond reach. Mind you, I don't say anything, or hint; but still you know best."

The punch was opening the heart of the detective, that was certain; and I don't know but what if we had asked that one of us should escape, he would have consented. The detective's confederates, who were in the room, and dining at their own expense, did not like the appearance of things, and cast angry glances at our captor, because he happened to be enjoying himself.

"We must make a move," said the detective, who was oblivious to looks until the last drop of punch was gone. "Time is on the wane, and I see that some of my fellows are anxious for a start. If you have no objection, gents, we will go up to the Castle, and see what the big wigs have to say. I wish that I could do better by you, hang me if I don't; for I have taken a fancy to you fellows, and think that you had ought to be in better business than lighting up the slumbering fires of Fenianism." And with this concluding remark, just eloquent enough to smell of whiskey punch, the detective got on his feet, and we followed his example.

When we arose, all the secret police in the room did the same. They pretended not to take notice of us, but we had seen enough of police life in Australia to understand all the little arts and tricks of the trade.

We passed out of the dining-room, and met the head waiter on the threshold. He looked a little serious, for he was an Irishman, and therefore hated the police. Perhaps he suspected more than he was willing to show, for he said,—

"Do ye slape here to-night, gents?"

We laughed, and replied,—

" That depends on circumstances. Keep our rooms for us, and you may see us come back."

"Thin, under the circumstances, yer honors," said the head waiter, with a look at the detective, "perhaps ye would jist as lives settle yer little bill afore ye goes. Ye may niver return, and thin, ye know, the house would be out so much."

We laughed at the man's shrewdness, and the detective also smiled.

"You think I'm a dangerous man — don't you, Jerry?" the officer asked.

"Faith, I could do without yer company, and niver feel lonesome. It's little sorrow I should have if I niver saw yer face agin. It's bad for Ireland when the likes of ye can roam round the streets and devour all who would see her free."

We saw that a row would soon ensue if the conversation continued, so went to the office and paid our bills, and, while slipping a gratuity into the hands of the head waiter, had the satisfaction of hearing him whisper to us, —

"Say but the word, and I'll get up a party of boys that will take ye out of the hands of the police afore ye reach the Castle. Bad luck to 'em, but they is a bad set, at any rate."

"Keep cool, Jerry," I replied. "No harm will come to us, be assured. They can't prove anything against us."

"Ah, ye don't know how the mane thieves can buy the evidence to convict," replied Jerry, with a sigh and a threatening look at the officer.

Fearful that the man would get into trouble, we left the hotel as soon as possible, and took a jaunting-car for the Castle, our escort following behind, with the exception of the detective, who rode with us.

We entered the Castle yard, and were received with considerable attention, for there were a dozen red-coated soldiers drawn up in line, as though they had expected us. Lights were seen in all parts of the Castle, and mounted orderlies entered and departed in hot haste, as if business of importance was before them.

"Are these the prisoners, Mr. Officer?" asked some one in authority, as we left the jaunting-car.

"Yes, sir; these are the persons whom I suspected of being head centres."

"All right. His lordship desires their presence immediately. Are they unarmed?"

"Yes, sir."

"Be sure on that point. This is no time for carelessness," the officer, who appeared to be an aid to the lord lieutenant, said.

"Don't be alarmed," cried Fred. "We did not land on these shores for the purpose of committing assassination; so his lordship can see us without the least danger."

"If you didn't visit Ireland for the purpose of committing outrages, why did you come here?" the aid asked, in a tone that showed he was a thorough-going Englishman, with a hearty contempt for all who were not so well favored as himself.

"We desired to see the country. As Americans, we take considerable interest in Ireland."

"More fools you," I heard the officer mutter to himself, and then aloud, "Ireland would be a prosperous and contented country if Americans would but let her alone, and not attempt to stir up revolutions."

"Suppose you Englishmen should make an attempt to see how prosperous Ireland could be by a few just laws and just treatment," Fred said.

The aid gave my friend a look of quiet contempt, which was intended to annihilate him; but it didn't, for some reason or other, and then, finding that Fred was not quite finished, or so ashamed as not to hold up his head, the aid said, —

"I'm not here to argue with you on state questions or political economy; but let me give you a piece of advice."

"We shall be very thankful for it, I'm sure," Fred replied, with a bow and a tone that it was impossible to tell whether he was serious, or poking fun at the Englishman.

"Well, sir, when in the presence of his lordship, don't pretend to argue such points with him. If you do, the worst for you. He is not in the habit of listening to such men."

"Take his advice," whispered the detective, who had stuck to us all this time, yet had not dared to utter a word, for fear of the consequences. "Get out of it the best way that you can."

"Suppose we compel his lordship to listen to us," Fred said, still keeping good-natured, and quite calm and cool.

"Sir!" the aid hissed.

"Don't talk in that way," whispered the detective. "For God's sake, be a little civil. You don't know what you are doing or saying. It's all my fault, in allowing you to drink so much punch. It has gone into your heads."

Fred took no notice of the detective's appeal.

"Yes," continued Fred, still addressing the astonished aid, "we shall tell his lordship some home truths, and perhaps they will make an impression on him. We have been molested enough, while in Ireland, to bankrupt your country, provided we were paid for all the trouble that we have experienced. Now, three of us claim to be honest American citizens, and the fourth one is a subject of the queen, and knows his own rights."

"Yes," cried Murden, in a sudden burst, "I'm an Australian, and know what is right as well as the next man, Yankee or Englishman."

"A ticket-of-leave man," suggested the aid, with a sneer.

"I'd break your cussed head for you, if you were outside the Castle walls, where you could not call for the assistance of the soldiers," Murden said, in a burst of mighty indignation. "D—n your eyes, who do you think I am?"

"By your language, an escaped convict," was the reply of the officer, short and sharp.

Murden sprang for the aid, and would have struck him,

if Fred and I had not held the indignant commissioner, and prevented the blow.

"Don't hold me," said the indignant Australian. "Let me alone. I want to revenge the insult that I have received. Why, the cussed popinjay! I could kick him from one end of the Castle yard to the other, with both hands tied behind my back."

"We know you could," Fred said, trying to suppress his laughter at the astonishment which the aid manifested at hearing Murden's outbreak, and continued: —

"Don't you mind him. He don't know you, or know of the important positions which you have held in Victoria. How should he? He will be glad to apologize after he understands who you are. Wait with some of your old patience. You remember the time when weeks were like hours to you."

"If he would but give me the satisfaction which one gentleman is willing to accord another," muttered Murden, "I would keep my hands off of him."

"The idea of giving a Fenian the satisfaction of a gentleman," the aid said, in so contemptuous a tone that Murden once more felt his passion stirred.

"Hang you and the Fenians, too," the ex-commissioner roared. "I'm no more of a Fenian than you are, and I'll prove it, if you will show us the lord lieutenant."

"You shall have your wish," replied the aid, in a cool tone of contempt. "Follow me, and let me give you a word of advice."

"We don't need it," said Fred. "Don't distress yourself about advice just at this time. We have our Yankee wits about us, and have had for some time."

"As you please," was the answer, curt and crisp, like all Englishmen's words when in a pet.

We followed the aid through various rooms and corridors, until we stopped in an apartment where half a dozen officers were lounging.

"Halloo," one of them said, addressing the aid who was escorting us. "You have been long enough to try and hang half the Fenians in Ireland. His lordship is devilish impatient, I can tell you; so you had better hurry them up. I never saw four men more fitted by looks for the gallows than the fellows with you."

"Perhaps our looks are merely a reflection since we entered the apartment," cried Fred, in one of his cool ways.

The officer roared with laughter at the sally, and then suddenly looked grave as they heard the tinkling of a bell.

"By Jove," one of them said, "his lordship has heard us, and his temper won't be improved by the noise. I don't wish your Fenians any harm; but I'll bet a sovereign that they are remanded to prison unless they tell all they know."

"And a little more, perhaps," muttered another officer.

"Yes, that is the only road to safety, nowadays. Tell all you can think of, and rewards and honors will be your portion instead of punishments;" and just as an officer had uttered these sarcastic remarks, a door opened, and an aid appeared.

"His lordship's compliments, and he will thank you to make less noise."

"Tell him the Fenians are creating the disturbance," one of the Englishmen said; and then all laughed, but in subdued tones, so that his lordship would not hear the noise.

"I'll tell him anything that you say," replied the newcomer; and then his eyes fell upon our party.

"Halloo," he said; "are these the Fenians his lordship is expecting? How long have you kept them here, when you know that it is important that they should be examined at once? I shall report such conduct."

The threat was received with a roar of subdued laughter, in which the party who threatened did not hesitate to join.

"Come," he said, "you must be examined without delay; and a word of advice. Hold nothing back if you wish to save your necks."

With these words the door was thrown open, and we were ushered into the presence of his lordship and half a dozen other persons, who were seated at tables, looking over papers and writing, as though they were reporters, and engaged in preparing copy for a morning paper.

His lordship was a man sixty years of age, heavy, sandy hair, and red mutton-chop whiskers, ten inches long. He was not a man remarkable for brilliant thoughts or deeds, and owed his position to the fact that he was of good birth, and could afford to spend money to amuse the aristocracy of Ireland with four balls or parties a year.

His lordship honored us, for a minute or two, by looking at us without speaking, as though he was seeking to probe beneath the surface, and bring to light all of our hidden thoughts. At last he spoke.

"Don't you feel ashamed to stand in the presence of royalty's representative, after outraging the queen's laws?" he said.

"We don't know why we should feel in the least ashamed," returned Fred.

"Put that answer down," said his lordship to one of the parties who was writing. "It shows how bold and defiant Fenianism is becoming."

"Will you allow me to make a remark?" said Fred, not in the least dismayed.

"A confession? Yes. Go on."

"Call it what you will," my friend said. "It does not matter to us, as long as we can make you understand our position. We assure you, in the first place, that we have no connection with Fenianism; and, in the second place, we desire to leave the country as soon as possible; for we have experienced only vexation and bother since we landed in Ireland."

"Can you prove your assertions?" demanded his lordship. "Is there any one who can satisfy me that you are not American head centres?"

"Yes, sir. Lieutenant Maurice can do so."

"Maurice — Maurice," muttered his lordship. "Why,

that is the officer who has been waiting for an audience so long. I had forgotten all about him. Admit him. We will see what he has to say about these people."

Some one left the apartment, and then the only noise that was heard was the scratching of pens and the rustling of papers, while his lordship stroked his whiskers and looked us all over.

CHAPTER XVIII.

A CONVINCED LORD. — HEZ AND HIS HAND-SHAKING. — DISCHARGED. — AN EXPLANATION. — A RUSE TO ESCAPE ATTENTIONS.

WE had no doubt but that Maurice could convince the lord lieutenant that we were travellers, and well-disposed ones at that; but if the lieutenant should fail, we could fall back on my father-in-law, or even the Earl of Buckland, both of whom could be reached by a telegraphic despatch directed to their residences in Lancaster.

While we were waiting, the lord lieutenant did not ask us to be seated, as he might have done, and as politeness dictated; so we took possession of chairs, regardless of the frown upon his lordship's brow.

"You people mean to make yourselves at home," his lordship said, in a tone that was intended as a sneer.

"We wish we were at home, or in some country where we should not be arrested every twenty-four hours, as suspicious persons, by suspicious rulers," retorted Fred, in a cool and unconcerned manner.

The head of Ireland frowned and pulled his long whiskers, but he never uttered another word until our friend Maurice came into the apartment; and very much surprised he was when he saw us in the presence of his lordship.

"Lieutenant, you have been waiting for an audience for some time," the lord lieutenant said.

"Yes, your lordship; I sent word that I had important information to communicate, but I suppose that message was never delivered."

"Yes, it was delivered, but I have been so pressed for time, that I could not see you. I have sent for you, now, however, to see if you could identify these persons, who have been arrested by our detectives as Fenian head centres. They have appealed to you for good character. Let me hear what you know about them."

"They could not appeal to one who knows them better than myself," was the answer. "I wish your lordship was surrounded by as good men as these four gentlemen, and that Ireland had no worse enemies."

"Explain," was the command; but the frown lessened from his lordship's brow.

"In the first place," said Maurice, pointing to Murden, "this gentleman has had the honor to hold a seat in the cabinet of Victoria, when Sir Robert Hardhead was governor. He left office when the colonial Parliament refused to vote supplies for the encouragement of the mutton-fat breed of sheep. If the design had been carried out, Australia would have been the greatest country in the world for its wool. But it failed, and Mr. Murden left the cabinet with the rest of the ministers."

His lordship looked a little surprised, and seemed to regard Murden with some interest.

"The others," he said; "who are the others? Can they give as good record?"

"Yes, your lordship. They are Americans. This one is the son-in-law of Sir William Byefield. You may have heard of his romantic marriage in Australia."

"Yes, yes, I have heard of it. Byefield is an old friend of mine. I remember all about his daughter, at the time she was stolen by that notorious prize-fighter, the Pet. So this is her husband — is it?"

"Yes, your lordship."

"I am glad to see him. Now give me some information especting the other two."

"This gentleman," pointing to Fred, "is one of the best men that ever settled in Australia. Had he been an Englishman, the highest positions in the land would have been open to him."

"I am satisfied. What about the next one?"

"That means me—don't it?" asked Hez, coming forward, just as though he was about to be introduced to his lordship. "How do you do, sir? Glad to see you, sir. Hope your wife and all the little lordships are well."

To our horror, Hez put out his hand and grasped the lord lieutenant's, and shook it as though really glad of an opportunity to show Ireland's lord that he could do an act of kindness in case he was so disposed.

The ruler of Ireland was as much astonished as if we had declared ourselves Fenians, and desired to make an attack on him and the Castle at once. He would have withdrawn his hand, but Hez held on to it as though knowing that, if he ever let go of it, he should not again obtain possession; so up and down he pumped the lord's arm, until the scene became so ludicrous that we were compelled to turn our heads for fear of laughing in the lord lieutenant's face.

"I'm darned glad to see one of England's nobility," said the wretched Hez, with all the gravity of a member of the Massachusetts legislature elected for the first time. "If you ever come to New Hampshire, you jist drop in on me, and you'll find a warm welcome, now I tell you. We ain't much on our show up there, but we are good on seeing that a man has a full belly and a good bed at night, and that's all a feller could ask for and be reasonable; now ain't it?"

His lordship, after the first surprise, seemed to comprehend matters at once, and to be rather pleased than otherwise with Hez. He smiled, and asked Hopeful if he was ever in Australia and that question set our friend at work.

"In Australia?" repeated Hez. "Well, I should think

I was. Didn't you ever hear of my quartz-crushers? They was considered a little the greatest thing out, at the time I set 'em up, and them who had ought to know said that I was the means of adding millions to the wealth of Victoria, — not the queen, you know, but the province of that name, — and one old lunatic, what I met in Melbourne, said that government had oughter to settle a pension on me for what I had done to develop the mines; but then I suppose the fellow was a little prejudiced, 'cos he wanted me to treat him to some gin, and I did."

Hez paused for a moment, to take breath, and we hoped that he had run down; but he hadn't, for he fired up and rattled on once more.

"If you think it is best for me to make application for a pension for what I has done for the gold mines of Australia, I'll do it, and hope you'll back me up, although I ain't confident that I shall get anything."

His lordship, with a smile, said that he should be happy to lend his aid if he understood the merits of the case, but that he did not just at that time.

"I suppose that your lordship is satisfied with the innocence of these gentlemen," Maurice said, for fear Hez would make another attempt at monopolizing the conversation.

"O, yes, perfectly satisfied," replied his lordship.

"Then you are willing that they should retire to their hotel — are you not?"

"O, yes, by all means;" and his lordship looked a little anxiously at Hez, for fear he would recommence his yarn about quartz-crushers.

We were about to retire, when his lordship suddenly recollected that Lieutenant Maurice had been waiting for some time, during the afternoon, to communicate with him.

"Did you wish an audience for any important business?" asked the lord lieutenant.

"Had my business not been important, I should not

have troubled you," was the response of the high-minded soldier.

"Of course — of course," his lordship said, and then looked annoyed to think that he had laid himself out for a rebuke.

Maurice then proceeded to state how it happened that his men were overpowered by whiskey, and their rifles taken from them. In fact, he gave a complete history of our proceedings, from the time we landed until brought before his lordship. ·I will give the ruler of Ireland the credit of saying that he became interested in the narrative, and manifested some enthusiasm when Maurice told how a rope was put round his neck, and the Fenians threatened to hang him unless a ransom was paid for his life.

"And these gentlemen actually offered to pay the sum of ten thousand pounds for your life — did they?" asked his lordship, with more surprise on his face than he ever before exhibited, except when told that the Fenians were dissatisfied with his rule.

"Yes, my lord, they proved their friendship on that trying occasion."

"I must shake hands with such gentlemen as you have for friends," his lordship said, in a moment of great enthusiasm.

"Certainly," cried that wretched Hez, pressing forward, and giving the lord lieutenant his hand, and a mighty shake at the same time. "We ain't a bit proud, and had jist as leaves shake hands with you as with any other man. Some people think we are stuck up 'cos we are Americans; but it ain't so, and we repel all sich blamed nonsense, and no mistake."

"I am happy to hear it," returned his lordship; and then he released his hand from Hez's powerful grasp, and rubbed it slowly and ruefully, as if he feared that he could never restore it to its original shape.

Seeing how his lordship was suffering, we pretended to take no notice of his request to shake hands with each of us, so retired from the august presence, and inwardly swore that we would give Hez some private instructions in etiquette before we were again introduced into the circles of English aristocracy.

As we passed through the doorway I turned to take a final look at his lordship, and to make him a final bow. He was not paying the slightest attention to us, but showing his hand to one of his confidential secretaries, and apparently explaining how much he had suffered by coming in contact with an uncouth American, who had New Hampshire ideas of what constituted heartiness.

Then the door closed behind us, and we found ourselves in the presence of the several aids, the gentlemen who had intimated to us that when we left the presence of the lord lieutenant it would be for solitary cells in the strongest prison in Dublin.

"Halloo!" said one of the aids, as soon as he saw Maurice, whom he appeared to be acquainted with; "you have got into new business — haven't you? What do you intend to do with these Fenians? Shoot them or imprison them?"

"I'll bet a sovereign that they are sent over the water if they are tried," remarked one young fellow, whom we afterwards discovered was the son of an English duke, and had been banished to Ireland on account of his debts and extravagances.

"Gentlemen," said Maurice, with all of his heartiness, — a relic of his Australian life, — "these are my friends, true and tried, and the man who insults them insults me."

Had a gang of Fenians burst into the room, and called upon the officers to surrender, I don't think the aids could have been more surprised than they were at the lieutenant's words. For a moment there was an oppressive silence. Then the duke's son said, with his habitual drawl, —

"D—n it, Maurice, you don't mean to say that you want to fight us all because we have had a little fun out of your Fenian friends — do you?"

"No, my lord, I have no desire to fight, but, at the same time, I will stand by my friends."

"A devilish good quality in a soldier," said one of the eldest of the aids. "I wish that I had some such friend."

"You would ruin him if you had," returned the duke's son.

"How?"

"Why, you would borrow all of his ready money and never pay him;" and at this sally all laughed, the victim as heartily as any one.

"It is true," the elder aid said, as soon as the laugh subsided, "I might borrow my friend's money, but, by Jove, I wouldn't get him to put his name to the back of a bill and then clear out to Ireland, and leave him to pay it. No, by Jove, I wouldn't do that."

This was a hard hit at the duke's son. We could see that the shot had raked him fore and aft, for his face flushed with anger, but recollecting that he had provoked the retort, he changed his show of rage to one of mirth, and laughed, apparently, as hearty as any one.

"Now, gentlemen," said Maurice, "if you have done stabbing each other, perhaps you will listen to me for one moment."

"Go on, Maurice. These two have sunk each other with their hot shot, so they will keep quiet hereafter," one of the officers said, and thus encouraged, the lieutenant remarked, —

"These four gentlemen have been friends of mine for many years. They have been tried and never found wanting in a single quality that goes towards making up all that is requisite in man. They just landed at Queenstown, and as they came from America, the whole population supposed that they were Fenian head centres. I was enabled to rescue them from the enthusiastic Irishmen who wanted their help and their gold, and from that simple circumstance the lord lieutenant supposed that all Ireland was about to break out in a revolt. He is satisfied, however, with my explanation, and my friends are at liberty to go where they please, and leave Ireland as soon as they please."

"I wish to the Lord he would give me the same privilege," muttered the duke's son.

"Maurice," said the aid, who appeared to be the first in authority, "your explanations are satisfactory, and if you will introduce us to your friends, we shall be happy to know them."

On this hint we were introduced in due form; and I will give the Englishmen the credit of behaving quite polite when they found out who we were. They invited us to remain and dine with them, and promised to show us something of the town in the evening; but our clothes wanted changing, after what we had passed through; so we were compelled to decline the invitation.

"Make it to-morrow, then," one of the aids said.

But we had made up our minds that Ireland was not a pleasant place for a residence just at that time; so declined, on the ground that we meant to leave Dublin the next day for England, where we hoped to find peace and freedom from the charge of Fenianism.

Our excuses were well received, and then we took our leave, with mutual protestations of regard.

In the court-yard of the palace we met our friend, the detective who had arrested us. He came towards us full of anxiety as to the result, and when we explained that nothing had been proved against us, he expressed some delight; but I fancy that he was disappointed, after all, for he had lost the rewards which were offered for head centres.

However, he shook hands with us, and then we left the palace for our own hotel, where Maurice informed us we should find all of our baggage, which had been taken from the station and sent to the house by the police, at the lieutenant's request.

No sooner were we outside of the palace gates than a ragged, beggar-appearing man came towards us, as if for charity. He held out his hand, and then looked us in the face.

I was about to hand him a shilling, when the supposed beggar uttered a shrill cry, and then began to give us specimens of an Irish jig, dancing around us, one moment advancing, and the next receding, until we began to think that the fellow was mad, or else was showing us a specimen of his skill for money. But the next moment we were undeceived, for his shrill yell brought forth from dark corners dozens of men like himself, poorly dressed, and with a wild, uncouth look about their eyes, and long, tangled hair over their necks and shoulders.

"Whoop!" yelled the dancer, "here they is, and now we must have 'em to ourselves."

The rabble gathered around us, and hard-looking customers they were. We did not know what their intentions were, but we were not long left in doubt, for they made a rush at us, and attempted to hoist us on their shoulders so that we could be carried in procession about the city, or to the places where Fenians congregated.

We struggled to free ourselves from their embraces, but they clung to us like leeches, and swore that their true-hearted American "hed centres" should never be separated from them.

The crowd was increasing, and we saw that we were likely to be again involved in trouble, unless we adopted some original method of getting out of it. Fred, who had a genius for just such a situation as the one we were in, put his hand in his pocket, and withdrew it filled with silver shilling pieces.

"Scramble for the money," he shouted, and dashed the silver to the pavement.

The wild-looking men left us in a hurry, and threw themselves upon the ground, scratching to the right and left for the money.

This was the moment Fred had looked for.

"The police are coming!" my friend shouted, and ran for the next street, as fast as he could; the rest of us following him, and shouting "Police!" as loud as we could roar.

This ruse had the desired effect. As we ran, we looked over our shoulders, and saw that the rabble and our devoted admirers had taken the hint and the money at the same time. They were scattering in all directions, but none of them came towards us; so we settled down into a walk, and at last reached the hotel, and were received by the head waiter with every demonstration of respect and approval. Not waiting for us to order it, he set a bottle of wine before us, and hoped that we would drink for the honor of the house, and to the prosperity of Old Ireland.

Rover was glad enough to see us. We had left the dog at the hotel while we were at the palace, considering that his company would not be wanted by the lord lieutenant.

While we were drinking the wine, the head waiter came along and announced that for our especial honor a serenade would be got up for us in the course of the night.

"Sure, we could do no less," he said, "for distinguished gintlemen from 'Merica, what had come all the way to Ireland to help the cause."

We looked at each other in despair. We had not ceased encountering troubles and trials.

"Waiter," I said, "what time does the boat start for Liverpool?"

"At eight o'clock to-morrow morning, sir."

"Send down at once and secure our passage. We have seen enough of Ireland to last us a year." And then we went to bed, only to be awakened in the middle of the night by a serenade got up in our honor.

CHAPTER XIX.

THE SERENADE. — A GRAND ROW. — OFF FOR LIVERPOOL. — HEZ AND A PRETTY GIRL. — DISAPPEARANCE OF HOPEFUL. — A REQUEST FOR MONEY.

It is not always agreeable to be awakened in the night, especially after a hard day's work. We had gone to bed tired, completely used up, mentally and bodily, and disposed to make the most of our last night's residence in Ireland by getting as sound a sleep as possible; so when we heard a roar in the street, and after the roar a few discordant notes of music, brass instruments and a drum, we uttered a few quiet curses, and then tried to sleep once more; and perhaps we should have done so if the head waiter (may he never live a thousand years) had not pounded on our door and requested the pleasure of a short conversation with us on business of the utmost importance.

"Go to the devil, you and your musicians," roared Fred, who occupied a bed in the same room with myself, while the next apartment contained Hopeful and Murden.

The only answer that was returned to such a salutation was a renewed demand to get up and hear what he had to say.

"The buys," said the head waiter, "is musterin' in force, and they won't go widout hearin' a few words from yer. They knows how to honor 'Mericans; so get up and spake to 'em, or they'll come up and spake to ye in tones that will prove how much they like ye."

Just then there was a roar, as though a thousand wild beasts were quarrelling. It was useless to attempt to sleep after that; so I sprang out of bed and looked into the street, while Fred admitted the head waiter, who brought lighted candles and charged them in the bill next day, and refused to strike out the item when we remonstrated.

In front of the hotel was a mob, or crowd, collected around half a dozen musicians, the latter unable to play the most simple tune, on account of the pressure that was brought against their elbows. The scene was wild and exciting in the extreme, because every one appeared to be talking, and none listening.

"Be still, now!" shouted one. "What in the devil do ye mane? Don't ye see that the music is bothered entirely by yer conduct? Let 'em alone, so that they can play to 'Merican gintlemen and show what tunes old Ireland produces. Whist, ye blackguards, while they give us the Piper of the Shannon."

The pleading did not appear to influence any one, for the noise continued, and the musicians had as little room as before.

A crowd of Irishmen cannot get together without having fun or fight. This crowd went in for fun in the most extensive degree. They cared no more for music than we did when first awakened from our sound sleep; so I was not surprised to see the instruments change hands in a short time, in spite of the remonstrances of their owners.

The new possessors attempted to use the instruments, but only produced the most discordant sounds and roars of laughter from the crowd; and at last one fellow seized the drum and dashed it over the head of the genius who was beating it.

This was the signal for a general row, and in a moment there was not a whole instrument to be seen. All were smashed over each other's pates, which occasioned a remark from the head waiter, who was still in our room, looking on in evident delight.

"Sure," he said, "the buys does know how to enjoy themselves. Ain't they as playful as kittens? But to bring 'em out real strong, yer honors has but to order some whiskey for 'em. Thin they'll show what they is made of."

We declined to order the whiskey for a thousand men, and in consequence the head waiter looked a little disappointed and grieved, as though we had done him some personal injury.

"Sure," he said, "I thought that all 'Mericans was true-hearted and liberal towards the down-trodden and oppressed of Old Ireland. I'm disappinted, it seems."

"It seems that you are, if you expected us to furnish whiskey to all the crowd in the street. We didn't send for them, and we don't want them to stay. They may go to the devil if they will but let us return to our beds and sleep."

The head waiter sighed.

"This is not the kind of treatment that the lads will expect," he said. "They s'pose that when they honor gintlemen with their attentions, that the gintlemen will at least do the handsome thing by 'em. It's lots of preparation I made for this serenade, and it seems that all of it is lost, and no one to pay."

"Pay!" repeated Fred. "Let those pay who drink."

"It's not the custom of the country, when they turns out to honor some distinguished visitors. Hark! Do ye hear 'em roar for ye?"

In fact the crowd in front of the house was roaring, but it was for the simple reason that some eight or ten of the most pugnacious were having a lively fight, and their friends were doing all they could to help the thing along, and involve others, so that the row would become general.

In this the most eminent success was the result; and while we were looking at the noisy, laughing, pugnacious, full-of-mischief crowd, which had smashed all the musical instruments, they turned upon each other, and then commenced a war with shillalahs. Heads were broken without the least regard for friend or foe, much to the delight of the head waiter, who still remained with us.

"Isn't it a pretty sight?" he said, rubbing his hands with gratification. "Ye don't often see the likes of this in 'Merica — now do ye?"

We thought not.

"Ah," the head waiter sighed, "if ye would but stand the whiskey, the buys would treat ye to a sight that would make Dublin howl."

Just at this moment, when the yells and the cries of rage and pain were the most powerful, some one raised the cry that the "sogers was comin'," and then the crowd began to thin out without much delay, but the most stubborn held on until the red-coats turned a corner and came towards the hotel on the double quick.

There were half a dozen savage yells from those who had been fighting, and then even the most obstinate turned and disappeared down narrow by-streets and lanes; and by the time the soldiers were on the ground, in front of the hotel, not more than a hundred civilians were to be seen.

"Ye see," sighed the head waiter, "the buys has gone, and not a drop of whiskey has wet their lips. It's little regard they'll have for 'Merica after this."

We could not help smiling at the remark, and thought that America would have to send over other representatives to recover lost ground in the estimation of the enthusiastic Irishmen of Dublin.

"Well," yawned Fred, "I suppose that, now the serenade is over, we can retire to our beds once more."

The head waiter looked a little severe as he answered, —

"And if ye can slape arter this night's work, it is more than most men could do. Niver was men so trated as the buys of Dublin this night; now I say it, who shouldn't say it, because there is no other one to spake it."

"Will you be kind enough to take yourself and your moralizing out of the room, so that we can go to bed?" asked Fred.

"Yes, I'll do it," was the reply, "for I no longer desire to remain in the company of sich 'Mericans as ye is;" and with that the head waiter washed his hands of us, and left the room, more in sorrow than in anger.

We once more turned in, and slept until aroused by

some one pounding on our door, and informing us that it was time to get up, if we meant to eat breakfast, and take the boat for Liverpool.

We lost no time in bathing, dressing, and eating our breakfast; and then came the hardest task of all, parting with Maurice, who had been to us more like a brother than a friend. He had been ordered to rejoin his company at Queenstown, without a moment's delay; so he could not accompany us across the Channel, as he hoped to, and as we desired.

However, he promised to do all that he could to rejoin us in Paris, and if that was impossible, we were to spend a week with him in Ireland, on our return from our tour.

The parting was sorrowful. The lieutenant went with us to the steamer, and there we shook hands for the last time, and then he hurried to the railroad station and took the cars, while we steamed out of the harbor for Liverpool.

There was the usual number of passengers on board — a miscellaneous lot they were. We saw no one that we knew, or cared to know, so secured our state-rooms, and turned in for a long sleep, to make up for the time that we had lost.

When we awoke it was afternoon, and dinner was ready for those who wanted it. We were of the wanting kind; and while ordering what we desired, suddenly missed Hopeful.

"Where is Hez?" I asked of Murden, for the two had roomed together on board the steamer.

"I haven't seen him since I turned out," was the response. "He woke up while I was sleeping, and went on deck, I suppose; and he is there now, unless he has jumped overboard."

I went on deck to find him, and I did. The son of New Hampshire was seated by the side of a pretty little girl, modest and as fresh-looking as a rose. To her Hez was paying the utmost attention, and the young lady was listening to him with every mark of interest and deference.

Hopeful was in his element, and so fearful that I should interfere with his pleasure that he would hardly take any notice of me. He thought that I might attempt to make love to the girl on my own account, although he should have known me better. I am not one to interfere in matters of that kind.

"Well, Hopeful," I said, with a look of admiration at the fresh-faced English girl, "you did not sleep late. Well, I don't blame you for preferring the deck to the state-room under the circumstances."

"Never you mind about that," returned Hopeful, with a sulky look. "I don't interfere with you when you has a gal, and don't you interfere with me."

"Why, Hopeful," I said, soothingly, "you don't suppose that I would interfere in your affairs — do you?"

Just at this moment the young lady looked up and gave me a sweet smile, as though she rather liked the turn of affairs, and hoped that the conversation would continue for some time, as it amused her.

"Look ahere," said Hopeful, in a tone full of wrath, "when you and Miss Goldthwaite was a flirtin', and a billin', and a cooin' on board the steamer, I didn't run up to you every time I seed your heads together — now did I?"

"No, Hez, you didn't. I'll give you some credit. When Miss Goldthwaite and I met, you kept in the background."

"That's so," Hez muttered.

"But at the same time you will do me the justice to say that I formally introduced you to the lady. Confess that."

"Yes, I confess that; but at the same time I don't mean to introduce you here; now you may believe it or not, just as you please. This young lady is all alone on the boat, and is under my protection, and I mean to protect her — you see if I don't."

"If she is under your protection, the best thing that you can do is to take her down to dinner, provided she is capable of eating any."

The young lady said that she was quite well, and never more hungry in her life.

"Then you shall come and have dinner with me," Hez said. "But mind," he continued, as he arose and offered his arm to the girl, which she took, although she gave me a glance that I could not or would not understand, "that I won't stand no blamed nonsense from no one."

"Don't be afraid," I said. "No one will interfere with you; and if they were disposed to, the young lady would not encourage it."

"No," said Hez, "I won't stand no blamed nonsense. The young lady looks to me for protection, and I'm the one to protect her, now you had better believe."

I saw that Hez was serious; and when he was in earnest about a woman, he was dangerous as a wild bull. I had seen that in Australia, when he fancied that he was in love with Amelia; so I determined to let him do as he pleased, and make as violent love as he wanted to, until he recovered his senses.

We went into the cabin together. Fred looked a little surprised when he saw whom Hez had for a companion; but I kept him and Murden still by a glance which they understood.

Down to the dinner table we sat. The young lady was exactly opposite me, so that I had a good chance to notice her. She had laid aside her hat, and I now saw her whole face; and a pretty one it was, with blue eyes, brown hair, and such sweet-looking cheeks, that I almost wished I had an opportunity to kiss them with no one to see me at such delightful work.

I did not blame Hopeful for wishing to keep such a delightful little prize of humanity all to himself. If I had been in his place I would have acted in the same way, for men are a little selfish with beauty, and like to own and protect as much of it as possible.

"I suppose that you are never seasick," I said, addressing the young lady, while we were eating dinner; but Hez interfered and prevented her from answering.

"Never you mind about that," he replied. "If she was sick she wouldn't be here, and I don't 'spose she wants to be reminded of seasickness every time she puts a mouthful of food down her throat."

Fred rolled up one eye to me, and I saw the corners of his mouth twitching as though he wanted to laugh, but did not dare to just then for fear of the consequences.

I didn't think the conversation very improving just at that moment, as it was attracting some attention, so said no more for fear Hopeful should get furious with jealousy.

The English girl smiled and glanced at Hopeful as if she sympathized with him in her defence; so I did not rate her refinement at so large an estimate as I might have done, had she shown a more fervent desire to get acquainted with Fred and myself, and left Hez to find some other lady of marked beauty.

The dinner was only tolerable. Fred ordered a bottle of wine, and sent a glass to the young lady; but Hez in her behalf refused it, and ordered wine on his own account, and they drank it until the bottle was emptied, and then all of us went on deck.

"What do you think of Hopeful's conquest?" I asked of Fred, while we were smoking our cigars.

"Faith," was the laughing response, "I think she is as pretty a girl as I have seen since I left home."

"With the exception of Miss Goldthwaite," I added, a little reproachfully.

"I accept of the exception," was the reply. "Miss Goldthwaite's style of beauty is more noble and refined, and with it is an air of coquetry that is perfectly irresistible, especially when she stands on the quarter-deck of a steamship, and laughs at her lover's misery."

It was now my turn to blush, and I did with a vengeance.

"Come, come," said Fred, while I was sucking my cigar in silence, with a burning face, "don't feel bad because the lady laughed at your sentimentality. I know by her actions that she is rather favorably disposed towards you, and if you will but exert one half your usual impudence, the next time you meet, she is yours."

"Thank you for your advice. Now let us talk of Hez's capture. What do you think of her?"

"I haven't made up my mind."

"She is pretty and looks innocent. Is she what she appears?"

"Who can tell? I am no judge of such matters. We must wait."

We did wait, and watched, and saw nothing that caused apprehension on our part, or heard a word that would have brought a blush to the cheek of the most refined.

As the steamer neared the docks, Hez left the side of the lady and came towards us.

"At what tavern do you propose to put up at in Liverpool?" asked Hez.

"The Queen's Head," was the reply, for that had been recommended to us.

"Wal," said Hez, "I've got to see the lady home, and then I'll jine yer thar."

We made no reply to this argument, and when the steamer entered the dock, we saw Hez and the young girl enter a cab and drive off, while we went to the hotel and booked our names and ordered supper.

We waited until nine o'clock for Hopeful, but as he did not come, we ate our supper, smoked our cigars, and then went to bed, determined to devote one or two days to Liverpool and its docks before we passed on to London.

The next morning we expected to see Hopeful, but he did not make his appearance. We were not surprised, although a little grieved, for appearances were not so favorable as we could expect from one who had had the advantages of our company and conversation for so long a time.

After breakfast we went to the docks, were gone till noon, and when we returned found a note and a message from Hopeful. The note was for a hundred dollars, and the messenger said that he was ready to take charge of the money, and convey it to our friend; but we were not to know where he was.

We met and consulted over the matter for a while, before we dismissed the messenger.

CHAPTER XX.

HOPEFUL IN A BAD WAY. — HIS MESSENGERS. — ROVER UNDERTAKES A DIFFICULT TASK AND ACCOMPLISHES IT. — A PROPOSAL.

THINGS began to look serious. Hopeful had left us the afternoon before, in company with a young and handsome girl, and had then stated that he should rejoin us in the course of an hour or two. Instead of doing so, he had kept away, and now sent an order, written by himself, for a hundred dollars in gold, or twenty pounds.

"What had we best do about the matter?" I asked of Fred and Murden.

"Send the money," both of them responded, "and with the money, a note asking Hopeful to join us without delay, as we want to leave for London."

We all suspected that Hopeful had been deceived by the pretty face of the girl, and that he was throwing away his money in her behalf. We knew how fond he was of a handsome face, and how easy it was for one to lead him from one folly to another.

I wrote the note and gave it to the messenger, with the twenty pounds. The fellow, who looked like a broken-down police officer, disappeared in an instant; and that was the last we saw of the man, or heard of Hopeful, until the next morning, when a second note was handed to me by a different messenger.

I opened the note with considerable anxiety, for I recognized Hopeful's handwriting. In a few lines he asked me to send him another hundred dollars in gold, as he needed the money very much. Not a word was said where he was or when he should rejoin us.

We didn't like it. If he kept on at this rate, the Bank of England would be needed to supply his demands. I showed the letter to Fred and Murden. They gave prolonged whistles, and thought that the joke, if it was one, had been carried far enough, and that we must now refuse to advance further sums, unless Hez appeared in person and demanded them.

"This mystery must be explained," said Fred, in a decided tone.

"How?"

"By following the messenger, and seeing where he goes."

"Does he look like a man who could be followed through the streets of a strange city?" asked Murden, alluding to the messenger, who appeared to take no notice of us, yet, I doubted not, was watching all our motions with the stealthiness of a cat.

"No," returned Fred. "He would throw us off the scent before we could turn half a dozen corners. He undoubtedly knows every twist and turn in Liverpool. We could do nothing with him. We must resort to other means."

"Appeal to the police," Murden suggested.

"And before we could get word to them, this fellow will have disappeared — hid himself in cellar or garret. No; we must let him go, yet be enabled to mark the place where he steps."

"How?" demanded Fred and Murden.

"Step into another room, so that the messenger cannot overhear us, or suspect what we are doing, and thus defeat our plans."

My friends took the hint, and much to the messenger's disgust, as expressed on his coarse face, we left the office and went to a side room.

"We must save Hopeful," I said, as soon as we had entered the apartment, and closed the door. "He has fallen into a trap, or bad company. A personal interview will bring him, but letters will have no effect. Now, neither of us can track the messenger through the streets of the city; so we must adopt another plan. We will let Rover follow the fellow, and return, and report to us where he goes."

"Can the dog do so much in a strange city? In Australia I should have no doubt of his sagacity. But here I fear the test will be too much for him," Fred said.

"I have confidence in Rover," I replied. "He is almost human in his understanding, and I have no doubt will do the best that he can to help us. We can but try him."

Fred and Murden were willing to try, but they did not have confidence in the plan proposed. I was willing to run the risk, so called Rover from the room in which I had slept. I took his massive head in my hands, and talked to him just as I would to a human being.

"Rover," I said, "Hopeful is lost, and you must find him. Follow the man you see me talking with, and then come home as quick as you can. Be careful and not let him know that you are watching him."

The hound looked me full in the face, and seemed to note every word that I said.

"You understand me, don't you, Rover?"

The dog wagged his tail and would have barked his expression of approval, but saw that such a course would not be just what I liked, so wisely refrained from giving vent to his joy that I had found something for him to do. He seemed to think that he had been idle long enough.

"He'll do it," cried Fred, in a low tone of approval. "He understands every word that you say."

We returned to the office. The messenger had waited for us quite patiently, for he came towards us and held out his hand for the money. Rover stalked into the room and lay down in one corner, his eyes fixed on the messenger, watching his every movement.

"Come," said the fellow, give me the blunt; I'm in a hurry for it."

"Wait one moment," I replied; "I have a few questions to ask before you leave us."

"Well, gov'nor," growled the fellow, "just put 'em to me, and then let me go, 'cos I've wasted time enough already for one mornin'."

"Where is our friend, Hopeful?"

"He's safe, I s'pose," was the reply.

"In what part of the city?"

"I ain't much acquainted with the pints of the compass."

"Then give me the name of the street and the number of the house in which he is stopping."

"That, gov'nor, is somethin' I can't do. Your friend told me not to let on where he was, 'cos he didn't want to be disturbed by your callin' on him."

"If I should make you a present of a sovereign, would you lead me to our friend's quarters?"

"No, gov'nor, I couldn't do it without your friend told me to. If he says yes, I'm your man to pocket the blunt; but till he says the word I'm mum."

"I'll double the amount if you will conduct us to the house where he is stopping."

The fellow shook his head. He wanted the money, but didn't dare to earn it in the way we proposed.

"I suppose that a woman detains him," Fred suggested.

The messenger grinned, and said that he supposed so too.

"Is she a young girl?" I asked.

"Well, your friend ain't the sort of a man to be detained by an old one. At least I don't think he is," was the messenger's reply.

The man once more held out his hand for the money and looked surprised when he did not receive it.

"No," I said. "You will get no more money from us until we hear from our friend, or see him. We do not know what he does with so much."

"I s'pose it is his'n — isn't it?" was the next question. "I s'pose he can do what he likes with his own. If he has the putty he can spend it — can't he?"

"Not foolishly, as long as he is in company with us," I replied. "We know his weakness, and intend to see that it is not abused."

The messenger uttered a growl of rage and disappointment, it seemed to me, and a minute or two elapsed before he spoke.

"Then I s'pose," he said, "that I must tell the cove what you says."

"Yes, tell him that ten pounds a day is expensive, and that he can't afford so much."

"Yes, I'll tell him, and a precious rage he'll be in when I does. It is strange that a cove can't use his own money."

We made no reply, and, after waiting for a moment, the fellow moved off and left the hotel, and then Rover got up and followed him.

I ran up stairs to an upper window, and looked out. The messenger was standing on the corner of a street, glancing back towards the hotel, to see if he was followed. Rover was looking at a picture in the window of a print-shop, and appeared deeply interested in what he saw.

The messenger remained on the corner five minutes or more, watching the door of the hotel, to see if either of us left it. Rover appeared to be satisfied with the artistic effect of the picture, and then stopped to exchange a moment's greeting with a stranger dog that happened along just at that moment.

Finding that neither of us was following him, the messenger turned down the street, and disappeared. Just at that moment Rover left his new acquaintance, the stranger dog, and followed the messenger. The stranger dog did not like to be left so unceremoniously, and so made objections; but Rover just turned his head and showed a full set of teeth. The sight was sufficient. The hound was not again molested, or requested to remain and idle away the whole afternoon in play.

. The parties disappeared from sight, and we sat down, and waited patiently for Rover's return. He did not come back for an hour or more. Then he stalked into the office, and came and laid his head on my knee.

"Did you track him?" I asked; and the hound responded "yes" by a sweep of his tail.

"Let us start at once and find the place where Hopeful is concealed," Fred said.

"No, let us wait and see what message he returns, after he learns that we refuse to supply him with more money. He may come to us, and so save us trouble."

My advice was agreed to. We took good care to be near the house all the forenoon, and towards night another messenger came from Hez.

This time we found that we had a Liverpool rough of the most advanced school to deal with. He was short-haired, broad-shouldered, pock-marked, flat-nosed, and bore a wonderful resemblance to some third-rate prize-fighter, who picks up a living by hovering in the vicinity of gin palaces and beer saloons, ready to fight or shake down a stranger, pick a pocket, or garrote a person whose appearance testified to the ownership of a watch, or a few gold pieces.

"I 'spects you is the cove what I wants to see," the short-haired fellow said, by the way of introduction.

"Well, if such is the case, what do you want of me?" I responded.

"Only this. A friend of yourn, what I happens to see to-day, axed me to make a call on yer, and speak a few words in yer ear."

He looked at Murden and Fred as though not quite certain whether they should hear his message.

"Go on," I said. "I have no secrets from these gentlemen. They know all my business. Say what you have to say before them."

This did not suit the fellow; so for a moment he rubbed

his short hair as if to raise an idea, and when he had found one, let it out.

"It ain't exactly accordin' to the articles, but as the money ain't up I s'pose we can talk a little afore we comes to time. Now this is what I has to say, and no more and no less. I ain't sparrin' for wind, so don't you think I is, I hits right out, as straight as I can, when time is called."

"Which means that you have a message for me that is rather plain in its language."

"That's the dandy, my boy; I has all that. Ye see, yer friend he says to me, this arternoon, says he, 'Bantam,'—meanin' me, what is called the Bantam Cock among the friends of the noble hart of self-defence and the prize-ring. He says to me, 'I jist want yer to run up to the hotel where the men what calls themselves my friends is a-stoppin', and do you say to 'em, from me, that they holds a precious sight of my swag,—a-meanin' money, of course,—and that I wants 'em to come down with some of it, jist as I writ for it to-day, and if they don't come down, I'll know the reason why.' Them was his words, jist as near as I can remember 'em."

"Can you tell us where our friend has concealed himself?" I asked, as soon as the Bantam Cock had concluded his long harangue.

"That, sir, is somethin' what I has nothin' to say about. When he wants to see his friends he'll come and pay 'em a visit; I has no doubt of it. He told me to keep dark till he had had his lark, and I ain't the man to turn my back on a cove what has axed me to keep mum for a while."

"Even the promise of five sovereigns would not induce you to bring our friend to us, I suppose?"

The Bantam shook his head, but in so feeble a manner that we saw the temptation to sell out was a great one.

"No," he said, with a mighty effort, as though collecting all his energies for the successful ending of a round. "No, I can't do it, although I'd like to oblige yer ever so much; I can't go back on **my backers.**"

"Come in here and let us talk this matter over," I said, for I thought I saw signs of weakness where I had expected much strength.

I led the way to a private room, and called one of the waiters.

"Let us have a bottle of wine," I said. "We can talk better over it."

"No wine for me," was the response of the Bantam Cock. "If you is willin' to stand somethin' handsome, why, jist tell 'em that I wants a go of brandy and water, with a little sugar."

I ordered his favorite drink, and then we once more proceeded to business.

"If you will recollect," I said to the Bantam, who appeared to enjoy his tipple, "I offered you five sovereigns if you would only restore our friend to us."

The Bantam emptied his glass and looked at the bottom with melancholy satisfaction. I took the hint, and ordered a repetition of the dose.

"Yes, sir; I know what you said," the Bantam remarked, after he had tested his new supply of liquor.

"And you can't accept the offer?"

"No, sir; I can't. I'd do most anything to accommodate you swells, 'cos I think you is trumps; but I can't take the money for that. I would if I could."

"Now listen to me," I remarked, in the most impressive tone I could convey. "You will lose by the rejection of the offer. We don't intend to send Hopeful another pound — no, not so much as a shilling — if he should send a hundred letters or a hundred messengers."

The Bantam looked into his glass of brandy, and said that it was rather steep to keep a friend out of what he had a right to.

"Not at all," said Fred. "Under certain circumstances it is right. We believe that Hopeful is under restraint, and not able to help himself as he should."

The Bantam said that he didn't know anything about

14

that. He was asked to do a message, and he had, and that was all he knew about it.

"Very well," said Fred, "remember this one thing. We leave Liverpool to-morrow. After we are gone, the parties who are now at work with our friend will find that there is nothing more to be made out of him. His letters of credit are with us, and can't be used without our consent; so you see we have the game in our own hands, and we mean to keep it."

"Does you mean to say that you don't care whether the cove is left without a penny or no?" demanded the Bantam.

"Yes, that is what we mean," I replied, although we did not mean it; but it was necessary to put a bold face on the matter when dealing with such people as the Bantam Cock.

"If I thought you coves was in real downright arnest," muttered the fellow, with a doleful look at his empty glass.

I touched the bell and the head waiter entered the room.

"Repeat what I said to you this morning," I remarked to the waiter.

"Yes, sir; I will, sir. You said, sir, that you should run up to London to-morrow, and to have your bills all ready, sir. S'pose you will alter your mind, sir, and stay with us some time to come, sir."

"That will do. Fill this man's glass with brandy."

The Bantam did not object. As soon as the waiter had obeyed the order I returned to the charge.

"You heard what was said. There is no attempt at deception on our part. We are in earnest in what we undertake. Besides, whether we have your aid or not, it don't matter. We know where our friend is."

The Bantam Cock was so astonished that he put his glass to his lips and drank half his brandy before he knew what he was about.

"You don't mean it," he said, when he had recovered from his surprise.

"We do mean it."

"You ain't had the peelers on the track — has you?" asked the man.

"We know where Hopeful is confined, and before you can give warning to remove him to another place, we shall be near him."

"Who stalked the messenger?"

"What?"

We didn't understand him.

"Who tracked the cove what come here this mornin'? It was Slippery Jim, and he isn't often gone back on. Was it a detective? We knows 'em all, and is on the lookout for 'em when we has a job of this kind. Come, tell a cove who it was."

"You shall know when we have secured the person of our friend, — not before."

"All right. Give me some more swipes and I'll peel the whole story for yer, on the ground that ye planks the dust arter I've come to time."

We ordered more liquor, and promised the Bantam that we would give him the money as soon as he had aided us to the extent of his power; but first he must tell us how it happened that Hopeful remained where he was, instead of joining us, as he promised he would do, when we landed on the dock at Liverpool.

The Bantam Cock winked one of his little fishy-looking eyes, and tipped his hat over his forehead, as he laughed at the question.

"A—," he said, "you don't know the games of Liverpool. This is one of 'em, and a mighty good one, too, now I tell you. In fact, I think it is the best one what we uses."

"Tell us all about it," Fred said.

"I will," replied the fellow. "Here goes for a last confession, as the man said what was to be hung. But mind, you won't blab on me, will you, and so spile our game?"

"No, we will not."

"Then here goes." But the yarn must be reserved for the next chapter.

CHAPTER XXI.

A PROPOSITION. — IT IS ACCEPTED. — IN SEARCH OF HOPEFUL. — THE SALOON, AND WHAT WE SAW THERE. — DAISY APPEARS.

We lighted fresh cigars — some that we brought from home, and not the miserable German things for sale at the hotel — and then prepared to listen to the Bantam Cock's account of the manner in which Hopeful had been taken possession of by the roughs of Liverpool, who were determined to bleed him to death before they let him go.

"The fact of it is," said the prize-fighter, with a grin, "I s'pose you know we're on it. That is, we is on our make, and we is on the lookout all the time for flats. Now, ye see, there's no sich thing in this world to rope a man in as a gal with a fresh face, and lots of good looks, and a devilish lot of art, — now is there?"

We all three bowed in silent acknowledgment of the truth of the statement. Alas, we knew by experience that a girl with a handsome face was more than a match for the hardest-headed man in our party.

"Well, gents, there's a party of coves what keeps three or four gals agoin' between here and Dublin, and they jist picks up the most promising men they can find on the steamers. One of us men goes with each gal to see that she does her duty, and to protect her in case things ain't square. I was on the steamer that brought you from Dublin."

"We didn't see you on board."

"Yes, but you did, though. You looked at me several times, but I wasn't quite so young lookin' as I am now. You see I had on a false gray beard and a wig, and that was the way I was disguised, and I could keep near my Daisy,—that's what we calls her, 'cos she looks so fresh and cosy,—and could post her a little on those who was on board."

"Do you mean to say that you could pick up some one each trip?" demanded Murden.

"Of course I could with Daisy. She is one of the best stools that we has. Sometimes she gets as many as two or three on a string, at one trip, and then it pays."

"But how did it happen that she hit on Hopeful?" Murden continued.

"Well, gents, I'll tell yer that, 'cos ye see the gal was a little wilful that day, and I had to speak kinder cross to her more'n once. She'd set her mind on havin' a different sort of cove from your friend, and I had some trouble to put her right. She's got a will of her own, has Daisy, when she takes a mind to show it."

"Who did she want to exert her fascinations upon?" asked Murden.

The Bantam laughed.

"Well sir, it wan't you."

"Who was it?"

"Well, sir, I don't want to hurt any one's feelings, I don't."

"Nonsense! just as though what you said could have any influence on us," Murden cried.

"Well, ye see," continued the Bantam Cock, "the gal put her eyes on you two gents," pointing to Fred and myself, "and said that she should like to have one of you come to time. She didn't care which, but she rather fancied this ere one," nodding to Fred, and causing that worthy fellow to blush in the most remarkable manner.

"You interfered in her choice — did you?" I asked.

"Well, I rather think I did. I could see at a glance

that you two gents wan't the kind to be bamboozled by a gal of her kidney, and so I jist told her to lay herself out for the green-lookin' one, and she did. He bit at the hook fast enough, and she landed him on shore, safe and sound; and -I must say that she has done well by him. We've got more than we ginerally do, but we did hope to do better by him than any one what we caught."

Of course we were not much shocked at the revelations made by the prize-fighter. We knew that vice existed in all the large cities of Europe, and we did not expect to pass through them without our eyes being offended by the sight of some of the degradations of women; but the entrapping of Hopeful showed us that all kinds of stratagems were resorted to by the fallen for the purpose of obtaining money through their shame. We each of us mentally resolved to keep a closer watch over Hez in the future, and to guard him against the wiles of the opposite sex. We knew that we assumed a task of no ordinary magnitude, but we were men determined to do our whole duty, regardless of consequences.

"Now," I said to the Bantam Cock, "you have told your story in a few words. We want to see the end as soon as possible. When can you undertake to deliver Hopeful into our hands?"

"You speak as though I could do it on time," was the reply. "Now I can't. We must play the double on the people at the house, and jist cut your friend out right under their eyes."

"We are ready for the job. Lead us to the house."

"What, jist as you is?" cried the fellow, in astonishment. "Why, you'd get your bloody heads knocked off afore ye knowed it. No, sirs, you can't go as swells and do much good, unless ye want to fight like blazes, and I don't s'pose ye do. Ye must change yer dress and appearance, and do jist as I tell yer to, and then I hopes we can come out all right."

"Do as you please about it. Furnish us with just such disguises as you desire, and we'll wear them."

"And allow a cove little somethin' for 'em?"

"Yes."

"That's comin' to time. Now we begins to understand each other."

"When must we start for the place where Hopeful is confined?"

"Not afore night. It's a lushin' ken where he is, and only at night does coves flock there. To be seen afore dark would make trouble. Jist be trained by me, and you'll come out all right."

We promised compliance, and then the Bantam Cock left us, to return in the evening with such disguises as we would require to protect us from inquisitive eyes.

About eight o'clock our man made his appearance, and to our joy quite sober. He evidently appreciated the fact that coolness and decision were necessary to carry us through the enterprise which we had undertaken.

"The coves is mad," he said, "'cos you don't bleed as free as they s'posed, and they swear that your friend can't leave the house till he comes down with more of the flimsies. But we'll have him out if things work well. Only don't be too fast. Jist keep your wind, and sail in when I tells yer."

As he spoke, the disguises were produced, and we went to our rooms to put them on. We found some wagoners' frocks, velveteen breeches, and rather rough-looking hats, which we had some delicacy about putting on, for fear of the consequences; but the Bantam assured us that no one had worn the clothes for many months, and that if they had contained live stock at one time, they must have died out for the want of sustenance.

As soon as the disguises were on, the Bantam exercised his ingenuity by disarranging our hair, making it appear as though it had not seen a comb or brush for several days. Then he commenced on our faces, smearing them with an ointment that rendered them rough-looking, as though they had been exposed to the weather for years, and had rarely known the advantages of soap and water

To complete our adornment, in which he was assisted by Murden, who had had much Australian experience in disguises, the Bantam painted a stain under one of Fred's eyes, as though a blow had left its impression by concealing some blood under the optic.

This was one of the Bantam's happy hits, and he prided himself on it, for he stood off like a landscape painter, and surveyed the result of his work with much complacency.

"That will take with the coves at the lushin' ken," he said. "They will know by that mark that you've ben game enough to stand up and take punishment like a glutton."

This was gratifying, to say the least.

"If any one should hax you about that ere hi, you jist tell 'em that you give the feller as good as he sent, and that you offered to bet him ten pounds that you could lick him in a fair fight. That will bring you up to the mark as a fightin' man, and make you respected."

We promised compliance with the directions, and then, slipping our revolvers into our pockets, we left the hotel, Rover remaining behind, for fear that he would incommode us with his inquisitive habits; and if he had once got scent of Hopeful, he would have excited suspicion by his desperate attempts to find him.

It was nine o'clock when we left the hotel. We passed through some badly-lighted and very dirty streets. Their names I do not remember, nor do I care to; but, after crossing Waterloo Street, we plunged into a thoroughfare more dark and slimy than any we had seen.

Here we saw two policemen standing on the sidewalk and talking together. We were about to pass them, when they stepped in our path, thus barring our passage, while at the same time one of them threw the light of his dark lantern into our faces; and as he did so, both officers scanned our features with considerable earnestness, as if desirous of knowing us again, should they ever see us.

"Well, Bantam, what is up to-night?" asked one of the

peelers, in a tone that showed no great respect for our companion.

The Bantam was humble, as he answered, —

"O, nothin' is goin' on what I know of. It's precious dull times jist now, and things won't liven up till a good match is made atween the Pet and the Slasher."

"Be careful that you don't miss seeing that match," was the warning of the officer, in a tone so ominous that it struck me the Bantam Cock was a little under suspicion for some gay freak.

"Don't you go for to fear for me," was the reply. "I'm all right."

"And your companions — how are they?" And the officer nodded to us.

"They is coves from Manchester, on a visit to see the Chicken."

The officers gave us another sharp look, and suffered us to pass on.

"Blast their bloody impudence," muttered the Bantam, whose self-respect and pride had been lowered by the interview. "What did they mean by blabbing to me in that ere way?"

As we did not know, we wisely refrained from answering the question; and when the Bantam Cock had said that he would like to punch their heads, and then kick the guardians of the law, he concluded to continue his journey; but as we walked along, we were somewhat shocked by his profanity, which found vent in the hardest oaths that man ever invented.

But all at once the Bantam stopped walking and cursing at the same time. He pointed to a sign that hung across the sidewalk, and we saw that we were nearly opposite the celebrated "Golden Horseshoe," a low tavern, or saloon, quite common in all the large cities in England, where women without virtue frequented, and men without honor or morals could be found at all times, desperate and hungry for crime, and little inclination for respectable employment.

"There's the ken where your friend is," whispered the Bantam. "We will go in and have a drink, and do you mind your eyes, or ye'll get 'em knocked out. Don't be gorpin' round, and thinkin' you can see the cove and his woman, 'cos you can't till all things is ready. Now you mind me — don't you?"

We said that we did.

"Now let me feel of yer hands, and see if yer is fluttered any at the prospect afore ye."

He felt of our hands and pulses, and expressed himself perfectly astonished at the coolness which we exhibited.

"Blast my bloody eyes," he said, "if yer ain't jist like lumps of ice; as cool as fellers what is certain to win a fight. What makes yer like this?"

"Because we are not afraid," I said; but I did not tell the fellow that we had passed through more dangers than those which now threatened us, and that we had faced bushrangers who were more like demons than men.

"I believes yer," was the response. "You'll make splendid coves for seconds in a prize-fight. I wish I could count on yer, now I tell yer."

We did not pledge ourselves to take the positions which he desired; so, after a moment's delay, the fellow led the way into the Horseshoe, and we followed him.

It was a narrow room, which we entered, but it was long, and at the extreme end, some way from the bar, was a platform, and on it was a piano. Along the room on each side were small tables, where four persons could be seated, and drink and smoke pipes at their ease.

Some dozen of the tables were occupied by females alone, and half a dozen by males and females, all drinking their half and half, and smoking long clay pipes. I don't mean that all the women were smoking as well as the men; but truth compels me to state that some of the women were blowing a cloud with considerable freedom, and as though they rather liked it. But they were the most hardened of all who assembled in the Golden Horseshoe

When we entered the place, half a dozen men were standing in front of the bar drinking, as a matter of course. They glanced at us as we entered, and one or two nodded their heads at our guide; but the majority of the company did not even take the trouble to salute the Bantam, for the simple reason that they looked upon him almost in the light of a sneaking thief, owing to his connection with women who fleeced susceptible strangers.

The Bantam did not look quite so important or pompous when he saw the roughs at the counter of the bar; and the reason why he did not was because the redoubtable Chicken, the great prize-fighter of Liverpool, was at the bar indulging in a pot of porter at some admirer's expense.

"Halloo, Bantam," cried some one, as we entered; "who have you got in tow just now? More victims for Daisy?"

The Bantam laughed in a sneaking manner, as he replied, —

"Does these coves look as though they was worth Daisy's notice? They hasn't got ten pounds, all told, in this world. No; they has jist come from Manchester to see the Chicken, and to know how to bet their shillin's when the fight comes off. I tell yer what, arter they has seen the man what is to win the fight, they will feel better."

The prize-fighter seemed to like this bit of flattery; for he grinned a little in approval at us, and when we asked him if he would take a drink with us, appeared to yield to our solicitations without much urging. He seemed to regard it as a tribute to his name and rank in the walks of prize-fighting life.

Of course we could do no less than ask those who were standing at the bar to drink with us, and this was too customary a proceeding to attract notice; for many a poor man, in England, would starve himself and family for the purpose of treating a celebrated bruiser.

"Well, mate," said the Chicken, as he emptied his glass,

speaking to Fred, and pointing to the stained eye, "some one has nearly closed one of your shutters."

"Yes; but the cove what did it got both of his peepers done up in mourning, to pay for it," was Fred's answer, in a tone that meant to convey considerable bounce.

"Do yer want to make a match?" was the eager question half a dozen of the fellows propounded; but to this Fred shook his head, and said that things were working all right in that direction, provided certain parties could raise money to put up.

The Bantam Cock was not easy in the company of the Chicken and his admirers, so soon retired to one of the tables and called for beer and pipes, and then we were joined by half a dozen of the female frequenters of the place, who were anxious that we should bestow some attention upon them; and we did select three of the best looking and cleanest, and treated them to beer and cheese; and the poor things needed all that they received, for they were full of misery and want, objects of pity to Americans, and abuse and ill treatment to subjects of her majesty.

At last we got rid of the females, and were left alone for consultation. We were impatient to begin our work, and commence a search for Hopeful; but the Bantam would not budge, or point out the course which we were to pursue, until the proper time.

"You jist wait," he said, "till I tells yer when time is called. We wants more beer; so now order it."

We did so; and before the pewter pots were emptied, crowds of men and women entered the saloon to listen to the singing and music which the proprietor of the Golden Horseshoe always served up to his guests at a certain hour of the night.

Just as the pianist took his seat, a short, stout-built man, with mutton-chop whiskers and the face of a brute, passed through the saloon, looking to the right and left, as though to see that all were helped, and eating and drinking with all their might.

I noticed that the women shivered when the brutish-appearing man looked at them; so I was satisfied that he was a tyrant, a scamp who would raise his hands against one of the opposite sex on the slightest provocation. Even the Bantam was not easy when the bully looked at him.

"That's the cove what we has to fear," whispered the Bantam. "He is the landlord, and keeps all these gals in his pay, so that he can send 'em off where and when he pleases. Daisy is his best card; and if he knowed we was here to block his game, he'd set all them coves what we seed at the bar on us; and then shouldn't we be marked?"

The Bantam watched the landlord until he left the house, in company with some of the roughs; and then our guide breathed easier, as though a load was removed from his mind.

"Now's our time," the Bantam whispered. "One of you get up and pass out of that door, kinder slow like, you know, as though you wasn't in a hurry. When you gets in the passage-way, jist wait for the rest of us."

Murden was the first one to start, followed by Fred, and then I passed out of the room and joined my friends. We had to wait five minutes for the Bantam, for he did not leave the saloon by the same door that we did.

"Come on," he said, as soon as he joined us. "We ain't got no time to lose, now I kin tell yer."

We passed through a long passage-way, out into a yard, which we crossed, and then entered a building that was separated from the houses near it by a high picket fence.

Here the Bantam told us to make as little noise as possible, but to follow him. It was dark; but we took hold of each other's hands, and moved along.

We passed up a flight of steps, and then saw a light under a door at the head of the stairs.

Here we made a little more noise than was desirable, when a door was thrown open, and Daisy appeared on the threshold, with a lighted candle in her hand.

CHAPTER XXII.

A STRUGGLE. — A PRISONER. — SEARCH FOR HOPEFUL. — THE LOST ONE FOUND. — A SURPRISE.

The sight of a pretty woman should not surprise any one, for they are rather common in England; but I must confess that I was a little astonished at the sudden appearance of Daisy in the doorway at the head of the stairs. To be sure, we had expected to see her, but we thought that we should have some little warning before we met her face to face.

We stopped the instant the fresh-faced girl confronted us, for we did not know what to say to her, and I am certain that she did not know what to say to us; so for a moment we stood looking at her as intently as she looked at us.

"Well," she said at last, without exhibiting the least tremor of alarm, "what do you want up here at this hour of the night?"

She looked directly at the Bantam Cock, and seemed to expect an answer from him.

"Why, Daisy," he said, "these here is some friends of mine, what I want to introduce to you."

"I don't want to see them," was the reply; and she cast one disdainful glance at the rough clothing which we wore, as though she was not in the habit of associating with men of our style of life.

"Not even for a moment?" asked the Bantam.

"No," was the decided answer; and the beauty turned away, as though to reënter her room.

At this moment, while her white, round shoulders were exhibited to our view in the most tantalizing manner, Fred stepped forward and laid one hand on her arm.

She shook him off as though he had been a viper, and her handsome face flashed the anger that she felt.

"You low-lived cuss," she said, "what do you mean by laying your paws on me?"

Alas! although Daisy was beautiful, she had a temper of her own, and could not command it on all occasions as well as she should. When she was angered she could not always use such choice language as one naturally expects in a pretty girl.

"I meant no harm," Fred said, by the way of an apology, although he was not so much startled by the flash of anger as one would have expected.

"Then keep your mawleys off me," returned the lady, who judged only by outside appearances. "If you don't want another peeper put in mourning, you just keep yourself to yourself."

She meant that, as Fred had one black eye, she would give him another to keep it company, unless he was more civil than she thought he was likely to be.

Once more the girl turned her back upon us, and was about to disappear in her chamber; but Fred again interposed.

As quick as a cat the girl raised her right hand and struck at our friend, intending to let her fist fall on his face, and thus carry out her threat; but Fred was as quick as she was, and easily avoided the blow.

"I wouldn't do that again," he said, in his most tender tones. "It is not lady-like, and does injury to your beauty. Let us be friends, not enemies."

"Who are you?" she asked, in some degree astonished at Fred's coolness and decision.

"I am a man, and would be your friend, if you would let me," was the answer.

Just at that moment we heard a volley of sharp oaths in the lady's apartment; and then who should come to the door but the landlord of the Golden Horseshoe — the bully whom we had noticed scowling at the women in the saloon! He was an ugly-looking brute at the best of times, but now he appeared more like a fiend than a human being.

"What's the row?" asked the landlord, in a sharp tone, and with a long string of oaths to make his remarks emphatic.

We looked for the Bantam Cock to answer him, but that worthy person had disappeared from sight as soon as he heard the landlord's voice.

"There's no row here," Fred answered. "We are only looking for lodgings."

The bully roared his rage at the reply.

"We don't allow lodgers in this part of the house. Who told you to come here? Who showed you up here? Clear out, or I'll kick you down stairs."

We did not turn and run, as the fellow expected. Murden and Fred uttered long-drawn sighs, as though testing their wind before the struggle, which they knew must come, sooner or later. We had faced more savage men than the one before us, so were not in the least frightened at the ravings of the bully of the Golden Horseshoe.

"We shall go down stairs when we get ready to go, and not before," Fred replied, in a tone that was well calculated to make the landlord madder than ever.

He was not accustomed to such plain-spoken words; so I was not surprised when I saw the fellow make a spring for Fred's throat.

"Look out," I said; but the warning was unnecessary, for Fred saw the contemplated movement as soon as I; and when the landlord made his spring, my friend stepped aside, and let his antagonist dash against the partition that was just behind us.

I don't think that I ever saw more rage and profound astonishment on one face than what appeared on the countenance of the landlord of the Horseshoe. He was not accustomed to such movements, and instead of grasping Fred's windpipe, he found that the bare wall was all that he had reached.

He turned on us like a snarling wolf at bay, and then made one step forward and put up his hands. We knew

The Liverpool Sporting Den.—Page 225.

what that meant, but still had no such fears as had inspired the Bantam Cock to run.

"Will you leave?" asked the bully, and drew back as though to hit out from his shoulder with his right arm; but his fierce little eyes showed a different meaning, and when the blow was aimed it came from the left shoulder, and was easily turned aside; and then Fred's opportunity occurred, and he was not the man to neglect it.

There was no feinting on his part. My friend was too prompt not to pay off all that he owed as soon as it was fairly due; so, as soon as the landlord's fist had been thrust aside, Fred's hand was sent out on a voyage of discovery, and, wonderful to relate, it found a tender piece of skin just between the man's eyes.

With such force and so unexpected was the blow, that the landlord of the Golden Horseshoe lost his perpendicular, and down he tumbled to the floor.

"Don't let him get up," said Murden, who rather enjoyed the excitement of the thing, it reminded him so much of Australia.

With a bound he alighted on the man's neck, and kept him from moving, in spite of his struggles.

Daisy, who had witnessed the whole scene, would have uttered a shriek and called for help if I had not interfered, and thus restrained her.

"We mean you no harm," I said, "but you must not make the slightest noise, or I don't know what will happen."

"Who are you, and what do you want?" she demanded, in a low tone, being warned by my words.

"We are not thieves or roughs," I said, "so you need not be afraid."

"I'm not afraid," was the answer; but her trembling lips told a different story, and then she turned and looked at the prostrate landlord, who was lying quite still, flat on his back, but mad all the way through, as one could see by his face.

"Don't hurt him," she said. "Do let him up."

15

"They don't dare to, the bloody cowards," the amiable host of the Horseshoe said, in response to the girl's appeal.

"We won't argue the point," was Murden's reply. "We have no chance to test your courage or our own; so please to give us a little time and much of your patience, for we shall need both."

The fellow responded by a kick, quite emphatic.

"Ah," said Murden, "you won't take our advice and keep still; so we must resort to force, and compel you to remain quiet;" and then the ex-commissioner put his hand in his pocket and produced some cords, without which he rarely travelled, and proceeded to bind the hands of the landlord.

It was a hard struggle, for the prisoner was a powerful man, and knew how to use his strength to the best advantage; but he had to contend with men who knew their business, and had managed just such fellows time and time again.

I will do the landlord of the Horseshoe the justice to say that he never opened his mouth to call for help. He fought fair, even if he did make several attempts to use his teeth while his wrists were being tied; but when he found that success had crowned the efforts of my friends, he only hissed out several oaths, and damned their bloody eyes.

"Swear away," muttered Murden. "It will do you good, and relieve your mind. Don't let the lady's presence prevent you from giving vent to your thoughts;" and then the ex-commissioner and Fred wound a few cords around the fellow's legs, and secured them so that he could not use them, even if he tried ever so hard.

"Now, d—n yer," cried the landlord, "jist put yer hands in my pockets, and take my money and watch, and then be off till the police nab yer."

"We are not robbers," Murden said.

"Then what in the devil's name are you?"

"We are friends of a poor fellow whom you have confined in this house."

"I suspected as much," Daisy said. "I thought I had heard your voices before. In spite of your disguises, I knew you were not laborers."

"Who is he?" growled the landlord.

"The man whom this girl picked up on board of a steamer a few days since."

"He ain't here," the landlord said.

"You know that you are not telling the truth."

"I am."

"No, you are not. We have come here for the purpose of finding our friend, and we shall not leave the premises without him."

"Then you'll have to wait a long time, for he ain't here."

"Is this man speaking the truth?" I asked Daisy.

She looked a little confused at the question. She feared to offend her employer, and yet did not really want to tell a lie.

"You know he ain't here," the landlord said, in a menacing tone, when he saw that the woman hesitated.

Daisy did not answer.

"He is here," I remarked, "and we'll find him."

"Then before we commence our search, let us remove this fellow from the entry to the chamber, so if any one passes, an alarm will not be given," Murden advised.

We dragged the landlord into the room, which we supposed to be Daisy's. It contained chairs, a lounge, and a work-table; but the latter was destitute of work, for Daisy had other things to think of.

We deposited the body of the landlord on the floor, and then Murden sat down to guard it; and, to prevent any unnecessary noise or confusion, our friend displayed a revolver to the wondering eyes of the landlord.

"We won't talk much," Murden said, as he showed his pistol, "because all conversation is unnecessary; but if you have a remark that you wish to address to me, now is your time."

"Do you want to murder me?" asked the landlord.

"Not unless you make a noise; then no one knows what

may happen. Keep quiet, and we shall be good friends, I have no doubt."

The landlord uttered subdued oaths, and then ground his teeth in his rage; but paying no attention to him, Fred and I turned our attention to Miss Daisy, who had sat down in a chair and waited for our movements.

"Now, young lady," Fred said, in a kind tone, "tell us where our friend is confined. You must know that we want to see him, and that it will be unprofitable to keep him any longer. You have made all that you can out of him. Throw your charms around some other man, and release our friend."

She did not answer us, but looked at the landlord for advice. We stepped between them so that their eyes could not meet, and once more appealed to Daisy. For a few minutes she was silent, as though thinking of the whole proposition; but at last she raised her eyes, dark blue, and full of expression, and then pointed to a curtain that hung against the wall, while at the same time she made a sign that showed she did not desire to let the landlord know that she gave the information.

We intimated to her that we understood her, and would be careful, so as not to involve her in trouble, and then we commenced searching for a door that would lead us to another apartment.

"You had better tell where our friend is," Fred said, so as to mislead our prisoner, who was still lying on the floor, bound hand and foot, but swearing in a subdued tone for his own benefit and relief. "We are certain to find him," Fred continued, "and if you can help us it will be all the better for us and you."

"How so?" demanded the bully, raising his head.

"Why, we might have rewarded the young woman for all of her trouble in the care of our friend."

"How much would you be willing to give?" asked the bully, in a tone that was a little more eager than any that he had yet used.

We did not answer him, for just at that moment Murden pulled aside the curtain, thinking that we had wasted time enough, and there we saw a door, with a key in the lock.

The landlord uttered several malignant curses, and attempted to kick at us, but did not succeed. He saw that we were on the point of a discovery.

We tried the door, but it was locked. We turned the key, and entered a small apartment containing two chairs and a bed. A candle was burning at the head of the bed. It was standing on a table, and threw enough light over the room to show us the form of a man reposing on the outside of the bed, with all of his clothes on, just as though he had thrown himself down for the purpose of taking a nap.

I rushed forward and raised the light, and looked at the features of the man on the bed. It was the one we sought. It was Hopeful, and in a deep sleep.

I was about to lay a hand on his shoulder and awaken my friend, when Daisy laid her hand on mine and restrained me.

"Don't be rude with him," she said, in a low tone, and with more appearance of sympathy than I had given her credit for. "He has suffered much in his mind the past few days, and has had but little sleep. Please let me awaken him. He will not be so much surprised."

We drew back from the bedside, and told her to do as she pleased.

"He has felt as though he was doing wrong all along, and at times has been violent; but I always managed to bring him to his senses, and then he has told me that he loved me more than ever."

The poor girl blushed when she made the confession, as though she was revealing the great secret of her life, instead of an acknowledgment of guilt.

"Perhaps," she said, as she was about to lay one of her light hands on the sleeper's shoulders, "you would not object to wipe your faces of the paint which they contain.

Looks like yours might startle him when he first opens his eyes. You will find water in the other room."

We thought the advice quite sensible, and so retired to remove some of the paint. It was lucky that the girl gave us the hint to do so, for we found the landlord had managed to loose one of the bands that confined his arms, and in ten minutes more he would have been free, and raised an alarm that would have done us no good.

"Just in time," Murden said, as he once more secured the bully's limbs. "I didn't think that you could start my knots; but it seems that you have. Now I'll do better;" and after our man was firmly secured, we wiped the paint from our faces.

The landlord watched the operation with much interest, and when we had concluded our toilets, he exclaimed, —

"D—n me if they ain't swells, arter all."

He had all along supposed us to be workmen hired to do a certain job, for which we were to receive large pay.

We could but smile at the man's exclamation, and then turned our attention to the scene that was going on in the chamber.

We saw the girl put her hand on Hopeful's shoulder, and gently shake him; but he did not wake very readily, for the reason that he must have drank considerable liquor before he went to sleep, as we saw a half-emptied bottle of gin at the head of his bed on the table.

Repeated shakings, however, at length aroused him, and he sat up in bed and stared rather wildly at Daisy.

"Ah, it's you — is it, Daisy?" he asked, in a low tone, that was really tender. "I've been dreamin', I s'pose, and it wan't no pleasant dream, either."

"I am sorry for that, Hopeful," she said, and smoothed his hair as tenderly as though she had known and loved him for years.

"Have my friends sent me some more money?" asked Hez, as he attempted to draw the girl towards him, so that he could kiss her lips.

She resisted him and held back, because she knew that we were near, and watching every motion.

"We have heard from them; but they won't send the money," was her answer.

"Then I'll go for it," Hez cried, in an impatient and angry tone. "My money is my own, and I'll do as I please with it, now you see if I don't. They shan't keep money for me, 'less they can shell out when I wants it. You has been a good girl to me, Daisy, and shall have jist what you wants."

He made an attempt to get off the bed, but she soothed him, and at last got him more calm. We still looked on, in pity for the fellow, and at no loss to account for his weak, irritable condition; for it was evident that he had been drugged with liquor and medicine, for the purpose of affecting his mind.

"You must recollect that your friends have known you for a long time, much longer than I, and that they would do better by you than I, or my friends," the girl said, with just a touch of sentiment in her voice.

"I deny it," cried Hopeful, in an excited tone. "I wouldn't give you for a dozen friends. I wouldn't give you for all the friends in the world."

"Do you mean that, Hopeful?" I asked, and then entered his room, and stood by the side of his bed.

The wretched man uttered a loud, despairing cry, and then buried his head in the bed-clothes as, though ashamed to look me in the face, while the girl glanced at me in a reproachful manner, as though I had come in upon them too sudden.

CHAPTER XXIII.

A WRETCHED LOVER. — A LITTLE PRUDENCE AND REA-
SON. — A RESOLUTION. — AN ESCAPE. — A GANG OF
ROUGHS. — THE OFFICERS OF THE POLICE.

HOPEFUL had buried his head in the bed-clothes as soon as he heard the sound of my voice. It showed that he felt a little ashamed of his conduct, and from it I argued a favorable response to our mission; for no one better than myself knew Hez's obstinacy when a handsome face had crossed his path, and obstructed his vision and warped his judgment. I had seen several instances of his perversity while with him in Australia, and it had indeed required all of my tact to keep him faithful to the vows which he had uttered to his New Hampshire fiancée.

To be sure, now he was a free man, a widower, and at liberty to marry whom he pleased; but it did not suit me that he should throw himself into the arms of the first artful woman whom he met, and whose face was handsome, but whose principles were not such as were commended in respectable society. I knew that I should have some work to perform, but not such serious business as really occurred.

"Hopeful," I said, laying one hand on his shoulder, and attempting to remove the clothes from his head, "look at me one moment; I want to see your face."

"But I don't want to see yourn," was the reply. "Go way and leave me — will yer?"

"No; I shall do no such thing. When I go, you must go with us. Come, don't be a baby; look up. Here's Fred and Murden, and they want to see you, as well as myself."

"Go away from me, gol darn yer," was the reply. "I'm content where I am, and ain't goin' to leave here unless the gal goes too; now I tell yer that."

Daisy, whose heart I began to think was not as bad

as her character, showed some signs of distress on her pretty face.

"Don't talk like that, Hopeful," she said. "I can never go with you or leave this place. It is better as your friends suggest. Go with them, and in a few days you will forget me."

"No, I shan't, either," roared Hopeful, in his anger and eagerness throwing the clothes from his head and sitting up. "I tell yer now, as I told yer a dozen times afore, that I won't leave yer, and no one shall make me. I'll stick to yer as long as ye'll stick to me; and now yer know what I mean, and it's no use for yer to talk any more. Either give me my money, or else let Daisy go with us."

"Neither proposition will be accepted," I said, in a tone that he understood at once; although I must confess that when I looked at the girl's sweet, fresh face, I saw much to apologize for in Hez's obstinacy, and so was inclined to excuse his temper and impetuous ways, for, perhaps, had I been situated as he was, I might have done the same thing. I hope that I should not; but I fear my nature is not made of cast-iron.

"I tell yer that I shall remain here," Hez said, with all the firmness and sullenness he could command.

"Without money you would not be allowed to remain a week," I remarked, and appealed to the girl for confirmation of my words.

"It ain't so," he muttered. "The gal don't care for my money."

"But if she does not, those who employ her are not quite so disinterested. Let him understand this, Daisy."

Hopeful looked at the girl with more eagerness than I had ever seen on his face.

"Tell me," he said, "is it me or my money what you care for?"

She did not answer him, but looked a little distressed, as though surprised at the turn which affairs had taken.

"Tell me yer opinion," Hez growled.

"I'm but a poor wretch, a tool in the hands of those

who bind me to their will. I was told to attract you, to fascinate you, and I did."

"But not for my money," cried Hez, with a piteous look on his face, that was enough to melt the heart of any one not lost to all feeling.

For one moment did the girl hesitate, as though reluctant to give more pain. Fred encouraged her with a look, and then she spoke out:—

"If you had been destitute of money, I should not have attracted you by my arts, for I preferred some other person on the steamer."

"But you have said that you loved me," murmured Hez, as his head sank, and the light left his face.

She did not answer him, but showed by her sweet face the pain that she felt at being reminded of her great sins.

"Didn't you lead me to think that you loved me?" repeated Hopeful, once more looking up, but with eyes all bloodshot, showing the struggle that had taken place in his mind.

"Yes, I did," was the candid answer.

"And didn't you say that if I had money enough with me, you would go jist where I wanted yer to go?"

"Yes; I remember to have told you so."

"And what did yer do it for unless you meant it?" Hopeful demanded, in an indignant tone.

She was silent, and once more looked the real distress that she felt.

"Answer me, Daisy. By some of the love that I have told you I felt for you, answer me," pleaded Hez, in tones so earnest that the girl looked more and more distressed, but replied,—

"You have been here three days, and in that time you must have noticed that I was selfish and wicked."

"No, no," came from our friend, in gasps.

"I was told to make you send for money," she continued. "You did so. I was told to ask you for it when it came. I did ask, and you gave me the ten pounds. The next day I told you to send for more money, and if you had remained here a month, the demands for gold would have been just as fierce as ever, until the last cent of your fortune was gone. Does love prompt a woman to act like that to a person whom she likes?"

There was no answer from Hez. He was suffering too much to speak. Fred nodded his approval to the frank-spoken girl, and thus encouraged, she continued:—

"You asked me for love. I had none to give, but much to sell, and I was compelled to make the best bargain that I could for myself and those who employed me to do the work that I have done for the past three years."

"How could you deceive me in this way?" asked Hez, with more firmness than he had yet manifested.

"Because you were wilfully blind, and would not see that I had a part to play. Come, let us separate and be friends. Go with those who have known you longest, and in a few days you will forget me."

"Never!" muttered Hopeful, and once more threatened to cover his eyes with his hands, but thought better of it, and conquered his weakness as well as he was able.

The girl smiled, as though she had heard just such words before; and I had no doubt but that she had, for she was one of that kind who would have made a lasting impression on some men, had she been as virtuous as she was fair.

"There ain't much use in snivellin', arter that," Hopeful said, as he got off the bed, and began to adjust his necktie. "I s'pose I may as well go now as to wait."

His voice choked a little as he spoke, and then, when he turned, and had a fair look at the girl's face, he again broke down.

"Daisy," he said, "if you will jist say the word I'll marry yer, and then let me see the man what will dare to look at yer exceptin' with respect, as my wife. I don't care what friends say or do, if you will stick to me."

"It cannot be," was the answer, kind but quite firm, as though she meant what she said. "I am not a suitable person to be your wife. Do not mention such a subject again, for if I consented it would only make us both miserable."

Again Fred thanked the young woman, with a look, for her noble conduct. It was better than we could have expected under all the circumstances.

"It ain't no use of my stoppin' here any longer," Hopeful said, in a hoarse voice. "Let's be off as soon as we can. I'm deceived in that woman."

She did not reply, or look the pain she felt.

"I'll never believe in a woman again, you see if I do," Hopeful continued, as he hurried on his coat. "From this time I renounce the whole of 'em."

Murden and I exchanged looks. We had heard the same kind of expressions several times, so did not tremble for the desolation that was about to fall upon the whole of womankind, in case Hez adhered to his word.

We left the bed-chamber for the sitting-room, and glanced towards the spot where the landlord had been reposing, bound with cords which were capable of standing a severe test. To our surprise we did not see our prisoner, and a slight examination showed us that he had managed to free his limbs while we were in consultation with Hopeful, and so escaped without our noticing the fact.

"The cuss has gone for a gang of roughs to clean us out," said Murden. "Shall we make a break for the lower part of the house, or stand here and endure a siege?"

"There may be time to escape," Fred cried. "Let us make the attempt, and so save the trouble of a row and a severe fight."

We opened the door and stepped into the entry; but we were too late, for we could hear the tramping of feet, as a crowd of men were hastening along the lower passage-way.

"They are coming," we muttered to each other, and then thought how we should defend ourselves, for we knew that we could hope for little mercy at the hands of the infuriated landlord.

We returned to the sitting-room and locked the door,

Daisy still being with us. In fact, she had not taken advantage of the confusion to escape, as we supposed she would, and when we had locked the door, to stop the first wild rush of the roughs, Fred had offered to let her pass out and join her friends if she desired to; but she said that she would remain with us until the disturbance was over, and expressed a hope that she might be the means of obtaining honorable terms for us, so that we could march out of the garrison with all the honors of war.

Hopeful now threw off his fit of depression and acted like a man. He could not quite forget his late sufferings, and every time his eyes fell upon Daisy's face, he would utter a deep sigh, and then turn away from a sight that so powerfully affected him.

"Let 'em come on," Hez said, in allusion to the roughs, who were now at the door. "I'll be gol darned if we don't serve 'em an Australian trick afore they is through with us; now you see if we don't."

"Bravo, Hez," cried Fred, slapping the son of New Hampshire on his back. "I knew you was made of the right kind of stuff, and would show your grit when the time came."

At this moment the landlord of the Horseshoe and his allies gained the door, and one of them pounded on it.

"Open," said the man whom we had knocked down and made a prisoner. "Open this door, or the wusser for you, now I tell yer."

We returned no answer.

"Do yer hear me?" demanded the landlord, with a kick at the door that threatened to take it from its hinges.

"We hear you," was our answer.

"Then let us in," the landlord said, and consigned our eyes to a very warm place.

"We don't desire your company," Fred replied. "We have had enough of it to last for a lifetime."

The landlord uttered some frightful curses, and once more kicked at the door as though determined to break through without the least unnecessary delay.

We saw that the roughs were bound to come through, at all hazards, and we had no authority to stop them, for we were but trespassing on the premises; but Murden, who knew something of the law, took a different view of the matter, and turning to Hez, asked, —

"Did you hire this room?"

"Yes."

"For any length of time?"

"Till I got through with it."

"And what were you to pay a week, as rent?"

"Five pounds, I guess. I know I promised to give jist what was axed: didn't I, Daisy?"

The girl acknowledged that he was right, but she was too frightened to do more.

"Then you have not given notice that you desired to leave the apartments?" Murden continued.

"Of course I haven't. How could I do so, when I haven't sot eyes on the landlord for a day or two?"

"Then we are not trespassing," the ex-commissioner said. "As invited guests, we have a just right to remain here, and we will do so in spite of the roughs outside."

"By the laws of England, this room is our friend's castle," Fred remarked, "and he has a perfect right to defend himself from any assault."

For a moment or two the fellows at the door had remained silent, in a sort of consultation, as to the best course to pursue, for, although they knew we were inclined to fight, they did not think we were armed with revolvers or other deadly weapons.

The consultation was soon over, however, and then came another rude summons to surrender.

"Halloo, in there," some one said, with an emphatic kick on the door.

"Well, what is it?" was our response.

"Let us in, or the worse for you."

"Don't you mean that it would be the worse for us if we let you in?" asked Fred, with a mocking laugh.

The roughs uttered some savage curses, and then kicked

at the door until it threatened to fly from its hinges under the fierce assault.

"What is the good of all that noise?" at length Fred asked. "Even if you come in, the tenant will warn you to leave as soon as you cross the threshold."

"Will he?" asked the landlord. "We shan't wait for that, for we shall throw you out of the window."

"It might hurt us," was the reply.

"For God's sake, gentlemen!" cried Daisy, now thoroughly alarmed, "don't aggravate them, for if you do they will murder you before you can leave the house. You don't know what savage men they are."

"We can imagine," was the answer; and then we knew that the moment had arrived for action.

We drew our revolvers, and retreated into one corner of the room, so that the roughs could not outflank us without some trouble. We placed Daisy close to the wall, so that we could cover her, and stand between her and harm, and by the time we had completed our preparations the door was torn from its hinges, and in rushed eight desperate fellows, inflamed with liquor, and the thought of giving four men an unmerciful beating.

The scamps dashed towards us, and did not stop until they were within a few feet of us. Then they halted suddenly, for they saw something that surprised them very much. In fact they retreated a few steps, and put their hands to their heads, as though to ward off a blow.

The sight which was so unexpected to the roughs was three men, in a corner, with three cocked revolvers, pointing at the crowd that was to thrash us without mercy.

We rather enjoyed the discomfiture of the fellows, it reminded us so much of life in Australia, when certain bushrangers supposed that they had us in their power, and yet found that such was not the case, we generally turning the tables at the most critical moment.

"Look ahere," said the landlord of the Golden Horseshoe, in a tone of extreme remonstrance; "what in the name of bloody thunder do yer mean by this ere kind of work, hey?"

"You see what we mean — don't you?" Fred asked, in his most pleasant, cool tones.

"No, I'm blasted if I do," was the reply.

"Well, then, let us explain. We mean that you have no right to enter our friend's room in this manner, and that if you don't leave it we shall shoot."

"What, fire at us?" was the astonished question.

"At you," was the short response.

"Well, this is a bloody go, I should think," was the muttered exclamation on the part of the crowd. "You don't mean it."

"You offer to lay your hands on us, and then you'll see that we do," was our reply; and the roughs appeared to be satisfied that we meant what we said, for after one or two long looks at us and our revolvers, they whispered to each other, and then quietly retired to the entry to consult as to the best method of obtaining an advantage over us.

As soon as they were gone we closed the door, but could not lock it, for the reason that the gang had torn it from its hinges when they entered the apartment. We did not put it up, thinking that it would keep the fellows out, but for the purpose of hiding our movements from the enemy

"Is there no way by which we can reach the street, except by passing over the stairs?" I asked Daisy.

"No," she answered. "You can't drop from the windows, for there is a picket fence beneath them, placed there for the purpose of preventing escape from this room. It would be certain death to drop on it."

"Then we must wait."

"And starve," added Murden; "for you may be certain that they will cut off our supplies, and thus force us into a surrender."

"Why not make a rush, and give 'em ginger?" Hopeful said.

"Because then we should suffer at the hands of the law, and we have had enough law in Ireland to last us for some time. No, that won't do, for the reason that we should have to kill somebody, or else get nearly killed ourselves. Let us wait."

And we did wait, and still we could hear the roughs in whispered consultation, advising certain schemes for our defeat. At last we caught the word "police," and then we knew that the landlord was about to bring a posse of officers into the house, and thus see if we could not be arrested on legal grounds.

We did not feel in the least terrified, but waited until the door was pushed aside, and four stout, uniformed officers entered the room, followed by only three of the landlord's crew.

CHAPTER XXIV.

ANOTHER SURPRISE. — A RETREAT. — A DEMAND. — MURDEN'S POINT. — DAISY AND HER FUTURE LIFE.

When the police officers of the commercial city of Liverpool entered the apartment where we were drawn up to receive them, they looked as fierce as men should look who are intrusted with the safety of the town, and have desperate characters to deal with at times.

It was evident to us that they had expected a fight of some kind; for they had their staffs in their hands, and seemed disposed to use them over our heads at the least sign of provocation on our part.

A slight look of disappointment passed over the stern faces of the officers when they saw that we were apparently unarmed, and not disposed to offer much resistance. They glanced at the landlord of the Golden Horseshoe for an explanation, and he was all ready to offer one on the impulse of the moment.

"Put the irons on 'em," shouted the man who was most

interested in our being locked up. "They is desperate customers, and threatened to make holes in our bodies with their pistols. They has 'em in their pockets now, and will use 'em agin yer, if you don't look out."

"Do ye give yerselves in custody?" asked the sergeant of the squad, stepping forward with a military air, and making a salute with his club.

"Let me answer him," whispered Murden. "I know how to deal with such characters better than you."

We had not the slightest objections to his doing so.

"On what charge," asked the ex-commissioner of the Australian mounted police, "do you arrest us?"

The police sergeant actually laughed in Murden's face, after a long and steady look at our friend, in the first place, and then our own persons in the next.

"Well," the sergeant muttered, as though a little astonished at our appearance, "if this ain't one of the jolliest goes that I ever did see in all my life, then I wouldn't say so — that's all."

Then he resumed his official stern look, as he replied to Murden's question.

"Look ahere, gents," the officer said; "I has been informed by a party what is in this room at the present time that you has offered to kill some one."

"Meaning me," said the landlord.

"Meaning you," said the sergeant; and then another grin passed over his face.

"And my friends what were with me at the time they makes the assault on me," added the landlord.

"You and your friends," said the sergeant, with more gravity.

"They threatened to kill us, and then mash us," the landlord added, for fear that he had not said enough.

"And it's a wonder to me that they hadn't done as they said they would, 'cos they look to me like men what would keep their word on all occasions. If they said they would mash yer, I don't see what prevented 'em, unless you run for it."

"We did," cried the landlord, quite eagerly. "When they pointed their pistols at us, we backed out into the entry in a hurry."

"And it was wise in yer to do so," said the police sergeant. "Never stand afore a pistol when a man means shoot. It's dangerous to do so."

"Perhaps, if you should hear our side of the story, you would think we were justified in our threats, and the course we took," Murden remarked.

"Don't let 'em stand there talkin' all night," the landlord said. "Take 'em away. I makes a charge agin 'em. Summons me to prove it to-morrow, and I'll do it."

"Don't let us hurry matters quite so much," the officer replied. "We must be a little cautious how we proceeds. This is a serious kind of business; this offerin' to kill a man can't be put out of sight."

"Will you hear our account of this trouble?" asked Murden. "I'll be quite brief in my statement."

" I think," replied the sergeant, in a tone that showed some deliberation of a mental kind, "that we had better hear what you has to say for yerself afore we do much more."

The landlord didn't like the turn of affairs; so he whispered to the sergeant long and eagerly; but he did not seem to change the latter's mind, for he repeated the remark that it was best on all accounts to hear what was said on both sides.

"Now, then," said the police officer, "let's open the case for the defendants. Fire away."

Murden stated his case in as few words as possible. He told how we had missed Hopeful on landing at Liverpool, and how he had been induced by a girl's pretty face to take up his abode among strangers, and to send for money to pay the exorbitant charges of the landlord. He then related how we had taken the trouble to hunt up Hopeful's quarters, in the hope of rescuing him from his bad company, and inducing him to go with us to London.

"And who does you know in London what will vouch for the truth of yer yarn?" asked the officer.

"Sir William Byefield and the Earl of Buckland will testify to the truth of our statements at any time," was Murden's reply.

The landlord and his crew uttered several ironical laughs when these names were pronounced, as though they considered it a good joke on our part. The officers, with the exception of the sergeant, joined in the laugh.

"Look ahere," said the landlord; "it won't do to utter no swells' names here, 'cos they won't go down with us, and we don't want nothin' to do with 'em. Now I'm a honest sort of man, and minds my own business; and when a cove comes here and says that he wants a room and grub, and a gal to keep him company, I has no objections, provided he does the right thing by me. I has no cause to complain of the man what they calls Hopeful. He has paid me for a week's lodgings; so I has no charges agin him."

"Then he had a right to the room for two or three days more?" asked the sergeant.

"Yes; I don't deny that he paid me for a week."

Then the officer turned to Hopeful.

"You call these gentlemen," he said, and pointed to us with an air of respect, although we were not dressed in gentlemen's habiliments, "your friends — do you?"

"In course," was Hopeful's reply.

"And you invited them to remain in your room — did you?" the sergeant continued.

"Sartin I did. They is the best friends I has in the world."

The police officer turned to the landlord with a look that was not quite as friendly as could be desired.

"I don't see how you can bring a charge against these parties," he remarked. "They had a right to be here as the guests of your lodger, and you had no right to break down the door when Mr. Hopeful told you not to come in."

"D—n sich law as that," was the response. "I could make better law any time."

The roughs who were in league with the landlord of the Golden Horseshoe reëchoed his opinion, and seemed disposed to punch the heads of the officers, and they would have done so if they had not feared the law.

"The question is not what you could do, but what is right," said the sergeant, turning on the landlord, and speaking rather sharply. "If you don't like what I says, jist go to headquarters and lay the case afore 'em, and see what they says; that's all."

"But don't you see," stammered the landlord, "that these men comes into my place for the purpose of robbing me, for all I knows of."

"Pooh! nonsense!" was the reply. "They wouldn't take a penny of what didn't belong to 'em."

"I ain't so sure of that ere," was the sullen response.

"But I am. I knows 'em, and has known 'em for years."

It was now our turn to look a little astonished, and to glance at the speaker with more attention than we had yet bestowed on him.

His face did not seem familiar. We did not recollect to have seen it before, and yet it was quite evident that the man had met us somewhere during our wanderings in various parts of the world.

"Where have you met us?" Murden asked him, after a pause, during which we scrutinized the man's face with the most marked attention.

"The sergeant laughed, as he asked,—

"Don't you recollect me?"

"No."

"Well, sir, I don't know as it is strange, arter all, that you shouldn't know my face; yet I once had the honor of servin' on the Melbourne police, and there I frequently saw Mr. Commissioner Murden and all the rest of you, gents; so you see I is quite well acquainted with yer all, and I is happy to serve yer if I can do so."

By the end of this long speech the landlord of the

Golden Horseshoe began to look as though he had made a mistake, and he would have retreated in company with his followers if Murden had not interfered.

"Hold on, my friend," he said. "Don't leave us in such a hurry. We have a little business to transact with you. Sergeant, my good fellow, I recollect you now as well as though you were my own brother. You did good service in Melbourne. When you arrested McCoodle the bushranger, who was seeking to escape in the disguise of a sailor, it was the crowning event of your life, and even the governor general spoke of the matter as being an honor to any man in the force. You see I know you. Now do me a favor, for old times. Just step in between the landlord and the door, so that the fellow cannot escape while I do a little business on my own account."

The police sergeant blushed with pleasure at being complimented by so distinguished a person as Mr. Commissioner Murden. He instantly complied with the request, and thus cut off the landlord's retreat.

"Now, my friend," said Murden, addressing the criminal, who was far from pleased at the situation of affairs, "we want some of that money which you have swindled out of Mr. Hopeful. He had ten pounds when he entered the house. He sent for ten pounds. You took the money. I want some of it."

"No, no," muttered Hopeful. "Blast the money. I don't want it."

"But I say yes. I want some of the money, and mean to have it," Murden continued.

"I won't touch a cent of it," Hez growled, with a blush and a glance at Daisy.

"I don't mean that you shall," was the prompt reply. "I want some of the money; but when I get it you shan't handle it unless you desire to."

Hopeful looked puzzled, and so did the rest of us. We did not comprehend our friend's meaning, and yet we knew that he had one of some kind or other.

There was a moment's silence. The landlord looked a

little irresolute, as though he did not know whether it was best to surrender at once, or to hold on to what he had got and hope for more.

"Daisy," said the Australian, "come here."

She obeyed him, in her usual modest and timid manner.

He took her hand, and she suffered him to retain it, just as though she was the most diffident girl in the city, and the most modest at the same time. It was hard to believe that she was wholly vile, while looking at her, as she stood by the Australian's side. I was prepared for any amount of sentiment, just then; but Murden had a harder head, and was therefore more practical than myself. He was enough to spoil the most delicate of woven romances.

"Daisy, my good girl," he said, "how much out of the twenty pounds did that man," pointing to the landlord, "give you for your part, in entrapping Hopeful?"

She hesitated and looked a little frightened.

"Don't be alarmed. That man shan't hurt you. Speak the truth though the heavens fall. Tell me the sum total, so that I can judge of his liberality."

All eyes were turned to the girl as she looked down, blushed more than ever, and replied, —

"He gives me a pound a week."

"Now," said Murden, "just hand over ten pounds. I want to use them."

"I don't want the money," muttered Hez. "Let the scamp keep it, and much good may it do him."

"Be quiet, will you?" thundered the Australian. "I'm managing this case in my own way, and I will have no interference."

Hez subsided, although he said that he didn't see what they wanted to make such a fuss for about a little money.

To the Australian's demand for ten pounds the landlord turned a deaf ear.

"No you don't," he said. "No man can rob me in my own house and four police officers standin' lookin' on. I've got the money, and I'll keep it, you see if I don't. Strike me blind if you can ride rough over me."

"You will give me the money," said Murden, in his most quiet tones. "I know you will."

"And I know that I won't. Who do you think I am, that you can bully me?"

"I think you are one of the most consummate scoundrels in Liverpool," our friend replied, still retaining his coolness.

"You may think so, but that won't give you the money," was the taunting reply.

Murden turned to the police sergeant, who still blocked up the door, and who had remained a quiet listener to the conversation.

"Sergeant," he said, "isn't there a city ordinance in force in Liverpool in relation to keeping disorderly houses?"

"Yes, sir."

"Wouldn't this house come under such an ordinance?"

"Yes, sir, if any one would make a complaint, and bring forward witnesses."

"I make the complaint," thundered the Australian, with all of his commissioner fierceness. "I give the man in charge for extortion and keeping a house of vile repute, noisy and disorderly."

"Where are your witnesses?" sneered the landlord, who began to look a little alarmed at the way things were turning.

"Here they are;" and Murden pointed to Hez and Daisey.

"I'll be d—d—" began Hopeful; but the Australian silenced him with a look and an oath of some magnitude.

"You'll do as I bid you," Murden said. "There is a principle at stake that we must not lose sight of. You will appear as a witness."

"Well, if I must—" began Hopeful.

"Of course you must. We can have no words on that point."

"But the girl. She will never dare to appear against me," the landlord said; and he gave her a threatening look, that meant something.

"She will appear against you, and do as I wish her."

Daisy trembled, and seemed undecided how to act.

"I dare not appear against him," she whispered. "He would murder me if I did."

"He will do no such thing," returned the Australian. "I will see that no one is murdered. If there's to be any killing, I'll have a hand in it."

"Will you protect me if I speak only the truth?" asked Daisy.

"Yes, with our lives and fortunes," returned the stout-hearted Australian.

"Then I'll do as you want me to. I'll appear as a witness."

"Daisy!" cried the landlord, in a tone that was meant to be threatening.

"I will do it!" she cried, with more energy than I ever saw her exhibit. "I am tired of the life that I have led, and would have abandoned it long since, had I known where to go or what to do. Here is a chance to escape from your power. I'll improve it, and then leave the city forever; and I pray God that we may never meet again."

"If we ever do —" muttered the landlord, with grinding teeth and a look on his face that was fiend-like.

"Come, come," said Murden, "don't threaten. We can do all the threatening that is necessary. Hand me ten pounds, and be lively about it, for I am in a hurry."

"I'll see you d—d first, and then I won't," was the sullen reply.

"Take him to the police station, sergeant. We'll follow and make the charge as soon as possible."

The officer laid a hand on the landlord's shoulder, and the touch seemed to melt the fellow's feelings, for he put his hand in his pocket and pulled out a roll of bills.

"Here's yer money," he said. "I hope it will choke you, I does."

"Thank you for the wish. We will risk it. Daisy, this belongs to you. Take the money, and keep it. I don't want any thanks. Now pack up your dry goods, and go with us."

"With me," cried Hez, starting forward.

"No, sir," frowned the virtuous ex-commissioner. "She becomes no man's property. She leads a new life from this time forth, and we will, by the blessing of God, see that she does not want for money while striving to reform."

Poor Daisy. She could hardly comprehend Murden's words, so great was her agitation and surprise.

For a moment she looked from one to the other, her fair face as colorless as a sheet of note paper; then the blood rushed to her cheeks and brow, and with a gasp she fell forward, and would have struck the floor with much violence, if Fred had not sprung forward and caught her in his arms.

CHAPTER XXV.

WHAT TO DO WITH A FAINTING GIRL. — ROVER AND THE LANDLORD. — MURDEN AND HIS PROTEGEE. — AN AWKWARD MEETING.

THE surprise and expressions of sympathy which Daisy had heard were too much for her. The thought that now she had a chance to leave the terrible life which she so much abhorred had come upon her so suddenly that she had fainted and fallen into Fred's arms, and the poor fellow did not know what to do with her, so concluded to hold on to her, and look at us with a most piteous expression upon his face, as though to deprecate any unpleasant feeling on our part, provided we were inclined to entertain it.

We did not know what to do with a fainting woman. Had it been a man, we should have forced open his mouth, and poured a glass of brandy down his throat, shaken him several times, and then told him to get up and do better in future; but one can't be so rude with a handsome female, unless all patience is lost, in which case man is capable of anything in the shape of bear-like manners.

However, as a preliminary step towards recovering her senses, I offered to take the girl into my own arms, and thus relieve Fred of his burden, which I feared distressed him. I was willing to encounter the ridicule, if any was offered; but to my surprise Fred seemed willing to bear the whole of the burden, without the least assistance on my part.

"You needn't trouble yourself," he said, as I held out my arms. "I can take care of her for a few minutes without much fatigue on my part. Just concern yourself by obtaining a little water and wetting the girl's lips. You will do more good that way than any other that I know of."

The water sprinkled on Daisy's face did the business. She soon opened her eyes and looked at the anxious-appearing men who surrounded her.

"I am better," she said, with a sigh, and then — quite properly, as I thought, and still think — quickly extricated herself from Mr. Fred's arms. "It was quite foolish in me to faint, I know; but I was so much surprised at what some one said, that all consciousness was gone in a moment. I hope I did not dream."

"Not a darned bit of it," cried Hez, coming forward. "It is all right, and if you has the least desire to begin all anew, with a real clean record and all that, I ain't the man to say yo shan't, not by a darned sight, now I tell yer. I may be a little weak in the head, when a pretty woman bothers me, but I ain't awfully wicked — now am I?"

We told Hez that he was one of the best fellows in the world, and that we always knew he had a good heart; and that pleased him so much that he was ready to agree to most anything we proposed.

"Well, g nts," aske' the sergeant, now speaking for the

first time, "what is to be done with this ere cove?" pointing to the landlord, who had been standing in the room, a cross witness of all that had taken place. "Do you want to make a charge against him?"

"No," answered Murden. "He has refunded the money, and now he can go to the devil, where he belongs. We want no more to do with him."

"One word before I goes to your relative what you seems to be on good terms with," the landlord said, with a sneer. "Will you oblige a cove by telling him who brought you here? Did the Bantam show you the way? That's all I wants to know. Jist tell me that, and I'll be satisfied; 'cos ye see I'll mash him in no time, you see if I don't."

We pretended that we did not know whom he meant; and just at that moment our noble old dog Rover, that we had left in our room at the hotel, stalked into the apartment, and wagged his tail as though he knew he should discover us with but little trouble.

Of course we were astonished to see him, and wondered how he had been able to find us, and how he had escaped from the hotel. We afterwards learned that one of the servants had entered the apartment where Rover was confined, and that the dog took the opportunity to dash into the street, and then had tracked us to the Golden Horseshoe.

"You want to know how we discovered the place where our friend was concealed?" asked Murden.

The landlord said that nothing would give him more pleasure; and he struck his fists together, as though to emphasize his words, and show what he could do with them on the body of an informer.

Murden pointed to the hound, which appeared to be quite at home in the apartment.

"The dog followed your messenger, and tracked him like a detective," he said.

"Then the dog may take that for his trouble;" and before we could interfere, the brutal landlord had raised one of his feet, and kicked the hound near his fore shoulders.

Rover, although somewhat surprised at such rough treatment from those whom he looked upon as friends, did not utter a howl or a whimper; but no sooner did he feel the scamp's boot than his lamb-like look was exchanged for the courage of a lion and the ferocity of a tiger. Up went the hair on his back like bristles, his eyes appeared like balls of fire, his lips were drawn apart, showing long white teeth, sharp as needles; and then, before we could or cared to interfere, he had launched himself full at the neck of the landlord, and bore him to the floor as easily as though a child.

Rover's motions were so sudden, so unexpected, that not one of us could raise a hand to hold the dog, and thus save the man's life, or some severe punishment; but the instant the landlord struck the floor, he put his hands around Rover's neck, and attempted to strangle the animal, or else choke him from his hold; but he might just as well have sought to destroy the life of a Bengal tiger famished for the want of food.

"Take him off, for God's sake!" cried the landlord, when he felt the hound's teeth, and found that he could not shake him off.

I made an immediate attempt to do so. I spoke to the hound, and called him by name; but the dog had received an insult and an indignity that he could not forget very soon; so I was compelled to lay hands upon him and drag him from the prostrate body of his foe.

"Curse the dog," cried the landlord, as he sat up and rubbed his throat, which was somewhat lacerated, but not in a dangerous manner, owing to the thickness of his neck-handkerchief and the collar of his coat.

"Don't swear at the dog, but at your own evil temper, which led you to kick him," I said. "It's a wonder that he did not kill you; for you deserve some punishment for what you have done. Rover is not to be trifled with, and he never forgets an injury. If he should meet you a year hence, he would show that he has not forgotten you."

The landlord looked at the hound with respectful fear.

The dog's prowess had won some of his esteem, although he still rubbed his throat and muttered curses at the treatment which he had received.

"I say," he cried at last, "you don't want to sell the dog — do you, nor nothin'?"

"No money that you could offer would buy him," was my reply; and Rover seemed to understand my words, for he crouched at my feet, and showed his teeth to the landlord.

"If you would like to sell the ugly devil, I'd buy him, and train him to fight a dog what I knows of, and what I think can be licked. If you didn't want to sell him, you might like to win a pile of money on him, and I can put you in the way of doin' it — I can."

We intimated that such kind of business was not in our line, and that we must decline to lend ourselves to dog-fighting; and then we made preparations for our departure, intending to take Daisy with us, although none of us knew what were Murden's plans concerning her. She was willing to go; and the landlord, after his punishment, did not make strong objections, but hinted that he should receive some compensation for loss of service — an idea that we laughed at.

"Now, sergeant," said Murden, after Daisy had gathered up her dry goods in a bundle, "you lead the way, and we will follow you out of this den and go to our hotel."

The landlord, still rubbing his throat, and scowling at the dog, did not object, because he knew that objections were useless. He went with us down stairs, where we found quite a crowd of his admirers; but they confined their actions to chaffing us for taking away the girl. The poor thing knew most of them, and shrunk from their coarse words as though each one had blistered her fair skin like a hot iron.

We would have shielded her from the billingsgate slang that was hurled at her head, but could not, for the simple reason that the ruffians were numerous, and we should have encountered much trouble had we bandied words with them, or knocked down one or two of the most offensive. Even the presence of the police could not have prevented our getting some hard blows.

One fellow, more inclined to be funny than the rest, thought that it would be a good joke to pinch Rover's tail, so that the dog would howl in anguish; but somehow the hound did not howl, but the ruffian did; for Rover, stalking along in sullen dignity, after his late bad treatment, turned on the fellow like a flash of lightning, and his jaws closed like a wolf trap on the very hand that touched his tail.

There was a shriek of terror, and then a prolonged "O," as the teeth met.

"You d—n fool," said the landlord, with his hand still up to his throat, "didn't you know any better than that?"

The fellow didn't appear to; for he swore some at the dog, at us, and every one near him; but no one appeared to care for his misfortune. A crowd of English roughs have but little sympathy for each other. More unfeeling men the world cannot produce.

We left the house as orderly as possible, and then the police sergeant dismissed his companions, and offered to accompany us to the hotel, which offer we did not refuse; for the officer had done us good service, and we desired to reward him in some way for his kindness towards us. We could not let an old Australian companion leave us without feeling glad that we had met.

When we gained the hotel, we compelled the sergeant to go to our rooms, while Murden ordered an apartment for Daisy, and sent her to bed, with the assurance that her new life. and a better one, had already commenced.

We had some supper brought to our room, and then made the sergeant sit down and enjoy himself; and when he left us that night, he had weighty reasons for remembering our first visit to Liverpool.

"Murden," I said, the next morning, after we had dressed, and while we were waiting for breakfast, "what do you mean to do with that poor girl, Daisy?"

"I intend to do well by her," he said, after a moment's thought.

"I have no doubt of it. But what do you mean to do? That is a question that I should like to hear answered on the girl's account, and more especially on Hopeful's account. You know how he feels on the subject."

"Yes."

"And in all your arrangements you will have an eye to his peace of mind, as well as to Daisy's comfort?"

'Yes, I have thought of all these things; and now I'll tell you what I mean to do. A ship sails this day for Melbourne."

"Yes."

"On board that ship Miss Daisy will take passage, with letters to some friends of mine, kind-hearted ladies, who will take care of her until I return and look after her in person."

"And you think she will be safe on board the ship?"

"Yes; for she will be put in charge of an aged lady and her husband, who have taken passage on the vessel."

"And how in the devil's name did you learn all this?"

"This morning, while you were sleeping, I was at the docks, looking for just the chance I have found. I was fortunate to find a ship that will sail at high tide, which will occur at one o'clock this afternoon. I was still more fortunate in discovering that the master of the vessel is an acquaintance of mine, one whom I befriended at Melbourne three years ago, when he was robbed of a large sum of money. I recovered his funds, and did not charge him anything for so doing. Ah, virtue has its own reward, after all."

"True; but I am surprised that you had virtue enough to refuse a liberal reward."

"Don't joke on so serious a subject. I did refuse, and now I am about to reap my reward for such a refusal. Here the captain turns up just when I want him. He is overjoyed to see me, and swears that he will feel everlastingly obliged if I will ask a favor of him. Could anything have been more fortunate?"

I acknowledged that he was in luck, but at the same time I hinted that I had my doubts as to the lady's compliance with his wishes in leaving England at such short notice.

"What?" he cried. "Not want to go to Australia? Not want to leave this old country, where every one will look at her with scorn? Not desire to see Melbourne, where she will be respected, and find a good rich husband in the course of time, so that she can go to work and have a family, who will in turn become statesmen, or wives of statesmen? Why, what do you think the girl is made of?"

"You have spoken to her about the voyage," I hinted.

"Not a word. I did not think of the project until after I had retired for the night. She will go. She must go. I shall pay her passage, and give her a good outfit of clothes."

"Can her clothes be got ready in so short a time?" I asked, knowing that some women require months of preparation for a week's trip to a fashionable watering-place.

"Of course they can. I shall take her to a ready-made furnishing store, where all kinds of garments are kept for sale. You'll find lots of such stores in England, and quite convenient they are to people in a hurry."

"Whatever you do," I said, "recollect that our company will share the expense. I rather like your project. If the girl is disposed to begin a good life, how much better for her that she takes a new country for her future residence!"

"Yes," cried the ex-commissioner, glowing with enthusiasm; "and such a country as Australia. Ah, who wouldn't go there if able to do so? What land can be compared to Victoria?"

I did not say that I had seen better countries, where the land was richer, the climate more agreable, the dust less dense, the wind not quite so fierce and cutting, and the rains not so heavy, and the bush more safe from depredations and desperadoes, because my friend had a weakness for the land in which he had lived and flourished, grown rich and popular. In Melbourne he was of some importance. In England he was unknown and of no account. We all like to be thought influential, and Murden was no exception to the rule.

"If she should kick in the traces," said my friend, after a moment's thought, "and refuse to go, you must do all that you can to help me persuade her that it's her duty to obey. You can tell her what a delightful country Australia is, and how much women are thought of there, and how quick they get good husbands. That will bring her to her senses sooner than anything else. Tell a girl that a husband is at the end of the world, and you see if she don't start after him."

"Do you mean that the previous character of the girl shall be known to those on board, or to those who have her in charge?"

"Am I a fool, or a man of sense? Answer me that."

"A fool, if you ask such questions of me."

"Well, then, don't you think that I should be in good business to advertise the history of the poor girl, and so set people to pitying and patronizing her, and broken-down theological humbugs holding her up as an example for all frail women to follow? Wouldn't it be a splendid thing for her to land in Melbourne, with the reputation of having been a fallen angel? No, sir; she shall go on board of that ship, if she goes at all, as an acquaintance of mine, and with no stain on her character that we shall mention, or that she shall allude to, for her own sake and ours. She shall change her name, and if any one should recognize her, she can set him at defiance, by alluding to my standing in the community, and her own innocent-looking face. There is no use in sending a town crier around to tell the people that Daisy has reformed. Better never let it be known that such reformation was needed. She can lock the secret in her own heart, and throw away the key."

"And wouldn't you advise her to find the key when she

round a chance to marry some good man? Shouldn't she unlock her heart before she changed her name?"

"What good would it do her or him?"

"He would then know all, and could never reproach her for concealing her past life."

"And so make both parties unhappy and suspicious of each other! The man would declare that he still loved her, perhaps, but he would never, never forget the blot that had rested on her name and fame, and he would be continually wishing that he had thought twice before he gave his name to one who had been so unfortunate; while the wife, knowing that her husband had lost some of his respect for her, would be miserable, and so much unlike her former self, that perhaps love would turn to hate. No; keep your family secrets. What a world this would be if all was known that is now so carefully concealed!"

Just at this moment the door was opened, and in walked Miss Goldthwaite and her father, whom we supposed in Paris; and just at that time Miss Daisy entered the apartment from an adjoining room, so that the two ladies found themselves face to face. It was all owing to the stupidity of the waiter, who had shown Mr. Goldthwaite and daughter to our parlor instead of the public reception-room.

This was not quite so favorable a situation as an ardent lover, who had never declared his love, could have desired when he met his mistress for the first time after an absence of several days.

CHAPTER XXVI.

AN EXPLANATION, AND ONE THAT IS SATISFACTORY. — AN INTERVIEW WITH DAISY. — HER CONSENT. — ANOTHER SURPRISE.

OF course I was delighted, and at the same time surprised, to see Miss Goldthwaite. I should rather have met her under more favorable auspices, for she had made a decided impression upon me on board the steamer, and I had looked forward to our meeting in Paris with much pleasure.

Miss Goldthwaite had stopped short when she saw Daisy enter the room. The latter, poor child, had done the same when she saw Miss Goldthwaite, and thus the two girls, both handsome as pictures, yet of a different style of beauty, — for one was a blonde and the other a brunette, — stood staring at each other with the most startling expressions of astonishment on their faces, for Miss Josephine Goldthwaite did not know what to say to Daisy, and the latter feared that she had intruded where she was not wanted just at that time, and so appeared rather embarrassed, and of course a little guilty.

Murden and I were as much in want of a little presence of mind as any two men that I know of, and for a minute, I think, we did nothing but stare at the ladies, without speaking a word. Then I recovered myself, and hastened towards Miss Josephine, and extended my hand; but the young lady did not seem to notice it. She was inclined to be sarcastic, for she said, —

"I am afraid that we have intruded on your privacy; but if we have, you must blame the servant, not us."

"Don't mention it," I cried, in as cool a tone as I could assume, and wishing that all of my impudence would return. "We are too glad to see you to find the least fault. This is our public parlor, and we have nothing to conceal."

And then I turned, and had a hearty shake of the hand from Mr. Goldthwaite, while the two girls still stared at each other in a rather defiant manner, at least on Josephine's part.

"I'm really glad to see you," said Mr. Goldthwaite. "We were in London when we saw an account of your troubles in Ireland, and also the news of your leaving Dublin for Liverpool. We thought that we would run down and see you, and that we could all start for Paris together."

"Father," said Miss Josie, speaking quite slowly, yet most emphatically, "I think that we have made a mistake, and we had better return to London."

"Why, my dear child, what reason —"

"Reason enough," she answered, in an impetuous manner. "I wish to leave this house without a moment's delay."

I telegraphed Murden to get Daisy from the room as soon as possible. He understood me, and made motions for his *protégée* to follow him, which she did without a word.

"It seems a pity that you should leave just after having found us," I remarked to Miss Josie, with all of my coolness restored, now that Daisy was out of sight.

"We shan't be missed, I think," with an indignant toss of her pretty head, and a flash of her bright eyes.

"There is where you wrong us. We should miss you very much, and if you knew how often my friend Mr. Hopeful had spoken of you since we parted, you would feel proud of the consideration which you have enjoyed."

"Mr. Hopeful's consideration!" she repeated, with another toss of her pretty head and a little scorn in her looks.

She was apparently a little astonished at the tone of my remarks, and evidently wondered that I did not mention myself as being concerned in her behalf.

"My dear," said Mr. Goldthwaite, who saw that his child was inclined to be angry at something, yet could not imagine the cause, "hadn't you better sit down for a moment?"

"How can you ask me such a question?" the lady retorted. "No; I prefer to keep my feet while I remain in this room."

"I don't understand it," said the father, in a perplexed tone, and then looked at me for an explanation; but I was not prepared to furnish it just at that moment. I did not want to bother the young lady, but I remembered that she had laughed at me when I landed at Queenstown, when I displayed a little sentiment on her account. She had taught me a lesson that I was disposed to remember for some time.

There was a large, comfortable-looking easy-chair in the apartment. I rolled it towards Miss Josie, and then politely asked her to be seated.

She hesitated, and looked at me with a glance that was intended to be penetrating, but I appeared unconscious of the power of her dark eyes.

"Answer me one question," she said, "or I won't sit down."

"I'll answer a dozen," I replied.

"Truthfully, sir?"

"Truthfully. I shall never speak but the truth to Miss Goldthwaite."

She pouted her pretty lips as much as to say that such kind of talk was man's talk, and hardly worth listening to; but still she asked, —

"Who is that handsome girl I saw but a moment since in this room?"

"That young lady," I began; but I could not help blushing a little, for I was about to tell a lie for the purpose of making all smooth and clear to Miss Josie's understanding.

"I want the truth, sir," she said, as she took the seat I proffered her, and then turned on me like an empress.

"And the truth you shall certainly have," was my

answer, blushing more than ever at the style of her questioning.

Now, I'll ask the reader how it was possible for me to tell the whole truth under the circumstances? Here was a virtuous girl asking questions which she should not have asked, and expecting the truth, the whole truth, and nothing but the truth, when the true circumstance of the case was the very thing I desired to keep from her for Hopeful's sake. I couldn't make her a confidant, just as though she was an old woman; so the only way for me was to mislead the young lady, and satisfy her with a yarn that would look plausible.

"Well, sir, I'm all attention," Miss Josie said, still looking at me most critically.

"For shame, Josie," said her father. "You have no right to ask such questions. I pray that you will desist."

She did not pay the least attention to him, which was wrong on her part. Children should always honor their parents with respect, in preference to a young man. It sometimes saves embarrassment.

"You see, Miss Goldthwaite," I began, "the handsome young lady —"

She interrupted me with an impatient gesture, —

"Is she a suitable person to be introduced to me? That is what I want to know."

Of course, Daisy, under the circumstances, was not a suitable person to be introduced to Miss Josie; but it would not do for me to acknowledge the same; so I had to talk around the subject, and avoid a direct question.

"I am astonished that Miss Goldthwaite should put to me, of all persons in the world, such an interrogation;" and then I walked to the window and looked out into the busy street, as though I was a little touched in my pride.

She followed me to my retreat with her eyes, and then, after a moment's pause, came towards me, and laid one of her little, white, gloved hands on my shoulder.

"Have I offended you by the directness of my questions?" she asked. "If so, forgive me."

"You did touch a sensitive chord by your interrogations," I replied, "for I can't endure the thought that Miss Goldthwaite should judge me capable of a bad action;" and so I looked as grieved as I could, just for the purpose of preventing her from asking more questions regarding Daisy.

"I didn't mean to offend you; so I ask your pardon;" and then, after a moment's pause, she added, "but I should like to know who she is; and I think you might tell me."

"You think her handsome — do you not?"

"Yes; if it is any satisfaction for you to hear me say so."

"It is a great satisfaction for one lady to do justice to another. I have no doubt but she would say as much for you if her opinion was asked."

"Thank you. Why not invite her in to meet me, and then we could compare notes."

But this was just what I did not desire, for if Miss Goldthwaite should ever discover the character of Miss Daisy, farewell to all of my hopes. I know that forgiveness would be an impossibility. Not that she was a prude, but she had a certain amount of dignity which she always took good care to maintain.

"Unfortunately," I said, after a moment's thought, to collect my scattered senses, "the young lady has but little time to spend in compliments. This very forenoon she sails for Australia."

"Indeed!" and I thought Miss Josie's face expressed a slight sign of satisfaction at the news.

"O, yes," I answered, with as much assurance as I could command, just as though I knew the matter was all fixed and settled. "Mr. Murden is a relative, or something of the kind, and has arranged that she shall go to his home in charge of the captain of the ship. But here is Mr. Murden, and he will tell you all about it."

"Of what were you speaking?" asked the ex-commissioner, coming forward, after exchanging a few words with Mr. Goldthwaite.

"Of your protégée, whom you are about to send to Melbourne. Miss Goldthwaite has expressed herself much pleased with the young lady's appearance, and desires an introduction."

Here I looked at Murden in a manner that he instantly comprehended. He saw what I wanted, and so acted accordingly.

"The young lady has already left the house," he said. "She has gone to a furnishing store to select some few things which she will need on the voyage. From the store she will take a cab and ride direct to the ship. If I had supposed for a moment that Miss Goldthwaite would have liked an introduction, I would have detained her for an hour or more, although time is quite precious to her, for the ship sails at high tide."

I don't know how much of this Miss Josie believed. At any rate, she appeared to think that all was correct, and turned to Fred and opened a lively conversation with him, which gave Murden time to whisper to me, —

"Steal out of the room for a moment, if possible. I want to speak to you."

I managed to slip out of the apartment with Murden, and as soon as we were in the corridor, my companion said, —

"Miss Goldthwaite evidently suspects something, and is on the watch to catch us foul. We must get Daisy out of the house, or she will know that I have told a lie. Heaven knows I have but few of them to answer for, but in this instance I shall be forgiven."

I had my doubts on the subject, but remembering that I had told one or two falsehoods for the purpose of screening my friend Hopeful, so as not to shock the ears of Miss Josie, I did not consider it worth while to dispute with him.

"Where is Daisy?" I asked.

"In her room, where she will remain until after your interview with her."

"My interview with her?" I asked. "What have I to do with her?"

"Much. You must see her at once, and tell her what arrangements we have made in her behalf, and induce her to accept of our propositions."

"But look here. I thought that you were to do all that."

"So I was, but I can't do it as well as you. My heart fails me in this respect; so, like a good fellow, as you are, undertake the job, and I'll keep Miss Goldthwaite in play while you talk with her. I should break down and fail, while I know you will succeed."

After such a delicious bit of flattery I could not refuse his request, and leaving Murden, I went to Daisy's room, and found her looking out of a window.

She was not surprised to see me, although I noticed that she was a little timid at finding herself alone in a room with one who was comparatively a stranger. At the same time I observed that the girl had been crying, and that her eyes were still damp with tears.

She put her hand in mine, and for a moment I held it, and admired the modest, subdued style of her beauty, and I did not blame Hopeful for his passion, or for feeling bad at the parting.

But it was dangerous to look at or hold so pretty a girl's hand; so I turned my eyes and relinquished her fingers.

"Are you very much offended with me for entering the parlor while that beautiful young lady was there?" asked Daisy. "I did not know that she was there, or I would not have disturbed you. Did she ask who I was?"

"She did."

"And you told her that I was different from her."

"No, Daisy, I told her no such thing. She is in ignorance, and will remain so all of her lifetime, as far as your personal history is concerned."

Daisy extended both her little hands, in her joy at my explanation.

"Thanks," she said. "You are more generous than some men. I wish that I could repay your kindness."

And once more I saw the tears well up from her eyes; then she laid her fair head on my shoulder and sobbed in a most distressing manner.

I tried to comfort her, and think that I succeeded in talking her into a state of calmness; and then she burst out with,—

"O, how I wish that I was good, and could live my life over!"

"Daisy," I said, in an earnest tone, "there is a chance for you yet."

She laid both hands on my shoulders and looked me full in the face, as though startled at the idea. At the same time her face flushed with surprise at my words.

"What do you mean?" she asked; and I thought that I saw hope in her face.

"Just what I say, Daisy. If you are so disposed, a great future is open for you."

"And the past can be forgotten?"

"Entirely."

She placed her fair head once more on my shoulder and appeared to think. For a short time I did not disturb her meditations, for I wanted her to reflect. Gently I put an arm around her slim waist and held her in a brotherly, fatherly, or some other kind of an embrace, I have forgotten which just at this moment, for I know I was tried almost beyond endurance, yet my stout, manly heart did not fail me in the emergency.

"Tell me what you mean," Daisy said, looking up from her refuge.

"Then listen to me attentively. You have no great ties to bind you to England — have you?"

"None. I am friendless."

"And you could leave England without a pang?"

"Yes, if I was sure of the future."

"You shall be assured of that. A bright future will be opened to you."

"And will you go with me, so that the brightness of

the future may not be dimmed?" she asked, in her child-like simplicity, it seemed to me.

"No; that is impossible."

She gently withdrew her form from my embrace, removed her head from my shoulder, and walked to the window, and looked out.

After a moment I followed her, and spoke to her.

"What are you thinking of?" I asked.

She did not answer me, but continued gazing into the street.

"Think as much as you please," I said, "only you must make up your mind what you will do, for Mr. Murden is expecting your answer."

"Tell me what you want me to do," she replied. "I am grateful for what you have done, yet I do not know what to do to secure your approbation."

"Then listen to me in silence, but at the same time look at me, and not into the street."

She raised her eyes to my face, and said I was to go on.

"Mr. Murden is very anxious that you should go to his home, in Australia, where you will find friends, until he returns. Your past life is to remain unknown. Your future life will be all that you could desire. Some good man will claim you as a wife, and then you can count on that happiness which you so much wish. On board the ship that is to take you, friends will be found who will look after your welfare. They will only know you as a relative of Mr. Murden, and that will be sufficient to secure you all due respect."

"The proposition is so sudden," she murmured. "If you were going with me, or if one friend was on board the ship, I should feel a little different."

"It is better as it is."

"Perhaps so."

"You must think and feel so. Only consider the honorable position in which you now find yourself, compared with what you were twenty-four hours ago."

"I know, I know; but O, it is terrible to part with friends whom you truly esteem."

"Do you feel the parting with Hopeful so keenly?"

"No, not with him."

I did not further question her.

"Forget that you ever saw us," I said, " or else remember us only as benefactors. We could not wrong you so much as to pretend to love where affection did not exist."

She raised my hand and kissed it, and covered it with tears, as she murmured, —

"I'll go; but I shall never, never forget your kindness, or the kindness of your friends."

I bent my head and kissed her thin, red lips, and then she drew back as though she feared I would repeat the salute. Well, the temptation was strong, but I conquered it, for I recollected my mission and the misfortunes of the poor child before me.

"We will call it a bargain, Daisy?" I asked, still holding one of her hands, and watching the tears that she could not entirely keep back.

"Yes, if you so will it."

"And you will write to us after you are in Melbourne, and tell us how happy you are, and how well you are succeeding in your new home?"

"Yes; I will do as you request me."

"And will you start this very day on the voyage?"

A moment's pause, a brushing away of tears, and then came the low answer —

"The sooner the better."

I stepped to the door to call Mr. Murden and announce the result. For some reason, Daisy followed me, and, when I opened the door, appeared at my side. Just at this moment Miss Goldthwaite left our private parlor, talking in a laughing tone with Fred.

She looked up and saw Daisy and myself, and then I noticed a change in her expression, that did not argue well for my interest.

CHAPTER XXVII.

DAISY AND HER VOYAGE. — EXPLANATIONS. — OFF FOR LONDON. — THE PRIDE OF ENGLAND. — A CALLER. — A LANDLORD'S ASTONISHMENT.

Miss Goldthwaite, as she appeared at the door with Fred, gave but two glances in my direction. The first one was directed to me, and the second one to my poor unfortunate companion, Daisy, whom I had just persuaded to go to Australia in a ship that was to sail that very day. Those two glances were enough to satisfy the proud, high-spirited girl that I had some motive in concealing certain things; and although she had no claim on me, yet she chose to appear a little resentful, as all handsome girls will appear when their pride is touched, or their confidence is not sought.

I saw that I had more explanations to offer and more lies to tell, and the latter did not suit me, for I wanted to be straightforward in my dealings with Miss Josie, and had not the least desire to deceive, as the reader well knows.

Well, I would not let Daisy see that I felt disappointed at Miss Josie's obtaining a glimpse of me, so put on a smile when our protégée once more commented on the remarkable beauty of Miss Goldthwaite.

"Ah," she sighed, "if I was only as handsome and good as she is, how happy I should be!"

"Remember the better days," I said. "Let us hope for the future, and be dead to the past."

Murden was in the corridor waiting the result of my interview with Daisy. I called him, and he hastened to us.

"Well," he asked, "what luck? Does she consent?"

"Yes. She will do as you require."

"Thank fortune. I was fearful that she would hesitate,

There is no time to be lost. Go to Miss Goldthwaite, and I will hasten to a store with Daisy, and provide her outfit. Meet us at the ship at eleven o'clock. I shan't come back to the hotel until the vessel sails."

I promised, and then turned back to take a look at Daisy. She had heard all that passed between Murden and myself, and now sat in a chair in her chamber, with her face buried in her hands and tears trickling between her fingers.

"God bless you, Daisy!" I said, as I laid a hand on her head.

"God bless you in return for all your kindness," was her answer; and then I bent down and kissed her forehead, and left the room.

I hastened to the parlor, where Miss Josie and Fred were engaged in conversation, and the lady's father was reading a morning paper which contained a brilliant description of the capture of some dozen Fenians by her majesty's troops. The account merely stated that several Americans were taken with the party, but they had represented themselves as tourists, and were discharged by the lord lieutenant.

Miss Josie did not look at me with favorable eyes as I approached her. Fred, who knew my weakness, like the good fellow that he was, vacated his place at the lady's side, so that I could take a chance at conversing with her. But to his surprise she asked him to remain, and brought her whole battery of attractions to bear on him, while I was unnoticed.

Fred telegraphed to me to know what it meant, and I returned an answer that I would explain at some future time.

"We shall be ready to take the night train for London," I said, as soon as I could get in a word.

"O, indeed;" and once more the young lady turned to Fred.

"Would you prefer leaving to-night, or waiting until tomorrow morning?" I asked.

"Really, it makes no difference to me. Perhaps you had better arrange the whole matter with papa;" and then she again turned to Fred.

"O, let me take the whole charge of the matter," Fred said, and started up to speak to Mr. Goldthwaite; but Miss Josie detained him.

"Pray, don't leave me. I shall be awful dull if you do, with no one to speak to."

"But here is my friend;" and Fred nodded to me and smiled. "He will entertain you."

"No; he has other business. He will exchange but a word, and then leave me for more congenial society."

"Miss Josie," I said, in a grave tone, "I won't quarrel with you, much as you may desire to. For all that I have done I have a satisfactory explanation, and you know it. Let us be friends as long as you are under this roof, and strangers after we leave it, if you desire it."

"I do desire it," she said, without a moment's thought or reflection.

Fred looked on with astonishment. He could not understand what it meant. He knew that something was wrong, but what it was he did not think it worth while to ask just at that time, knowing that I would explain everything as soon as I could find an opportunity. Therefore, like the good discreet fellow that he was, he bowed to the passionate young lady and turned away from us, so that we could settle our quarrel to suit ourselves, without his hearing what was said on either side.

"Miss Josie," I said, "are you in earnest in what you say?"

"Yes, sir; I am."

"Will you give me your hand on it to prove your sincerity?"

"No, sir; I will not. You have just been holding the hand of a young lady in her private room; so I don't care to place myself on a level with her."

Now, if I had had more experience with the sex, I should have known that she was a little jealous; but at the time I imagined that she was boiling over with virtuous indignation at the idea of finding a suspicious female in our apartments, whom I was endeavoring to conceal from her sharp eyes.

"The young lady whom you allude to has left the house with her relative, and will return no more. In a few hours she will be on her way to Australia."

"Of course you were taking leave of her in her room?"

"Yes, because I could not induce her to enter the parlor and encounter you, on the simple ground that her dress was not good enough, and that she looked like a fright in her hurried toilet, compared to your elaborate and tasteful display."

Women like to have their toilets complimented, even if they pretend that they don't like to be praised for their beauty. Miss Josie was no exception to the rule. She tossed her pretty head in disdain, apparently, but I saw that she was mollified by the compliment, and that her eyes softened a little. She managed to murmur the word "Indeed."

"O, yes; and Mr. Murden thought I had better shake hands with her where she was, before she left the house. I did so, and you saw me in the act."

She could not stand up in the presence of such a cool, plausible yarn as the one I had told, and with so many backers as I had; but she did rally a little, and asked, —

"Did Mr. Fred part from the lady in the same manner?"

"Of course. Just ask him. Here, Fred."

"It is of no consequence," the lady said. "Your explanation is quite satisfactory."

"And you will shake hands on the strength of it?" I asked.

"Yes."

She gave me her little hand, and allowed me to squeeze it just a bit, and then to press it to my lips, for the reason that I was not quite prepared to kiss her.

"Before we are complete friends," I said, 'let me make one more explanation."

"Yes, half a dozen of them, if they are all satisfactory."

She was getting in good humor — that was evident. I could see by her eyes that she felt better.

"Well, the ship that the young lady sails in leaves the dock at one o'clock. I am going to see her off at that hour."

"Can't I go too?"

"Of course you can, if you desire it. I will have a carriage ready, and we will all start together — your father as well as yourself. I shall be delighted with your company."

"I do believe you are a real good fellow," she said, and once more gave me her hand, to prove that the assertion came from her heart.

"Then we are really friends once more," I said.

"Yes, and will continue so until you provoke me to quarrel with you."

I thought that was cool, considering that I had done nothing but fib a little to screen a friend. However, I was too happy at the turn which affairs had taken to find much fault, and mentally hoped that so particular and exacting a young lady would never discover that I had deceived her.

So Miss Josie and I sat down and had a long and pleasant chat. She told us all that transpired on board the steamer after we had left her at Queenstown, and how kindly the Earl of Buckland and his countess had spoken of us, and how much care they bestowed upon my son, whom they took charge of.

Thus engaged in pleasant conversation, time passed so rapidly that I was not aware that twelve o'clock had arrived, until Fred came in and told me that a carriage was at the door, ready to take us to the dock.

"Hopeful," he whispered, "is still in bed, and refuses to move. I have not told him that Daisy is to leave us, for he is miserable enough without the information. Besides, if I enlightened him, he might make a fool of himself, and that is not desirable just at this time. I have put Rover in his room, so they can keep each other company until we return."

He had done just as I could have wished, and I pressed his hand in token of my appreciation of his course.

Then Miss Josie got ready in a few minutes; she took my arm, and down stairs we went to the carriage, all as happy as we could be, and full of plans for the future, when we should meet in Paris.

We drove to the docks, and found the ship that was to sail for Australia. Fred went on board, and discovered Daisy and Murden, the latter hard at work fitting up a state-room and stowing away her baggage so that the lady could find it when wanted.

As for Daisy, she was sitting in the cabin, and crying as bitterly as she had in the morning; and all of the ex-commissioner's sympathy was lost, as far as attention was concerned.

The ship was crowded with passengers, most of them belonging in the steerage; so all was confusion, receiving stores and taking leave of friends. But, amid all the bustle, Murden worked on with a purpose, and transformed the state-room into a comfortable chamber, where the girl could have as much light and air as she pleased, and would not be rolled out of her berth the first night at sea.

"He said that he would come and take leave of me," Daisy remarked, as soon as she saw Fred.

"He will, if you desire it," Fred replied; and then he came and told me that Daisy wanted to shake hands before she sailed, and as Miss Josie was willing to excuse me for a few minutes, I went on board.

"You will think of me sometimes?" she asked, when I had encouraged her with a few words.

"Yes, I shall hear from you quite often. Who knows but that we shall return home by the way of Melbourne? and if we do, what pleasure we shall find in meeting!"

"If I could only think so,' she sobbed; but before I

could offer a promise to that effect, a call was made to clear the vessel, as she was about to leave the dock.

The poor girl heard the cry, and knew that the hour of separation had arrived. She got up and put her arms around my neck, and kissed me, and thanked us for our kindness, and promised to pray for us; and then we left the vessel, and poor Daisy was soon sailing down the Irish Channel towards her home, so many thousand miles distant — an unknown land, where the wanderer has looked for a paradise and been wrecked upon a desert.

We all went back to the carriage, feeling a little melancholy at the parting, yet satisfied that we had done our duty towards an erring but not a wicked child of the world.

"I gave her a letter to our old friend Smith and his wife," Murden said, as we reached the carriage where Miss Josie and her father were waiting for us quite patiently. "They will do the right thing by the child, and perhaps take her into their family; for I hinted that I should regard it as a favor if they would."

Then we entered the carriage and drove to the hotel, where we found Hopeful still in bed, despondent, and dependent upon gin and water to keep from giving way to the wildest despair.

We compelled him to get up and dress himself, and then, when he hinted about Daisy, we told him that she was miles away, and that he would never again see her unless he visited Australia.

To our surprise, this information, instead of casting down New Hampshire's favorite son, seemed to raise him up. He put away his grief in the same manner that he put away a glass of gin. He seemed to swallow it, although he swore that it was a darn mean trick to let her go and not tell him of it; but when we explained that we wanted to save his feelings, he appeared satisfied and reconciled to his loss.

And now let me say one word about Daisy, and then dismiss her from my record. She had a pleasant passage to Melbourne, and was treated, on the voyage, with the utmost distinction by the captain of the vessel and all the cabin passengers. It was reported on board, that she was a relative of Mr. Murden, the rich Australian member of the cabinet; so she had advantages not often allowed to a poor girl. Her society was courted by the best on board, but still she was not spoiled by the flattery that met her on every side. She was modest, unassuming, and made friends instead of enemies. Her dreadful secret was not discovered, or even suspected, by any one on board, for which she was thankful.

On reaching Melbourne, she found Smith and his wife on the lookout for her. Murden had written by steamer, announcing the event of her sailing, and our old friends went to the city expressly to invite Daisy to make her home with them. She did so, but had not been in Victoria more than six months when she was married to one of the largest stock-raisers in the province. He was a magistrate, a member of Parliament, and quite a prominent man in the colony.

It was a good match on both sides. He had money and position, and was quite a cultivated man, and loved her dearly. She had beauty, health, and good common sense; and I have reason to believe that she had a real attachment for her husband. Two children have blessed the union, and there is not a family in Victoria more respected. Murden, in his letters to me, always speaks of them, and Daisy, once in a while, writes to me, but never of the past; nor do I allude to it. The subject must be too painful for one like her to recall. Her secret is safe in the hands of her friends. She never revealed it, thus following the ex-commissioner's advice. Such a course is not always to be recommended, but the reader must remember that Daisy commenced a new life in a new country, and deserved all the happiness that awaited her. May Heaven continue to bless her and all who call her mother!

The last time I heard from her she sent congratulations

on the eve of my approaching marriage, and in the letter was an elegant diamond ring, containing five stones, and valued at one thousand dollars. It was a present to my wife, but would not have been accepted, had I not known that Daisy's husband was so rich that he could not spend the interest of his money; and each year but added to his wealth. So much for the fortunes of Daisy; which proves that our stay in Liverpool was not entirely devoid of interest.

After dinner we packed, and took the train for London. We had a compartment to ourselves, and I had the honor and pleasure of sitting by Miss Goldthwaite's side, and talking with her all the way to the city, while Fred and Murden occupied the father's attention so that he could not interfere in our chat.

Perhaps the reader would like to know if I advanced my cause on the journey. I can't answer that question with any degree of certainty, as I had a peculiar young lady to deal with. One moment she would appear as though absorbed in all that I had to say, and the next would manifest such indifference that I was more than half inclined to leave her and never look on her face again.

But the instant she saw by my face that I was angry, she would dazzle me with her brilliancy and kindness; and so we entered London, on my part charmed and angry, delighted yet half indignant at the pretty girl who was leading me a dangerous game.

We all went to the same hotel, — the Pride of England, — where we found the most eminent respectability and high charges; where the waiters acted as solemn as parsons, and disdained a smaller piece of silver than a shilling for handing a person a napkin, or giving him a cup of tea. It was the most dignified establishment that I ever entered, and it did all that it could to turn away plebeians who desired to enter its doors. The landlord was inclined to look upon us as a suspicious set, and was rather scant in his attentions; but in the course of the forenoon, after we had changed our travelling costumes, and donned suits a little more becoming, he even suffered a friendly look to appear on his fat face, and asked us if we were quite comfortable in our rooms.

But the blow that broke his pride, and turned him from a haughty despot to a cringing, fawning landlord, was received when a carriage stopped in front of his house. It was a plain vehicle, yet on the panels it had the coronet of an earl, and a coat of arms beneath, while on the box were a coachman and a footman in livery.

This establishment created the most intense excitement in the Pride of England. All the servants were ready to welcome the owner of such a carriage, and when the footman entered the hotel, with a card in his hand, and inquired for me, a revolution of feeling took place in our favor. We were acquainted with an earl. Our eminent respectability was established in a moment.

Half a dozen servants dashed up stairs to find me, while the landlord took charge of the card to hand to me in person. There was the most intense astonishment on the host's face as he said to me, while I was chatting with Miss Goldthwaite in the parlor, —

"Good 'eaven, sir, 'ere is the Earl of Buckland's card, and he is axin' for you in his carriage at the door."

I took the card, and looked at it in so cool and calm a manner, that the landlord almost fainted through nervousness.

CHAPTER XXVIII.

AN INVITATION FOR LANCASTER FROM A LIVE EARL. — MEETING WITH RELATIVES. — A BIT OF ADVICE. — A SCENE UNEXPECTED.

I WILL confess that I felt some little pride to think that a live earl was at the door, in his carriage, and anxious to see me. I should not have been human unless I was a little elated; but I would have suffered death rather than have shown it to the thick-headed John Bull, who now stood humbly before me, with a silver salver in his hand, on which he had borne the bit of pasteboard containing the earl's name.

Never had I seen such change in a landlord. From a fuming, pompous, pig-headed brute, of the real English species, he had developed into the slimy Pecksniff breed, all humbleness, as far as outward form was concerned.

"The earl," said the landlord, "is at the door, and his ludship would like to see you."

"Then be kind enough to ask his lordship to come in."

"But he may not have the time, you know," cried the landlord of the Pride of England. "The earl might not like it, you know, if you was not down to the door to receive 'im, you know."

"O, tell him I'm in, and that I should be happy to see him," I answered; and then, to show the landlord that I was not so forcibly impressed as I might have been, I just turned to Miss Goldthwaite, and resumed a conversation which our host had interrupted.

John Bull gave me one look of bewilderment, and then left the parlor under the impression that I must be somebody of importance, or else such a stranger to English manners as not to know that an earl was a great man in that part of the world, provided he had large rent rolls to back up his position.

"It is really kind on his lordship's part to call, and I should have thought that you would manifest more interest in the visit," said Miss Goldthwaite, as soon as Pecksniff had left the room.

"I am aware that it is an act of kindness, Miss Josie; but to become frantic over the subject, in the presence of that old slimy Englishman, would have lessened his respect for us in a great measure. Keep cool, and make him think that we see earls and noble lords every day of our lives. That is the only way we shall receive any attention in this hotel."

"And he will charge all the more in his bill," laughed Fred.

"Perhaps; but then, with lots of aristocratic acquaintances, don't you see that we can better afford to dispute his bill. We shan't tremble at his frown, but make him do all the quaking. But here comes the earl. Let us give him a warm, and, at the same time, dignified reception."

The door was thrown open with a crash, and then the landlord and two servants backed into the room, bowing in the most obsequious manner, while the earl looked as though he would like to kick the parties who impeded his progress, but was unable to get at that position of their persons which nature intended should be kicked.

"The Earl of Buckland," shouted the landlord, by way of announcement; and as he spoke, he turned half round, and this enabled his lordship to get past his tormentors and to come towards us with outstretched hands.

We gave him a cordial greeting, because it was a sincere one; and then Fred turned the landlord and his servants out of the room, although they were dying to hear what was said, and to know what business the earl had with us.

"I am glad to find you at home," said the earl. "I feared that you would be out exploring some of the mysteries of smoky London."

"Pray, how does it happen that you knew we were in London?" I asked, as soon as the earl had shaken hands with all of our party, and paid a compliment to Miss Goldthwaite, which caused her to blush like a red rose.

"Why, my man saw you driving from the railroad station, and so followed you to this hotel. He informed me of the circumstance this morning; and I took the liberty of calling on you thus early, for the purpose of assuring you that your son is well, and that he is with your father and mother-in-law at Lancaster. Of course they are impatient to see you, and have been much concerned about your adventures in Ireland. Sir William would have started and hunted you up, if he had not read in the paper that your party had left Dublin for Liverpool. What possessed you to mix with those absurd Fenians?"

"For the simple reason that we could not help ourselves," I replied. "All our protestations would not avail. All Ireland was ready to swear that we were head centres, and so we left the country to avoid the honors they would thrust upon us. It was lively for us while we were there; but we had no desire to become martyrs for the cause of Fenianism."

"It was absurd in landing at Queenstown; but it is past, and now I have come with a proposition which is full of sense. I want all of you to run down to my place at Lancaster, and stop with us as long as you can make it convenient. Lady Frances is quite anxious that Miss Goldthwaite should pay her a visit, and in her name I invite you all, with the understanding that I will not take a refusal; so make up your minds as quick as possible, and then pack, and we will be off."

"You know that Sir William would not permit me to remain away from his house," I remarked.

"Well, I really don't think that he would; but I'll exempt you on the ground that you dine with us every day when we don't dine with Sir William, and that you make yourself just as much at home at Elmwood as at the Oaks. Is it a bargain?"

"It is, as far as I am concerned." And then, after a short consultation, the rest of the party agreed to become guests of the earl, and to leave for his place that very day.

This was all settled to our satisfaction, and then the earl left us to attend to some business, but agreed to meet us at the station at three o'clock, at which time trains left for Lancaster.

In the mean time we drove about the city, and saw a few of its sights; but our stay was too limited for only a glance at the parks and a few of the public buildings. We promised ourselves a more thorough pleasure at some future time, and then settled our bills and left the Pride of England, and the landlord, and his high charges, never to see either again; for when we returned to London, we had the good sense to put up at a hotel where there was much comfort but little ceremony, and where they did not kill their guests and then suck their blood like famished vampires.

At the station we found the earl waiting for us. A compartment was secured for our party, and we were off, prompt to time, whirling through the best tilled country that we had ever seen.

Past villages, through towns with quaint-looking houses, by ruins that were venerable with age long before our country was settled, on we thundered, our journey enlivened by pleasant chat, until the cars stopped at a station, and his lordship informed us that we were in Lancaster, and that his country-seat was but a few miles from the road.

I looked out of the window and saw several carriages in charge of servants in livery. I recognized one or two of Sir William's people, and then I caught a glimpse of my respected father-in-law, holding by the hand his grandchild.

In an instant I was out of the car and had my son in my arms, and after a long embrace I had time to turn to Sir William and receive his welcome.

My respected father-in-law had changed but little since I saw him last. His hair was white, but his face was as fresh as when we met in Australia, some years before, and his form was as vigorous and straight as when I first knew him.

Hopeful, who had recovered some of his lost spirit, was warmly welcomed by Sir William; and then Rover came in for his full share of attention, and the noble dog received it as graciously as a human being.

The rest of the party were introduced to the baronet, and after the usual compliments we entered carriages and drove to the earl's residence, where I found my respected mother-in-law, who had agreed to spend the afternoon with Lady Frances, so that she could see all of my friends at the same time, and give them a hearty welcome, and invite them to the Oaks as soon as they could come.

Dinner was ready for all of us, and no sooner was it concluded than Sir William insisted upon returning home. All knew that he and his wife were anxious to be alone with me, for the purpose of speaking of family matters; so no objections were made when we withdrew; but I promised to ride over to Elmwood in the morning and take breakfast, and then lay out some plans for the amusements of the day.

I dreaded being alone with the parents of Jenny; but I knew that there was no help for it. I feared that they would ask certain questions which I was not prepared to answer; and sure enough, the interrogations came as soon as we left the earl's grounds.

"Who is that young lady that belongs to your party?" asked my mother-in-law, in a tone that showed she was about to begin her cross-examination in lawyer-like style.

I pretended not to hear, for I looked out of the window of the carriage and admired the timber, and the deer which were lying in the shade.

There was a long pause; but Lady Byefield could not remain quiet. Like all mothers-in-law, she felt anxious when she saw me in company with a handsome lady. She renewed the attack as follows:—

"Who is that young lady whom I saw with your party?"

She made me hear, for she put her hand on my arm, to attract attention.

I looked up and saw that Sir William and his wife were devoting their entire attention to me; so I summoned all of my coolness and self-possession, as I answered, —

"O, she is the daughter of the old gentleman whom you were introduced to, I think."

"We know that; but who is she?" continued her ladyship, with some animation.

"We met her on the steamer, and Lady Frances appeared quite pleased with her. She belongs to a very good family, I believe. Her father is rich, and they are on their way to France, where they mean to reside for some time."

"She is quite handsome," remarked Lady Byefield, in a gentle tone, and with another earnest look at my face.

I did not quail in the least, but returned her glance with one so vacant that she must have thought me stupid, for the moment.

"Yes," I said, "she is called quite handsome by those who know her. On the steamer she was a belle. I think her very entertaining."

"Your friend Fred appears to be very attentive to the lady," suggested her ladyship.

"He would naturally be attracted by such a frank, fresh-looking young lady," I observed.

There was a moment's silence, and then Sir William, as though he had considered the subject, said, —

"Yes; I should think Miss Goldthwaite would interest most any man. I hope she will make us a visit before she leaves England."

Her ladyship did not reëcho the wish, for some reason or other. I really think that she suspected I had a warm attachment for Miss Josie, and so began to hate her as most mothers-in-law do their daughters' successors.

However, she did not discover by my looks or words

that I was partial, for I did not wish to mar the happiness of her ladyship during my visit to the Oaks. She had not seen me for five years. During those five years I had lost a wife, and she a daughter. There was much for me to speak about, much which a mother would like to hear; and I could not pain her by letting her think that I was not devoted to the memory of the dead, and during my stay in Lancaster I did not let her see that such was not the case.

I found but little change at the Oaks. The same servants were there, and they welcomed me with all the enthusiasm which favorite servants usually display on such occasions; that is to say, I received a smile and a bow from each, and the butler said, " Glad to see you, sir, and I 'opes you is well, sir, and I'm pleased to think that you wasn't killed durin' the rebellion, sir, as I feared you would be, sir."

He had about as clear an idea of the rebellion as he had about the Danish and Prussian troubles; and once, while I was at the Oaks, asked me if the rebels were not all black, and if they hadn't licked the whites every time there was a battle. He had heard that such was the case, and believed it.

I was up early in the morning, and, with Rover at my heels, took a long walk in the park, and had some trouble in convincing the hound that the deer we met were not lawful prey, to be pursued and run down whenever he fancied. The dog thought that it was the meanest arrangement that he ever heard of; and I had to talk quite plain with him before he comprehended that the animals were ornamental inhabitants of the park, and that Sir William would be likely to scold if his pets were molested.

After breakfast I mounted a horse, and cantered over to Elmwood. Sir William refused to accompany me, as he had some business with his steward that required special attention, while my respected mother-in-law was not up when I left the house; so I missed her usual greeting and kind inquiries concerning Miss Josie.

I found my friends on the lawn, playing croquet, with the exception of Lady Frances, who was in the library; and to the library I went, to pay my respects to her ladyship.

She held out her hand when she saw me, and made me take a seat by her side.

"I am glad that you have come to keep me company," she said, "for I was unable to join the croquet party, having a few domestic matters to attend to."

I bowed my appreciation of the compliment.

"Why didn't you bring your son with you this fine morning? Little Alice has been asking for him ever since she was dressed."

"He was to follow me in the course of an hour or two, with the nurse."

"That is right. Now give me your attention."

"I am listening with all my might."

"Which had you rather have — a heavy dinner party or a ball? The earl is determined to give one or the other in honor of his guests. Let me know your feelings on the subject."

"We are sufficiently honored without either party or ball. Do let us remain here in quietness, for we are not ambitious of putting you to the expense or trouble of summoning the whole county for the purpose of meeting us simple Americans, who do not care for display, and would willingly avoid it."

"But we wish to show to our friends the two gallant gentlemen who risked their lives in Boston harbor for the purpose of saving little Alice. We have not forgotten the circumstance, if you have."

"Then dismiss it from your mind, if you think to repay us by inviting to your house a number of friends who can have no interes in us. Believe me, Lady Frances, it is my sincere wish that you will not give either a dinner party or a ball while we remain here."

"What are you afraid of?" the countess asked, with a smile. "Do you fear that some of our titled county friends will carry off Miss Goldthwaite, and so cause you to lose the prize upon which you have set your heart?"

"Yankee like, let me answer a question by asking one. What makes you think I have looked in that direction?"

"My judgment and my eyes. A woman is seldom in the wrong in such cases. She can tell by a thousand little tokens the state of a man's heart."

"Indeed."

"Yes; so I know that you care for the girl, and your pretended indifference does not deceive me in the least. Come, make me a confidant; for I should like to see you married and happy. I know that you deserve to be."

"When I have anything to confide, I will do so," I replied; "so you must believe me when I tell you that Miss Josie and I have not exchanged a word on so serious a subject as marriage; and, to tell you the truth, I don't think it would be of any use for me to aspire to her hand."

Her ladyship looked at me for a moment, as though to judge if I was in earnest; and when she saw that I was, she merely smiled, and said that I was a modest man, and did not come up to her idea of a modern lover.

"Can't you help me?" I asked.

"No, you must do without my assistance. If you are in earnest, and desire to succeed, I have no doubt but that you will; but will you let me give you one word of advice?"

"Certainly. I should be delighted to listen to you."

"Then do not test Miss Goldthwaite's patience too far. She is an amiable and beautiful girl, but she is impulsive, and apt to be rash while under a momentary fit of impatience. You might lose her if you should provoke her too much, and that would cause both of you unhappiness. Be gentle, yet firm, with her, and she will be your wife."

For ten minutes we sat silent, each pondering on the subject that had been discussed. At last Lady Frances arose and came towards me. She laid one hand on my shoulder, and said,—

"You are not offended at my words?"

"Heaven forbid. They were meant in kindness, and in the kindest spirit I take them;" and I took the little white hand that rested on my shoulder, and kissed it; and just as I did so,—in fact while my lips were touching her fingers,—who should enter the library but the person of whom we had been speaking—Miss Goldthwaite.

She stopped on the threshold of the door, apparently astonished at the scene before her. Then, as she realized what I had done, the proud girl turned away with a haughty toss of her handsome head, and went up the broad oak stairs to her room.

"You see the result of your good advice," I said, with a short laugh, for the scene was so ludicrous that I could not help it.

"Yes, I see that somebody is jealous of a poor married woman, and from this I argue success to your cause. But you must excuse me now, for I will go and see the abused girl and laugh some of her nonsense away;" and then the countess smiled and left me, and I went out to meet my son, who had just arrived in Sir William's family carriage with his nurse and grandfather.

CHAPTER XXIX.

A DECLARATION OF LOVE ON THE PART OF HOPEFUL. — THE DEPARTURE FOR PARIS. — OUR PLANS. — AN ARREST IN THE NAME OF THE EMPEROR.

I DID not see Miss Goldthwaite again during the day, and the countess informed me that the young lady had kept her room on the plea of indisposition, but at the same time she intimated that it was not of a serious nature, and that I need not worry myself as to the result, which was conclusive proof, I thought, that the countess had had an explanation of a convincing nature.

After luncheon our party mounted horses and rode over the earl's vast estates, and saw something of English farming — a subject on which our cousins can give us some profitable lessons, as far as crops are concerned, while our people would laugh to scorn their farming implements, which require the strength of giants or several horses to move.

But we admired the crops, the hedges, the rich lawns with the most velvety of grass — short, soft, and green as emeralds; and when we returned to Elmwood we had appetites sharpened by pure air, a long gallop, and scenes which were well worth examining.

But I must hasten to the day of our departure for France; and yet I like to look back to the two weeks' residence at the Oaks and the earl's place with real pleasure, for they were the most quiet and satisfactory of the whole time I spent abroad. The only thing that disturbed me was the fact that Miss Josie had seen me kiss the hand of the countess, and consequently had sulked for a day or two on the strength of it; but she had got over it in some manner, and I think that Lady Frances laughed away her jealousy.

Sir William gave a grand dinner party as a parting testimonial of the estimation in which he held us. All the nobility and gentry of the county were present, and to my confusion and dismay I found that I was the centre of attraction on account of my romantic marriage with the baronet's daughter. Most of those present had heard of our Australian adventures, and were eager to listen to more; so I had a fine opportunity to bring forward a man who liked to shine in just such society. My friend Murden was fond of talking, as he was of action; and when those who were introduced to me made inquiries respecting life in Victoria, I managed to invite the ex-commissioner to participate in the discussion, and then retire to some other part of the drawing-room. If others assailed me I made Fred lend me a helping hand, while Hez paid his respects to the ladies, and fell deep in love with the daughter of the Marquis of Bute; and as the young lady was handsome and full of fun, she took it into her head to encourage him, and actually led the poor fellow along, made him talk and relate some of his exploits in Australia, and when she saw that he had a mechanical mind, induced him to explain the peculiar workings of his quartz-crushers, his patent rat-traps, and butter-making machines.

He forgot Daisy and everything excepting the beautiful being before him. He talked loud, earnestly, and eagerly, and the young lady enjoyed her fun, and smiled to think she had so much power in her beautiful face.

At last I feared for Hez's peace of mind, and got the countess to speak to the young lady and attract her attention in another direction. Lady Frances did so, and remonstrated with her friend, while I took charge of Hez, and led him into the library.

"For Heaven's sake," I said, "don't let that young lady make a fool of you. She is only playing with you, and will laugh at your eagerness as soon as she has a chance."

To my surprise Hopeful became indignant at once.

"I wish you would mind your own business," he said, "and let me alone. Can't I speak to a gal but you must come and put your face in between us? I don't serve you that way — do I? When you are sweet on some one, I don't try to take her away — do I?"

"No."

"Then I wish you would let me alone. I've met a gal now that takes to mechanics, and all that. She is interested in me and in what I say, and whose business is it?"

"You won't give me credit for my friendship," I remarked. "I thought that I might save you a pang or two; for don't you know that the young lady is the daughter of a nobleman, and the greatest coquette in the county?"

"Well, what of it? Don't most coquettes find their

match, arter a while, and who knows but her ladyship has found hers?"

I could not help laughing, much to the disgust and indignation of Hopeful, who could see nothing to smile at. He flattered himself that there was a chance for him in the affections of the lady, and that he had made an impression.

"So you have forgotten Daisy so soon, — have you?" I asked, as soon as Hopeful had explained to me his position.

"I wish you wouldn't mention that young woman's name here in this house," Hez said. "It ain't just the thing, and you know it. She and I have separated for good, and I've turned over a new leaf."

"Very well; I won't speak of her again, although you will acknowledge that I prevented you from making Miss Daisy your wife."

"It's no sich thing, now I tell yer. I hadn't any sich idea. I guess I could do better than marry her;" and off Hez went to find and flirt with the daughter of a marquis, engaged at that time to be married to the Duke of Peppergrass, one of the youngest peers of the realm, and at the same time one of the richest.

I thought that my friend was like mankind in general, so considered that I had but wasted my time and words in talking with him. If he wanted to be singed by the fire of the lady's eyes, I had no objection, after the caution.

After dinner Fred, and I, and Murden left the house, and walked through the gardens, for the purpose of smoking our cigars. The night was warm and pleasant, with a full moon overhead. We sat down in an arbor and talked of our departure, and while thus occupied we heard footsteps, and then low voices. We kept still, but peered out, and saw that Hopeful and the daughter of the marquis, Lady Alice, were near us.

"Let's go in thar, and set down," said Hez. "It's a real good place to talk."

No; the lady preferred the open air. Besides, she would have to return in a few moments, or she would be missed.

"O, they are too busy to mind you, even if you are gone," Hopeful pleaded. "Let's go in and rest a while. I've got something to tell yer."

"Then tell it to me here," the young lady said. "This is as good a place as any."

"Well, I don't know about that. I reckon I has a place in Hillsboro' County, New Hampshire, United States of America, that would make you open your eyes; and if we was thar I guess we could talk a little better than we can here. I ain't no nobleman, as I has told yer afore, but I is a downright honest man, now you had better believe, and you might go a great deal further and fare much wusser than me."

The lady appeared to have some slight idea of what was coming, for she mildly hinted that the house was the best place to talk.

"No, it ain't either, not what I has to say," returned Hopeful, in a tone that showed he had made up his mind, and would not be put off. "I have been waiting for a chance all the evening," Hez continued, "and now that I has it, I ain't goin' to be put off any longer."

"But, Mr. Hopeful," pleaded the lady, who didn't know whether it was best to laugh or be angry at the determined man, whom she had been playing with all the evening.

"Yes, I know jist what you would say," replied our New Hampshire friend, "but we ain't got time to talk of that now. You jist listen to me, now, 'coz I'm in earnest."

"Good Heaven," whispered the horror-stricken Murden, who was an intense worshipper of rank and all its privileges, "if he ain't making love to the daughter of a marquis, may I be blessed."

He started to his feet as though the British constitution was overthrown, and the nation tumbling to pieces.

"Sit still," whispered Fred, holding the excited man, so that he could not run out and interrupt the fun. "Don't disturb them for the world. Who knows but that she will accept?"

"Accept!" repeated Murden; "why, she is the daughter of a marquis."

"What of that?" Fred asked, with a low chuckle of delight. "Isn't Hopeful the son of a sovereign, and a sovereign in his own right? According to such reasoning he is superior to her in rank."

"Pshaw! what blasted nonsense! you know," was all that the Australian deigned to bestow upon such reasoning.

But Murden sat down, nevertheless, and looked through the rose-bushes, and watched the love-making, with as much interest as the rest of us. Occasionally, however, he would utter a groan as he thought of the sacrilegious depravity of Hopeful in uttering burning words to a nobleman's daughter.

"Look ahere," said Hopeful, as soon as he had cut off the lady's retreat; "I jist want to tell yer what is on my mind, and I know you'll listen to me when ye hear what it is."

"Please don't," said the lady. "I beg of you not to say anything more."

"O, but I shall," cried the impetuous son of New Hampshire. "I want to tell yer what a gol darned handsome gal you is, and how much I should like yer for a wife. I tell yer there ain't nothin' what money could buy but you should have, and there wouldn't be a better lookin' wife in all Hillsboro' County."

"Pray, say no more," the lady said. And we saw her glance at the house, as though she hoped relief would come.

"O, but you must hear me," Hez continued, after he had taken breath. "I've talked with yer all the afternoon and evening, and now I want to tell yer that I never loved a gal as I love you, and if you'll say the word, I'll marry yer jist as quick as you can get ready."

"My dear Mr. Hopeful," stammered the young lady, "I am sure —"

"Say you accept me," cried the excited Hopeful. "It's all right. I'm my own master, and I have got money enough to support yer. I'll ax yer father to-night, afore he goes, and I know he'll say yes, when he hears that I'm well off. Don't you be afeard but what it will come all right. We'll talk it over on the quiet, you know; and now give me a kiss, to make me feel that I'll soon be married to the prettiest little gal in this part of the world."

Here we saw Hopeful stretch out his arms, as if to enclose her, but the lady started back; and just at that moment Murden, who could hold in no longer, uttered a half-suppressed groan.

Hopeful's arms fell to his side at once, and he glanced around to see where the noise came from; and at that moment Lady Alice took advantage of his confusion, and ran towards the house, and we could not tell whether she was laughing or crying, as she tripped along.

For a moment Hopeful remained quiet, as though listening for the repetition of the sounds that had disturbed his love-passage. We knew how angry he would be if he should see us and was aware that we had overheard his passionate declaration; therefore we concluded to keep still, and not reveal ourselves.

Hopeful stood for a few moments in deep thought, or else listening to Lady Alice's retreating footsteps. After a while he roused himself, and exclaimed, with a shout of triumph and a species of double shuffle, as a fit accompaniment to his state of mind,—

"Wal, by thunder, they can't say but what I've had a shy at a lord's darter, now I tell yer; and darn me if I don't believe she wants me."

We were compelled to keep our handkerchiefs up to our mouths to prevent our laughing, and thus revealing our presence. We managed in some way not to make a noise; but thankful were we when Hez returned to the house and left us to laugh and talk at discretion.

"Well, of all the d—n Yankee impudence that ever I heard of, this is the worst," cried Murden, as soon as he could give vent to his indignation and astonishment. "To think that a man like Hopeful should ask one of the first ladies in the land to marry him beats my time."

"There's nothing so astonishing in the declaration," remarked Fred, "although I am surprised at it so soon after he had vowed that his heart was broken because we separated him from his Daisy. He is an impetuous sort of chap, and when he sees a pretty face, goes in for winning it at all hazards. I commend his choice; but confound his impudence. With true American spirit he supposes that he is fit to associate with most any one; and I don't know but that Lady Alice would make a good bargain in taking him."

"What blasted nonsense you talk!" was the Englishman's reply; and as we saw that the subject was one that he did not relish, owing to his prejudices for rank and title, we bothered him until our cigars were consumed, and then returned to the house.

"Where have you fellers bin?" asked Hez, a little suspiciously, as soon as we entered the drawing-room.

"O, out for a long walk," was the answer; and then we separated for the purpose of escaping a cross-examination.

I went direct to Lady Alice, who was talking with Miss Goldthwaite. Both ladies looked good-natured, as though they had had a quiet laugh together over some subject which I could guess.

"Can't you let me into the secret of your good humor?" I asked; but they declared that they could not, as it was not intended for masculine ears.

"There seems to be some mystery going on," I said, with a smile. "I just saw my friend, Mr. Hopeful, leading the way to the library in company with your honored father, the marquis."

The young ladies exchanged looks of consternation and surprise.

"O, they must not meet," Lady Alice said. "What will papa think of me?"

"Can I be of any assistance?" I asked, with real enjoyment of the scene.

"O, yes; do give me your arm, so that I can go to the library and see papa. I would not have them meet for the world."

"Why, one would think Hopeful was about to ask your hand in marriage," I said, in a bantering tone.

"I should be ashamed to think of such a thing!" Miss Josie exclaimed, coming to the rescue of her friend, who was covered with confusion.

"I am sure I didn't think that there was any harm in asking a lady to become a wife," I said. "If such is the case, I shall have to remain single."

The girls exchanged glances, and then Lady Alice accepted my arm to be escorted to the library, where, sure enough, I found Hopeful and the marquis. My friend had not, however, opened his mind on the subject; for he had not had time to speak. He was talking on other topics, and thus the young lady interposed.

"I do wish, papa, that you would order the carriage and go home with me; for I assure you that I am not quite well. The heat has affected my head, and I shall be grateful for a little cool air."

"I suppose that our conversation can be deferred until some other time?" the marquis asked, with a bow to Hez.

"Wal, I ain't so sure of that," was the reply. "We is off to-morrow; but if the lady is willin' to lose a good chance, I s'pose I am;" and before Hez could say any more, the young lady had induced her puzzled father to leave the room and prepare for his departure.

"What did you have to say to the marquis?" I asked.

But Hez was not communicative, and refused to confide in me. He was mysterious, too, and hinted that if everything had gone right, some people that he knew would have been astonished at his good luck; but not for many days did we let him know that we had overheard his auda cious proposal to one of the richest heiresses in the kingdom of Great Britain.

The next day we all took our departure for London. We had had a most pleasant visit; and our hosts had done all that was in their power to make us happy. We promised to return to the Oaks and Elmwood as soon as we had finished our trip to the continent; but no definite time was set, on account of the uncertainty of our movements.

I left my son and Rover in charge of Sir William and his wife; of course I knew that they loved the boy better than themselves, and that the hound held a place in their affections next to the child. It was hard to part with the child, and almost as hard to part with the dog; but we could not travel with him in France without danger of losing him; so I thought it best to let him remain at the Oaks, where he could have the best of care, and a large park to run in when so disposed. Rover whined a little at first at the idea that we were to be separated; but when I told him that he must watch over my son and look after him, he made no further demonstrations.

We remained but a few days in London, and then started for Paris by the way of Dover and Calais. Our passports were all right; we made no attempts to smuggle; and as four of our party spoke French with some degree of correctness, we found no trouble in getting through the custom-house without much detention.

On reaching the city we separated; for we did not think that it was desirable that all of our party should remain together. Mr. Goldthwaite and his daughter took possession of their old quarters, at the head of the Rue Rivoli, while the rest of us found splendid accommodations on the Boulevard Sebastopol, where we had front apartments, an accommodating porter and wife, and no one to care what we did as long as we paid our bills promptly and never grumbled at the charges or items. We brought with us numerous letters of introduction from Sir William Byefield and the Earl of Buckland; but, after a consultation, we agreed not to deliver them for several reasons.

"The fact of it is," said Fred, "we are under an engagement with Mr. Goldthwaite which we cannot repudiate. I distinctly remember how, on board the steamer, we promised to join him in the attempt to find his eldest daughter, who is supposed to be confined in some convent in the city."

We all remembered the promise. Of course I was not likely to forget it, for the reason that Miss Josie had spoken to me several times on the subject; and each time I had vowed with all energy that I would never give up the search; and whenever I had made a new vow I was rewarded with a little pressure of her hand and a glance that was eloquent of gratitude.

"I take it," continued Fred, "that none of us will forget the promise we made. We have months before us in which to work. Even while surrounded by pleasure, let us remember our vows, and seek for some method by which we can discover the lady and rescue her from her living tomb."

"We are all agreed on that point," Murden said. "We must work, and work in a secret manner. Once let us discover in which convent Miss Goldthwaite is confined, and I'll warrant that we have her out;" and after arriving at so important a conclusion, we dressed and left the house for breakfast at the nearest restaurant, and after that to see something of the city.

While we were sipping our coffee and eating our rolls and fresh butter, a person in plain clothes entered the saloon and took a seat at a table near our own.

We did not pay him much attention, but continued to chat on various topics until we were ready to leave, and then the person in plain clothes arose and put one hand on Murden's shoulder.

"Pardon me, monsieur," the stranger said, "but I arrest you in the name of the emperor."

CHAPTER XXX.

UNDER ARREST. — AN EXAMINATION. — A REMARKABLE MAN. — AN EDICT. — A SURPRISE. — THE EMPEROR.

The mild-looking, quiet little gentleman, with a soft voice and gentle manners, who had sat near us in the restaurant, and sipped his coffee with infinite relish, and when he had finished it, pocketed the lump of sugar that was left, had laid one of his hands on the shoulder of Murden, and informed him, without the least excitement, that he was a prisoner.

For a moment we could not comprehend the Frenchman, so stood staring at him in the most absurd manner, while the officer — he was an officer, one employed in the detective department — beamed on us in the most engaging manner, as though he had just performed for us an important service, and did not wish any thanks.

"Gentlemen," said the detective, still smiling at us, "you are surprised at your arrest, I have no doubt."

Murden admitted that he was a little astonished at what had taken place.

"Ah," said the Frenchman, "I have been looking for you more than a week, and now, thank God, my search is rewarded. I saw you go into the restaurant. I followed. Nothing more natural than that, you see. You talk, I listen. Good again. I do not understand what you say. You speak English, except when you talk to the *garçon*. I listen. You talk of Ireland, the Fenians, and then you laugh. *Eh, bien.* I still listen and sip my coffee. Presently you talk of Italy, of Garibaldi, of the emperor;" and here the little Frenchman removed his hat. "When you speak of Napoleon, you all laugh. Then I think *gens de même famille*, and I know that I have the right man before me; so I wait till you have eaten, and then I arrest you. Have I not done well?"

We could but smile, in spite of the seriousness of the arrest of our friend, to think of the difference between French and English police officers and detectives. Here was a little fellow, standing before us and talking as confident as an emperor, and without the least sign of fear that we should knock him down or attempt to run away. We also laughed in a subdued manner, when we recollected that we had talked, while at breakfast, of our exploits among the Fenians of Ireland, and we had all laughed at Hopeful when he had boldly stated that he meant to seek the Emperor Napoleon, and introduce to his notice and the attention of the empress the patent rotary gun which Hez had invented in a moment of inspiration. We had asked him how he expected to make his way to the emperor's presence, and he had hinted that he could find a way; and then Murden had laughed long and loud at the idea of the son of New Hampshire obtaining an audience with the ever-busy Napoleon.

The French detective understood enough English to think that some plot was going on; so he thought he had found a celebrated conspirator in the person of the bluff ex-commissioner, who was guiltless of plots against the emperor or any other sovereign, for he was too firm a believer in the divine right of kings to intrigue against them.

"Look ahere," said Murden, turning to Fred; "what in the devil's name does this polly vowdedingdon mean, any how?"

In spite of the position in which we found ourselves, we could but laugh as the extent of the commissioner's French rolled from his lips in one continuous stream, like the Falls of Niagara, while the face of the detective assumed such an expression of astonishment, as he heard Murden's words, put together without meaning, that it but added to our amusement.

As soon as we could subdue our mirth, we managed to inform Murden that he was under arrest.

"Nonsense," was the reply. "I've done nothing that

should warrant an arrest. This is one of your confounded jokes."

"The gentleman will not find it a joke unless he can prove himself innocent," the Frenchman stated, as soon as we had explained to him what our friend said. "The laws of France are all very strict on the subject of conspiracies against the emperor."

"Look ahere," thundered Murden; "ask the darned frog-eater whom he takes me to be."

In reply to that question, the detective took from his pocket-book the photograph of a man who looked enough like Murden to be his twin brother. If a stiff beard had been added to the picture, the resemblance would have been most complete.

"I'm blest if it don't look like me," Murden admitted; "and I don't blame any first-class officer for making a mistake. But I know I never sat for that photograph, and I know I ain't the man; so what does he mean to do about it?"

"You have made a mistake," I said to the Frenchman; "but it is quite a natural one, and until we can prove that you have blundered, I suppose you will hold the prisoner."

"Yes, I shall do that, and you had better go with me to the prefect of police, and satisfy him that your friend is all right. Then I shall have done my duty, and the blame will not rest on me. I speak plain — do I not?"

"Yes."

"Then let us go. Shall we walk, or will you engage a carriage? Here is one. Enter, gentlemen."

He had held up his hand, and a carriage suddenly appeared from around the corner, as though the driver had been on the watch for a signal such as was given. At the same time two police officers in uniforms left a doorway in which they had been standing, and walked down the Boulevards towards the tower St. Jacques. They had received a signal that we were not desperate, nor disposed to offer resistance, and would submit to the arrest in the most lamb-like manner.

"*Allons*," cried the detective to the coachman, "to the minister of police."

We rather enjoyed our ride through the busy streets of Paris, in spite of the disagreeable position in which we found ourselves. The detective was kind and communicative. We offered him a good cigar, a prime Havana, one that we had brought with us, and had got through in a way that all tourists understand, and that simple act won his heart and opened it at the same time.

"I hope your characters will prove as good as the cigar," he said; "and the more I see of you, the more I think you are all right. Come, tell me who you are."

"Do you really want to know?" I asked.

"Yes, *mon Dieu*, I should be delighted."

"Well, this gentleman, whom you have arrested, at one time had the honor of being chief of police of Victoria, Australia."

"Ah, the devil! you don't mean it?"

"It is true."

"So that we are comrades."

"Yes."

The detective extended his arm and shook hands with Murden, and then he once more consulted the photograph.

"Ah, thunder, but the likeness is wonderful; and yet I must admit that there is a difference, now that I look at it by the light of friendship. Yes, you never sat for this picture."

"Then why take us to the minister for examination?"

The Frenchman shrugged his shoulders, as he answered. —

"I must take you before the minister, because he knows by this time that I have made an arrest. If I should release you, I should be suspected of receiving bribes. A Frenchman must be above suspicion."

We had no intention of offering bribes; but I really don't think that the detective would have accepted money even if we had offered it.

"You may as well tell us, now that you believe us innocent: of what is our friend charged?"

"I can tell you now; but say nothing to the minister. He wishes to take people by surprise, and make them confess by an overwhelming charge, like that of the great Napoleon at Wagram."

We promised compliance, and the detective went on:—

"Two days since, I received orders to look after four men who had left London for Paris, with treasonable designs against the emperor. They were friends of Garibaldi. The picture of one of the men was given to me. I took up my station at the depots, and watched; but I could see nothing of those I wanted. Eh, did I get discouraged? No; I waited, and at last saw you arrive. I followed you to your rooms. I kept watch of all your motions. I saw one of you throw a kiss to a pretty girl in the street this morning."

At this we laughed and looked at Hopeful. He was the man who did it.

"When you went to breakfast I followed you, and heard all that you said. I understood the French, but could not master the English. It is such a terrible language. So harsh, and hard, and such dreadful words, I should never learn it. It is impossible."

"Why do you not arrest us as well as our friend?" I asked the Frenchman.

"Because only one is dangerous. So it was said. The others were only friends, and would do nothing. They cared nothing for the Italian plots, and they loved the emperor. Why should they not? He is a great man, and has made France the greatest nation in the world. See what he has done for Paris. Is there any city like it?"

We acknowledged that there was not, and as our cigars by this time were consumed, the driver was directed to pull up opposite the building occupied by the prefect of police, where the minister was to be found when important cases required his personal attention.

We entered the building. The detective reported himself, and we were told to sit down, while two stout fellows, with cocked hats, and swords by their sides, guarded the door, so that we could not pass out without their consent.

For half an hour we sat in the outer office, silent and thoughtful. Not a loud word was spoken all the time we were there. In one corner of the room was an old man busily engaged in writing; in another corner a young man, who seemed to be looking us over and making memorandums of our personal appearance in a large ledger, which must have contained some curious names and remarkable records of crimes.

Every few minutes a gendarme would enter the office, make some whispered report to the old clerk, and then retire in pursuit of new adventures. Each of them gave us a sharp look, as though to recollect our faces in case we ever again met, which we had no desire to do.

After waiting until we had almost lost patience, we heard a bell; and then the old clerk nodded to the detective, while at the same time a door, leading to an inner office, opened, and a gendarme with sword and cocked hat appeared.

"Enter," the last apparition said. "The prefect and minister await you."

The detective touched Murden and pointed to the door; but just then something suggested itself to our guide. He recollected that Murden could not speak a word of French, and his superiors not a word of English. He sent the gendarme to the prefect, and asked that Fred and I might also appear at the examination, as we had important testimony to offer.

The officer returned with permission; so we followed him to another room, where we found more clerks and half a dozen gendarmes, who seemed to be in waiting. As soon as we appeared, they came towards us, and laid their hands upon our persons.

"It is useless," said the officer who had arrested us. "They are unarmed, with the exception of pocket knives."

"We must have them," was the answer. "The prefect will take no risks from strangers."

We gave up our penknives without a word of remonstrance, for we knew how careful the officials of France always are in their interviews with political offenders; then once more we were moved forward, and in a minute found ourselves in a small, neatly-furnished room, and in the presence of three gentlemen.

All of them looked up when we entered, and we felt their eyes on us in the most searching manner. One of the gentlemen, a stout-built man, with a heavy-looking face and long, waxed-end mustaches, calm, fish-like eyes, put his hand to his mouth just as the detective was about to make some kind of a salute. It may have been a signal, for all that I knew; but at any rate, our friend the officer neglected the salute for that person, and saluted the other two in military form.

"You made the arrest, Augustus?" asked one of the gentlemen, with his little black eyes on Murden's face.

"Yes, monsieur. The person who corresponds with the photograph is here."

"Have you asked him any questions?" continued the man with the black eyes, whom I took to be the prefect of police.

"Yes, monsieur, I have asked him questions, and also his companions."

"And what do they say for themselves? Do they acknowledge anything?"

"No, monsieur, nothing." And then, with another military salute, added, "I fear, monsieur, that I have made a mistake, and arrested the wrong man."

"Impossible," cried all three gentlemen; and then each looked at a photograph which they held in their hands.

"Yes, it is the same," they all said. "There can be no mistake."

Then the prefect opened a book and took up a pen.

"Your name and country?" asked the prefect, still speaking in French.

"You can talk to him in that language all day, and you will get no answer," said Fred, in French. "Our friend does not speak your tongue."

The three gentlemen exchanged smiles, and the prefect said, —

"The last time you were in France you could speak French, and when plotting in England you could speak French. How does it happen that you have forgotten so soon?"

"I think, monsieur," Fred said, with a smile at Murden's look of wonder, not understanding a word that was said, "that you had better be convinced, in the first place, that you have secured the wrong man. Our friend is as innocent of plots as the emperor himself."

The gentleman with the dull, fish-looking eyes suffered a grim smile to pass over his face at Fred's words, while his companions stole a look at his countenance, as though to see how he liked it. But they did not smile, perhaps fearing that they would compromise their dignity by such a proceeding.

"Do you know the emperor by sight?" asked the minister.

"No, sir. We never saw him. This is our second day in Paris," said Fred.

"And when were you here before?" asked the prefect. "Be careful; for I have access to reliable records."

"This is our first visit to Paris; and your records must contain much that is false, if they state that we were ever in the city until the present visit."

At this retort the prefect frowned, and the minister and the gentleman with the peculiar eyes smiled.

"Don't you be too sure," said the prefect. "I have caught smarter birds than you, as you will understand before I get through with you. Now listen to me."

"We are all attention, monsieur," was our reply.

"Then answer my questions," addressing Murden, and nodding his ead to Fred; "do you interpret my words to your companion, and be sure that you make no mistake, for some of us can speak English as well as yourself."

"Then why employ one of us?"

Again two of the gentlemen smiled, while the prefect frowned, as in duty bound.

"Because," the official answered, "it pleases me to test your honesty in any way that I see fit."

"Thank you," returned the bold Fred; "but you could have tested us in a more simple manner. If you had asked us who we are and what we are, we should have told you in a few words."

"It is not too late now," the man with the eyes remarked, in English, and in a tone so quiet and dignified that we could not repress a grateful bow to the individual in question.

The remark was given to the prefect in French; and I noticed that he colored and flushed up as though he felt the rebuke. He paused for a moment, and then asked Murden, —

"What countryman are you?"

"An Englishman; but now a true son of Australia."

"You are sure that you are not a native of Italy?"

"Quite sure."

"And I suppose that your name is not Guilippo Murtano?"

"Yes; tell them that I'm confounded sure of it," was Murden's reply.

"And you never conspired against the life of the emperor?"

"No; I respect Napoleon too much to desire any harm to him," was Murden's prompt reply. And I saw that it pleased the man with the eyes.

"Why do you respect him?"

"Because he has proved himself an able man and a good ruler for France. Why should I, a stranger to the country, desire the emperor's death?"

"We can't answer that question, because man's ways are mysterious," was the prefect's answer.

"Gentlemen," asked the man with the eyes, "what brought you to Paris?"

He spoke in English, just as though he was familiar with the language all his lifetime, and knew how to use it to advantage.

As the gentleman looked at me, I felt called upon to answer.

"We desired to see Paris, the emperor, and France."

"And you wanted to see Paris more than the emperor?"

"No, sir; but we have little hope of seeing Napoleon, unless he invites us to his receptions, and we do not suppose that he will. So, as Paris is free, we class it first."

"What countrymen are you two gentlemen? Not English?"

"No, sir; we have the honor to be Americans."

"I thought so. Have you letters to, or an acquaintance with your minister?"

"No, sir. We are about to wander through Europe in our own way, and so do not desire such influential acquaintances."

"But you have passports?"

"Yes, sir; and they were examined, and found to be correct."

"Can you bring any proof that you are what you assume to be?"

We thought for a moment. Mr. Goldthwaite was in the city, and could sustain our statements; but I did not wish to call on him. Suddenly I recollected that the Earl of Buckland and Sir William had given me letters to certain influential English parties in Paris, with the understanding that I could use them or not, just as I pleased.

I produced the letters, and handed them to the person who was questioning me. He glanced at them, and then a smile passed over his face, as he said, speaking to the minister and prefect, —

"You have made a great mistake. These gentlemen are not conspirators. My old friend, the Earl of Buckland, recommends them in the warmest terms. Let them be discharged instantly, and no more molested."

The man with the eyes here folded up the letters, and came towards us, and put them into my hands; and as he did so, he said, —

"You want to see the emperor — do you?"

"Yes, sir. It is one of our ambitions."

"Well, then, look at me. I am the emperor."

CHAPTER XXXI.

HOPEFUL AND THE EMPEROR. — THE HOPPER GUN. — AN INTERVIEW APPOINTED. — CONVENTS. — A DINNER. — AN APPOINTMENT.

WE were so much surprised when the gentleman with the peculiar looking eyes announced himself as the Emperor Napoleon, that we could only stare at him in astonishment and doubt.

But soon we began to recollect the stern face that had been photographically impressed upon our minds in every café which we had entered in Paris, and also in every room in the house in which we lodged. There could be no mistaking the long, waxed mustache, the heavy, full face, the short legs, and the long, stout body.

As the fact forced itself upon our minds that we were in the presence of the emperor, the man who ruled the destinies of France and Europe, and whose word was potent for peace or war, we bowed our respect, and were just about to say something handsome and complimentary, something that would have made a lasting impression upon the mind of Napoleon, and thus drawn the lines of friendship between the United States and France closer than existed at that time, when we heard a slight noise at the door, and, turning our heads, we saw, to our infinite horror, Hezekiah Hopeful struggling with two gendarmes, who were trying to prevent his entering the apartment.

"Let me alone, gol darn yer picters," shouted our friend, very red in the face, and very indignant at the restraint put upon him.

The gendarmes looked appealingly at the prefect of police, as much as to say that they could not prevent the stout Yankee from making a noise, unless they resorted to serious means, which a French officer does not like to do, only as a last resort.

"I'm goin' to see if my friends is imposed on, or what is the matter with 'em," Hopeful continued. "If you lays a hand on 'em in violence, I'll stir up the whole of New Hampshire but I'll have redress, now I tell yer. Let me alone — will yer?"

The last remark was addressed to the officers, who still clung to Hopeful, and wanted to remove him; but Hopeful would not be removed. He had caught sight of us, and was bound to join us and see how we had been treated.

I rather think that the prefect of police must have signalled the officers to release our friend, for they suddenly quit their hold, and the next instant Hez was shaking hands with us in the most enthusiastic manner.

"I rather thought that the dedongs had shut yer up," said Hez; "so I guessed I'd look arter yer a little myself. It won't do for 'em to fool round us Yankees, unless they is ready for trouble, now I tell yer."

The emperor saw that we had a character for a companion; so he suffered just the faintest possible smile to pass over his face. He did not appear in the least offended at Hopeful's words, which I put down to his credit.

"For Heaven's sake, hush," whispered Murden in Hopeful's ear.

"Hush! What for?" demanded the son of New Hampshire, not in the least abashed. "Ain't this a free country? Ain't a man a right to say what he likes, and not be took up for it?"

"For gracious sake, stop your noise," Fred whispered. "Can't you see that you are in the presence of the Emperor Napoleon."

Hopeful opened his gray eyes to their widest extent, as he started back.

"You don't mean it?" he gasped, in a tone so loud that the emperor heard it, and once more smiled at our friend's eagerness.

"To be sure I do; so now act like a rational being," Fred continued to whisper; but Hopeful, with his eyes fixed on the emperor's face, seemed lost in wonder and astonishment.

"You don't mean to tell me that this is Louis?" our wretched friend cried, in a tone so loud that the emperor heard every word he spoke.

We were so ashamed that we could have kicked our faithful friend for his gushing impetuosity. Of course we made no answer to Hez's question, and the wretched fellow continued, —

"I've long wanted to see the greatest man in all creation, and now you mean to tell me that this is him?"

The emperor smiled. He rather appeared to like this sort of thing, as a novelty in the way of being addressed.

"Louis," said the wretched Hez, in a gushing, confidential manner, "I'm devilish glad to see you, now I tell you. Let's shake hands."

To our surprise and consternation, Hopeful pushed us one side, and walked boldly up to the emperor, and gave him his hand; and Napoleon did not refuse it. No; the emperor, the man who commanded a million bayonets, whose word in France, Italy, and England was supreme, shook hands with the son of New Hampshire in as hearty a manner as though they had been old friends, and had just met after a long separation.

"Louis," cried Hopeful, still retaining the great man's hand, as though reluctant to give it up, "I like to meet a man of genius, and one what appreciates genius."

The emperor smiled, and bowed to the compliment; but still he looked a little puzzled.

"You see, emperor," Hez continued, dropping the familiar name of Louis, "I can invent machines what can do the work of a thousand men, and do it well, too; and I have just thought that you are the man to take hold of my hopper gun."

"Hopper gun?" repeated the emperor.

"Yes, sir. I call it a hopper gun, 'cos all you has to do is to put the bullets into a hopper, and then you turn a crank and out they fly, and with one you can knock down more Prussians in an hour than a dozen of your best regiments with rifles."

I saw a look of interest pass over the emperor's face, and he even turned to the minister and prefect, who were near him, and explained to them what Hopeful had said; and a laugh was the result of the reference to the Prussians, and a more respectful glance the reward which our friend received from those in authority.

"Have you a model of the gun?" asked the emperor. "I take some interest in fire-arms, and should like to see what you have so well described."

"But if I show it to yer, you won't come the rough over a feller — will yer?"

"I do not understand you," the emperor said, in a tone that sounded a little stern.

"What I mean, emperor," continued Hez, "is, that you won't take a fair look at my model, and then go for to experiment with the principles — now will yer?"

"Do not fear on that account. I have no wish to deprive you of your honors."

"Now, that's what I call the right kind of talk, and just what I would expect from a man like you," cried Hez, in a burst of confidence. "You shall see my model of the hopper gun, and if it pleases yer, we'll strike up a trade, and make it all satisfactory; or I'll take a contract to kill off yer Prussian enemies at so much per hundred, arter you has declared war."

"May the day be distant before France and Prussia engage in war," was the quiet answer. "France means peace — an honorable peace, and no other. There is no fear of war."

The emperor bowed, as though our interview was at an end; but Hez was not quite satisfied. He wanted something definite and clear; so he once more returned to the charge, in spite of our winks and hints.

"Emperor," he said, "when do yer want to look at my hopper gun? Can't yer appint a day to examine it? I want yer to have a look at it afore some one else snaps it up."

"Bring it to the Tuileries to-morrow," the emperor said. "I will devote the hour of eleven to looking at your invention. I should be happy, gentlemen, to see you also;" and this time the emperor bowed as though he was in earnest in dismissing us; so we left his presence with the kindest of smiles from the emperor, the minister, and the prefect.

The detective, the man who had arrested Murden on suspicion of being Guilippo Murtano, accompanied us to the street, and there shook hands with us in the most harmonious manner, and congratulated us on our discharge; but we were not inclined to let the officer off in that manner. It was near our dinner hour; so we proposed to him that he should acccompany us to the Three Friends restaurant, and there dine with us — an offer which was accepted in the same spirit that it was tendered.

We walked through the streets, and our companion, who knew every inch of Paris, pointed out the most notable objects on the way.

"There," he said, calling our attention to a dark, sombre-looking building, that stood on a by-street, surrounded by a high wall that bristled with spikes and broken glass, "is a convent."

We became interested at once, and exchanged glances. In some convent in Paris Mr. Goldthwaite's daughter and sister had taken refuge, and to get the former was one of our objects in visiting Paris.

"And do young ladies still bury themselves in convents in the heart of this great city?" I asked.

"Large numbers of them," was the reply. "When a young lady of good family is without dowry (and you know here men do not like wives without money), owing to the poverty of her parents, she goes to a convent, for the simple reason that marriage is impossible. Once in a convent, a young girl is safe, for she gives no further trouble."

"Does she never leave the convent after she has entered it?"

"Rarely. Once in a great while a girl escapes by the aid of outside friends, and sometimes through the law, which can reach even the interior of a convent. But he who fights the pope must have a long purse, for all manner of obstacles are thrown in the way of those who would remove one of the saints."

We did not stop while speaking of the convent. We sauntered on, and Fred asked, in a careless tone, —

"The name of this convent is —"

Fred hesitated, as though he could not recall the name.

"The Saint's Rest," was the reply. "Some hundred nuns are in that convent, and it is one of the richest in Paris."

We passed on, but the conversation made an impression on my mind, and I thought that the information which I had gained would be of some service at future periods.

We had a glorious dinner at the Three Friends. Every one of us enjoyed it, and none more than our new friend, the detective. He swore, over bottles of the coolest of champagne, that he was our friend for life; and just as he was relating the most thrilling of adventures, the waiter ushered into our apartment a gentleman dressed in plain clothes, and who looked as meek as Moses; for not a particle of beard could be seen on his face, and but little resolution on his lips.

Our friend the detective and the new comer were acquainted. They shook hands, and then we were introduced in due form. The stranger was another of the mysterious combinations of Paris by which the people are kept in subjection, and all their feelings known to those in authority. He was named Dupont, and considered one of the ablest officers in the department; for, in spite of his lamb-like look, he was as brave as a lion and as crafty as a fox.

"My child," said the new comer to our friend Farenti, "I heard that thou wert here. One of the gendarmes saw thee enter this place; so I made bold to follow, for I have work for thee that must be done."

"And no man is more willing to work with Dupont than I, my friend. But is there much occasion for haste? Canst thou not find time to drink a cup of wine with my new friends? Three of them are Americans, and the other is a born Englishman, who has seen much service in that strange country called Australia, where the convicts are fierce for blood, and the wines all sour, and the winds parch the skin until it looks like the head of a drum, and the women have fashions that are two years old. Ah, my child, he has suffered in that part of the world, and now sees enjoyment for the first time in la belle Paris. Shake hands with him, for he belongs to our noble profession."

We gave Murden the substance of the conversation, and then had the satisfaction of seeing the Englishman and the Frenchman shake hands in true fraternal manner; and it needed but a word of mine to place M. Dupont at the table, with a fresh glass in his hand, and some remains of the dessert in a plate before him.

"I drink," said M. Dupont, "to that America which our Lafayette loved and served." And we honored the toast in fine style, although Hez insisted upon replying to it on the ground that he once knew a Gideon Lafayette, a farmer in Hillsboro' County, New Hampshire, who had the crossest bull of any man in those parts; and then the wretched Hopeful proceeded to tell several stories of the bull; certain bad boys who provoked him to desperation, until the great Lafayette would be awakened by the noise and rush out of his house to stop the strife.

At last Hez concluded. The Frenchmen, who did not understand a word that was said, sat and listened with a gravity that promised well in the way of courtesy, if not comprehension. If they did not understand a word of the English language, at least they tried to, and that is saying much when a fellow is boring you with tales of a cross bull.

"Hez," I said, as soon as he had concluded, "the Lafayette whom you mean and the Lafayette whom the gentlemen mean are not one and the same person."

"Wal," that genius replied, "'tain't my fault if they ain't — is it?"

No answer was returned to the question, for the simple reason that an answer was impossible. Who could argue with Hopeful, after he had made up his mind?

"My child," said Farenti, as soon as Hez had concluded, "what business hast thou on hand which requires thy attention? I know that something is up, and I am curious in such matters."

"Thou art a war-horse, and snuffest the battle from afar. There is work for thee and for me, and no time must be lost in preparing for our mission."

"Explain," cried Farenti, as he filled his glass.

"Before these gentlemen? Can I do so?"

"They are as true as Frenchmen, and I answer for them," replied Farenti.

"Enough; I am convinced. Listen to me, for what I have to say is worth your attention. To-day the prefect sends for me. He compliments your friend, and then he compliments my friend Farenti. I tell him that Farenti is worthy of his regards, and that few can equal him in courage or endurance. Ah, you see that I never forget you — never; we have been friends too long for that."

Here the two detectives, overcome with friendship, enthusiasm, and a little heated by wine, arose and embraced.

"Gol darn their picters, if they ain't kissin' each other," cried Hez, with such an expression of disgust on his face that I nearly laughed outright. "I can kiss a woman, but 'll be darned if I can kiss a man. It would make me sick. I'll be darned if it wouldn't, now I tell yer."

We were ready to take his word for it, well knowing his feelings.

The Frenchmen, after their embrace, emptied their wine-glasses to each other's health, and then to our own.

"Now, Dupont, thou must tell the remainder of thy story. What said the prefect?"

"He told me that to-night there would be another party at the hotel of the Countess de Lorenzo."

"Again?"

"Again, my friend."

"Sure? Why, it was but a few nights since the countess gave a party."

"Yes, and but few ladies were present."

"It is true."

"The countess and her two lady friends."

"I have seen them. They dress like the *demi-monde*."

"Ah, thou hast noticed them. It is well. Now listen."

"I am all attention."

"The prefect instructs me to be present at the party."

"Ah, he suspects the countess — does he?"

"You shall see."

"Tell me more."

"'Let Farenti go with you,' the prefect said."

"He said that — did he?"

"Yes, or I would not be here."

"True. Tell me some more."

"'Go to the party to-night,' said the prefect, 'and take Farenti with you. Your eyes are sharp, and you will see what is going on. Your ears are open, you will hear what is said.'"

"*Morbleau,* I should think so. Did we ever fail the prefect in such cases?"

"I think not. But listen."

"Go on."

"'You will mix with the crowd,' said the prefect. 'Here are tickets for your admission to the hotel. Don t be the first to arrive, and don't go together.'"

"He need not have given us such advice as that, — the prefect."

"No, but the prefect is particular."

"True. Go on."

"'When once in the hotel, cast your eyes about you.'"

"As though we would not."

"'Drink but little, and partake sparingly of the refreshments.'"

"Who would eat after such a dinner as this?"

"True. But listen."

"I am all attention. Faith, the prefect is particular."

"He is, as you see. 'Note,' he says, 'all those present.'"

"Of course."

"'Watch the countess, and see where she places herself, and what she does when high play commences.'"

"Ah, that is it — is it?"

"It is."

"The prefect suspects the countess — does he?"

"Yes; for a young friend of the emperor has been bled at the hotel, and his majesty now thinks it time to stop it."

"He is in earnest."

"Never more so. We must watch the play, and see where the cheating is, and then make our arrest."

"What, the countess?"

"Of course, and those who are confederates. The emperor's friend has lost much money, and it is desirable to see where it has gone to."

"Do I know the young gentleman?"

"Of course."

"His name is —"

Dupont looked at us.

"They are honest, my child. Do not fear," said Farenti.

"The name of the young gambler is Prince M——."

"*Bien*, I suspected it. What is to be done with him?"

"Nothing. He is to go. The emperor will attend to him after we have attended to the countess."

"Well, I am ready for the job. We shall give a good account of ourselves, I have no doubt; and now, *bon Americanos*, what will you do this evening?"

"Faith," said Dupont, with a laugh, "why can't the two who speak French like a Parisian go with us and take a look at the countess?"

"An excellent idea. Will you go?" demanded Farenti.

For a moment we took counsel with our friends, and they insisted that we should go, just to see a little of the high, dissolute life of Paris. They wanted a little rest, and were willing to remain at our rooms and sleep all night, so as to be prepared for the theatre on the following evening.

"We will go," we said, "but we have no cards of invitation."

"Don't fear on that account. We can obtain as many cards as we please." And so we planned to go to the hotel of the countess, and see what means she adopted to fleece strangers and young Frenchmen, or whoever fell into her net, which was a large one.

CHAPTER XXXII.

THE INTERIOR OF A FRENCH HOTEL. — HOW A COUNTESS CAN PLOT AND PLAN TO ROB THOSE WHO HAVE MONEY. — AN INTERRUPTION.

AFTER we had dined, we left the Three Friends, and spent a short time in the gardens of the Tuileries, and at nine o'clock we were at our rooms dressing for the party which the Countess de Lorenzo was to give at her splendid hotel, situated near the Place de Concorde. Dupont and Farenti had promised to call for us when they were ready; so we dressed and waited until such time as they chose to appear.

It was past ten o'clock when two cabs stopped in front of our lodgings, and the porter's wife escorted the two detectives to our rooms.

At first we did not recognize them. The officers had left us young men, about twenty-eight years of age, and they came to us looking all of fifty. Their hair was sprinkled with gray, their skin was wrinkled, and age had settled near their eyes. But their clothes were of the most fashionable cut, the finest material, and their linen glistened as though it had come fresh from the hands of an artist. Each of the officers wore magnificent diamond pins, single stones, which could not fail to attract attention; but no other jewelry could be seen on their persons.

We had ordered in coffee and cigars, and then, with Murden's and Hopeful's best wishes, we were off, Farenti and I in one cab, and Dupont and Fred in the other, so that we should not arrive together.

"Tell me," I said, as we rode along: "do you feel the least nervous on account of the adventure before you?"

"Feel my pulse. Does it beat rapidly?"

"No; it is as calm as my own."

"*Bien*, I supposed so. There is but little danger to

encounter to-night. It is only a question of wits. I should prefer other service; but a Frenchman in detective service must go where he is sent."

"You have encountered more dangerous adversaries than a gambling countess?"

"Ah, have I not? I was near the emperor when the Italian conspiracy was consummated, and came near being a victim. I made two arrests that night, and desperate men they were, half maddened at the thought of failure."

"And the night of the explosion was the first news that you had of the conspiracy?"

"The devil! no. A hundred times no. I was one of those who had followed Orsini's track from the time he entered France. Sometimes I was in one disguise, and sometimes in another. I had urged that he be arrested a few hours before the explosion. But no. The prefect said that the plot was not ripe. I knew that it was ready to burst, and said so. But I was told to wait. I did wait, and the emperor nearly lost his life. But the conspirators lost their lives and the prefect his place."

"And what reward did you receive?" I asked.

The detective pointed to a ribbon in the button-hole of his coat. It represented the badge of the Legion of Honor, so much coveted by all Frenchmen.

"The emperor gave me this with his own hands. *Mon Dieu!* but it was the happiest day of my life when he placed it on my coat. He spoke to me, too, and uttered words of praise for what I had done; and then I told the emperor that it was not my fault that the plot of the miserables nearly succeeded."

"And what did he say to that?"

"He told me that he knew it. Ah, the emperor knows everything. Can you blame me for loving him, when he is so generous to reward and so prompt to punish? He has made France and Paris the first in the world. He is a great man."

I was not disposed to dispute the assertion, for before my eyes was evidence of the emperor's greatness. Whole streets had been made out of narrow alleys. Palaces had gone up where hotels formerly stood. Trees and gardens, fountains and vases, statues and flowers, now existed where formerly there were waste places. No wonder Paris was called the finest city in the world. It deserved the title, for evidence of beauty and refinement was seen on all sides. All that was vulgar, coarse, or immoral were kept out of sight, or else seen only by gas-light.

After half an hour's drive, we stopped and alighted in front of a large house, the residence of the Countess de Lorenzo.

My companion dismissed the carriage, and then the doors of the hotel were thrown open by a man in livery, and we entered the house, merely handing the servant our cards of invitation; but I noticed that he did not glance at the names which they bore, apparently satisfied that we were regularly invited.

We passed up a flight of broad stairs, and were ushered into a room, where we laid aside our hats and arranged our toilets before being presented to our hostess of the evening.

A dozen gentlemen were in the apartment when we entered. They were all young, and bore the marks of Paris life upon their faces. Late hours and dissipation were telling on them, as it does on every one who is so foolish as to seek for pleasure at the expense of health.

Every one in the room nodded to us, although there was not a single person present, except the detective, whom I recognized. The company supposed that we were of the same social rank as themselves, and so exercised the usual courtesy of Frenchmen.

One man, whom I heard addressed as marquis, spoke to me, and knew at once that I was a foreigner.

"You are not an Englishman?" he asked, with a polite bow and a smile, as he offered his snuff-box.

"No; an American."

"Ah, *mon Dieu*, I am glad of that. I like the Americans and hate the English. They killed our emperor, but never defeated him. No, sir."

I bowed and murmured something about the emperor's being a great man, and the greatest general that ever lived; and just then Fred and Dupont arrived; but according to agreement, we did not speak, although we exchanged signals, and then passed through to the drawing-rooms, where the countess was arrayed in all the pride of an elegant toilet, to receive her guests, and bestow a smile upon each one as he passed before her.

It was a little singular, but the countess was the only lady present in her large rooms; and I noticed that none of the gentlemen brought ladies with them, and they did not act as though they expected to meet the opposite sex, or were disappointed in seeing only the countess.

I imitated the rest of the company, and, without waiting for the formality of an introduction, pressed forward and presented myself. The countess looked sharp at me as she extended her little hand, exquisitely gloved, with heavy bracelets on each arm.

"Ah," she said, "I've seen your face before — have I not?"

"I should have been unfortunate not to have seen yours before to-night," was my reply, and pressed to my lips the little hand.

She looked pleased, although she did tap me on the arm with her fan, as a punishment for my flattery.

"You are welcome, monsieur. I am pleased to see you at my house; you must come often." And then I was dismissed with a bow, so that the next person could have a chance to pay his compliments.

I saw Fred and the two detectives pass under the observation of the countess, and I noticed that the lady looked long and earnestly at the two officers, as though she had seen their faces before, and was trying to recall the time and place of meeting. But they were so well disguised that the lady was baffled in her endeavors to recall their features; and so, after a few words, Dupont and Farenti were taking snuff with the gentlemen present, and listening with much attention to the political talk of those who would discuss politics.

Presently there was a sensation caused by a new arrival. It was the important personage whom the detectives were to look after and see how he lost his money.

"Ah, mon prince!" exclaimed the countess, advancing a few steps to meet the new comer, "I feared that you were not to honor us with your presence to-night."

"The emperor detained me later than usual," was the reply. "I dined with his majesty, and then went with him to the opera. But I stole away as quickly as possible, and feel rejoiced that I am once more in the presence of so fair a lady as the Countess de Lorenzo."

"Who is the prince?" I asked of Farenti, in a whisper.

"Prince M——, the grandson of the once king of Naples."

Here was an historical character, and I lost no time in taking a good look at him, for I had a great admiration for his grandfather, the greatest cavalry leader that ever lived.

The grandson was a good-looking Frenchman, careless, dissipated, and did not come up to my ideas of a man who bore a great name. He was not one who would have worked his way from a stable to a throne, and charged an enemy, armed with but a riding-whip.

"Come," cried the prince, "let us get to work. I long for my revenge. I lost so heavily the other night, that I am entitled to it."

"Fie, prince," cried the countess, in a tone that was intended to be languishing and seductive; "you have but just arrived, and yet you would quit me for those horrid cards. I did not think it of you."

"Then sit beside me, and woo luck with your smile. I am sure the goddess could not resist it."

"I consent, for your sake," was the reply.

And then I thought that I saw the countess exchange a quick glance with one of her guests. It looked to me like an expression of triumph, and I turned to the two detectives to see if they noticed it. It seemed not, for they were discussing some great question that was before the Institute at the time, with two oily Frenchmen, who wore bits of ribbon in their button-holes.

The countess touched a bell, and servants brought in card-tables. The scene of the evening was about to commence. All the amusement of the party was to be concentrated on the gambling operations of the gentlemen who were present.

Cards were produced, and down some of the people sat, and undertook various games. The prince and three gentlemen, taking seats at a table, commenced what I supposed to be whist. The countess, with a smile of the most killing sweetness, assumed a position by the side of the prince, and tapped him on the head, face, and hands with her fan, when she felt so inclined.

"Monsieur," said a soft voice in my ear, "will you honor us by taking a seat at our table? We shall play for but low stakes."

Turning, I saw Dupont. He had managed to get Fred and Farenti at the same table, and wanted me to make up the party.

His object was simply to make a show of playing and betting, so that sharp eyes could be kept upon the movements of the countess; for the table at which they proposed to play was within a few yards of the prince.

I accepted the proposition, and was introduced in due form to Fred by the Frenchman. Then we chose partners and commenced whist, at small sums for stakes. No one seemed to care for us, and that was just what we liked, for our detective friends were inclined to devote their whole attention to the countess and her illustrious visitor, by whose side she sat, and into whose hand she glanced to see what cards he held.

The whole thing was revealed to me at a glance, inexperienced as I was in detective business. I saw that the countess was in league with three of the men who were seated at her table, and that those three men had combined to fleece the prince. It didn't require much talent to discover that, I thought.

But for all that, I watched the countess in such a manner that she would not notice me, or know what I was about, and I saw her tricks at once. She had signs to her confederates, and could telegraph to them how to play so that they could win or lose, just according to the money that was at stake.

And all this was done by so simple a method that I was lost in admiration of the skill and audacity of the woman. I did not understand her telegraphing, until one of the detectives let me into the secret by a word. As he dealt the cards and noticed my looks, he had said, with a smile, in reply to a look of interrogation, —

"The fan."

"The fan," I muttered; and then the scales fell, and the countess and her arts were revealed.

With a wave of her fan she could show what cards the prince held. With a tap of her fan she indicated what cards the opponents of the prince should lead, and when she opened her fan or flirted it, signals were made which her friends understood, to the infinite injury of the prince's pockets.

The play grew interesting, and the stakes heavy. The prince doubled his bets and lost, and he continued to lose until the countess announced, in reluctant words, that supper was ready, and that gambling must be suspended for a while for the sake of eating.

All arose at once, and went to the apartment where supper was served. The wines were abundant, and the viands rich and rare. The hostess was unremittent in her attentions to her guests, and more than once she filled the prince's wine-glass and made him pledge her in bumpers. The liquor restored the prince to his good humor.

"*Mon Dieu*," he said, "I hope the wine and the supper will give me better luck than I have had."

"Ah, mon prince, have you lost to-night?" asked one of the guests.

"As usual, yes."

"Fortune is against you."

"Yes, but the countess still smiles on me."

"That is fortune itself," replied one bald-headed Frenchman, with a face that looked sensual enough for a stock in trade of vice. "I would be willing to lose if she would smile on me."

"*Tres bien;* then we will exchange places, laughed the prince; and some of the company joined in the mirth; but the lady tapped the prince with her fan and called him an *ingrate*, which he received with much composure, as though the reflection did not harm him.

Supper was soon over, for the company were impatient to return to their play. They had come to the house to gamble, and they meant to do their work in a thorough manner.

Once more we sat down to the cards. The prince was flushed with wine, while the countess and his opponents were cool and collected, as though they knew how much depended on their understanding all the signs that the lady made. We watched the parties with but little fear of detection. They were too absorbed in matters that transpired at their own table to notice us.

Suddenly the prince threw down a handful of bills.

"One hundred thousand francs on this game," he cried. "If I win, I recover all my losses; if I lose, I play no more."

The countess looked at his cards, and her face grew white with suppressed emotion, as she raised her fan.

Tap, tap, tap. She struck him three blows on the shoulder. They were light blows, and would not have hurt a fly. Then she waved her fan in the form of a crescent, and again in the shape of a cross. Not until she had made these signs did she deign to speak.

"Fie, mon prince," she said; "I fear that you are gambling. Take back one half the stake, I beg of you."

"The whole or none," was the reply.

Tap, tap, tap, went the fan, and the eyes of her conspir

ators followed every movement, for there was too much at stake to allow of trifling. The detectives looked on with the calmness of martyrs. Not a movement escaped their eyes, or showed that they were interested in what was going on.

"You won't cover the prince's money?" cried the countess, in an imploring tone, to the men with whom he was playing. "He is mad, and must not stake so much."

"The money is the property of the prince. *Mon Dieu*, if he is disposed to risk it he should be humored. We are willing to meet him," was the reply.

"I ask nothing better," cried the prince. "Put down a sum equal to my own. Let us make or break each other."

The conspirators watched the movements of the lady's fan. She was telling them every card that the prince held, just as plainly as if they could see his hand.

We looked on and awaited the result with some anxiety.

Two hundred thousand francs were placed on the table, and the game began.

Parties at the other tables stopped their games and crowded around the prince. The stakes were so high that every one was interested.

The two detectives kept their seats and looked on.

"Has the prince a chance for his money?" I whispered.

"Not the slightest," was the reply. "You shall see in a moment. Have patience."

It was all very well to ask us to have patience; but we could not bear to see a gentleman cheated of his money in the manner in which he was being cheated by an artful woman and three designing men. We were in favor of instant action, but the French detectives did not think that the time had arrived for such a course.

We saw the cards played, and then there was an exclamation, for the prince had lost, just as the officers said he would.

The conspirators uttered sighs of relief at the turn

which affairs had taken, and the countess showed by her looks how pleased she was at the result.

Still the detectives did not move. They waited until the prince had started from his seat, dashed down his cards, and uttered several exclamations at his ill fortune.

"The devil," the prince said. "Was there ever such frightful luck? Two hundred thousand francs gone in a week's time. *Mon Dieu*, it is enough to make even a Frenchman swear in the presence of ladies."

The countess motioned to her confederates to take the money, and they were about to do so, when Farenti and Dupont arose to their feet, and said,—

"Let the money remain, monsieurs, if you please."

CHAPTER XXXIII.

DEATH IN THE MIDST OF LIFE.— AN ASTONISHED GROUP. — GRUMBLING COMPANIONS. — AN INTERVIEW WITH MISS JOSIE.

IF one of Orsini's hand grenades had been thrown into the apartment and exploded, I don't think that there could have been greater astonishment manifested than when the two detectives stood up, and, in a quiet tone, requested the plunderers of the prince to let the money remain on the table.

The attention of every one in the room was attracted to the detectives, and I think that even the countess began to suspect that she had more among her guests than she had bargained for; as she turned deathly pale, and had to clutch the table to support her trembling form.

"Messieurs," said the gamblers, with looks of astonishment, "why do you tell us to let alone that which belongs to us?"

"Because," replied Dupont, "you have won the money from the prince by cheating."

"Cheating!" was the general exclamation; and the countess trembled worse than ever.

"Do you know what you are saying?" asked the prince. "Take care. These are all Frenchmen, and men of honor. They are my friends."

"Friends do not usually swindle one out of two hundred thousand francs," was the detective's reply.

"Who are you that speak thus?" demanded the prince.

The detectives turned back the collars of their vests, and there was revealed the emblems of their authority. All looked and all shuddered. The countess gave a little shriek, and sank into a chair, putting her hands, white and well decorated with diamonds, to her eyes.

"Prince," said Dupont, "you have been most shamefully cheated every night that you have played cards in this house."

"I have discovered nothing, and I am not a man that is easily deceived," was the haughty reply.

"Perhaps not; yet you have been cheated by a band of sharpers, with the countess at the head. You had no show for your money as long as she was at your side."

"How! Is it possible, madame, that you would stoop to such meanness?" demanded the prince, in a stern tone.

"No; the charge is false," the woman replied. "The play was fair."

"Be careful what you say," replied Dupont. "We know you."

The countess once more covered her face with her hands, and I saw that she trembled. I began to pity her, for she was handsome, and it is natural for a man to pity a handsome woman.

"Prince," said Farenti, "take up your hundred thousand francs. They belong to you."

"I have lost them to those who played with me," was the reply.

"You were cheated. Take your money and then we shall see if the rest cannot be returned."

The gamblers who had won the prince's money began to move uneasily in their seats. The countess suffered a sob to escape her.

"I cannot take money which has been won from me," the prince said; and at this the faces of the gamblers brightened.

"Then listen, and see if the parties who have plundered you, mon prince, are worthy of your generosity."

The countess looked up with a glance that was beseeching. The detectives took no notice of it, but went on.

"This woman"—and the officer pointed to the countess —"has long been known to us. She came from the provinces to Paris ten years ago. For two years she was the mistress of the Marquis de Tocqueville. Then he married, and found a place for her on the stage at the François. She was in the ballet, and attracted the attention of the Count Lovinski, a Pole. With him she left Paris, and the next that the secret police hear of her, she is in the employ of a Russian princess. One day her highness, the princess, loses a set of diamonds, and they are found on the person of the Count Lovinski, just as he is attempting to sell them to a pawnbroker. The count, in the most ungallant manner, swears that madame gave them to him, and that he knows nothing more about them."

"The mean, cowardly dog of Poland," hissed the countess when the detective reached this part of the narrative.

"As madame pleases," Farenti said, with a shrug of his shoulders. "He was a vile dog, I have no doubt, and he received his pay for some of his vileness. He is now at Toulon, and will remain there for ten years to come, a galley slave, with a black mark against his name. *Ma foi!* he is not much to be envied, for they lead no idle life at Toulon."

"Curses on him; I hope they will work him to death," cried the countess, with a look that showed she had an immense amount of bitterness and ill-feeling at her heart towards the adventurer who had betrayed her.

Dupont waited until the burst of passion had subsided, and then he continued his revelations.

"Madame will recollect that she was arrested for the abstraction of the diamonds, but that she was acquitted of the charge through some influence which it is not necessary to allude to here. Since that period madame has lived in Paris, and supported herself by entrapping rich men. As long as she confined herself to people of little account, the police did not interfere; but when she struck for such game as a prince, the prefect opened his eyes, and the result is now before us. Madame will please give up the two hundred thousand francs which were lost in this house within two weeks."

The prince began to pick up the money, which was still lying on the table, and truly he rather appeared to like the idea of getting it back.

"The money is gone; I have none of it," said the countess, who uttered a deep sigh as she saw the prince put the bank notes in his pocket-book.

"It must find wings and come back, and quite soon, too," was the detective's answer, so quiet that not a show of temper could be noticed.

"It is impossible. The money is spent. Part has gone for the supper to-night."

"Madame shall be paid for her supper, but the money must be produced."

The countess bit her lips and folded her arms. She had made up her mind what to do, and was determined.

Farenti stepped to a window, threw it up, and whistled. From the dark shadows of half a dozen trees, figures of men in uniforms stepped out and came towards the hotel. The front door was opened, in obedience to a signal, and into the drawing-room came a squad of gendarmes, quiet and respectful, yet resolute, as men who knew their duty.

Dupont pointed to the countess and the three men who had sat at the same table with the prince.

"Arrest them," he said.

The police moved forward and laid their hands on the shoulders of the three men. The countess waved them off.

"Do not touch me," she said. "I don't want to be polluted with the hands of a common thief-taker. *Mon Dieu!* there is an escape, and here it is."

She thrust one hand into the bosom of her dress, and drew out a small phial with a glass stopper.

"The devil!" cried Dupont. "She means mischief."

He sprang forward, but was too late to stay her hand. She had raised the phial to her lips and drank the contents before he could seize it.

"God forgive me!" she murmured. "I am now beyond your reach. Even the police of Paris will not dare to follow me to that unknown world, where I shall find darkness or light."

"Quick, quick!" cried one of the detectives to the gendarmes. "A doctor! We must save her life. *Ma foi!* I had no idea she was so desperate."

One of the gendarmes rushed from the house in search of a physician, without waiting for a second bidding.

"It is useless," murmured the countess, whose face already began to show the effect of poison. "I shall be beyond the reach of all human aid in less that ten minutes. All the doctors of Paris could not save me."

She trembled and staggered as she spoke, and had not Fred sprang forward and caught her in his arms, she would have fallen to the floor.

But even with death the pride of the countess did not desert her. She sought to remove Fred's arms from her waist, as though there was contamination in the embrace.

"Ah," she gasped, "you are a *mouchard*, and I hate you."

"No," cried Fred, with some eagerness, "I am a gentleman, and in no way responsible for this."

She made no further resistance to his assisting her to a lounge, where she could lie down at ease; but the poison had begun to do its work. Her eyes grew glassy, and lost the look which health and success had given them a few minutes before. Her face, full and handsome when we entered the house, now began to show signs of dissolution, for the features began to contract, and a death-like pallor stole through the rouge which was laid on her cheeks in small quantities. A cold, bead-like perspiration appeared on her forehead and lips, while her hands, pressed upon her bosom, began to tremble and to turn blue, and the dark blood to settle under the nails.

"For God's sake, will the physician never come?" demanded Fred. "Let some one else go in search of a doctor."

Dupont made a motion, and another gendarme disappeared.

"I know where the celebrated Ducrow resides," said one of the persons who had fleeced the prince. "He can save her, if any one can."

He started up, and was about to hurry to the door; but Dupont stopped him with a bow and a word.

"Monsieur," he said, "will be kind enough to take his seat again. We must do without his assistance. We shall want monsieur in a short time, and we fear that if he leaves us now, we shall find some trouble in again catching sight of his face. Monsieur is under arrest, and must not escape."

"But if he can find the great Ducrow," suggested the prince. "*Sacre*, but it seems to me that a life saved is a life gained. I will be responsible for the man's appearance with the physician. You know me, officers."

"Yes, prince; but not well enough to take your security for the return of a man who has passed two years of his life in prison for cheating."

The prince muttered an exclamation that sounded like an oath, and then turned to a window and looked into the street, so that he should not see the dying face of the woman who had tempted him and led him on the road to ruin.

I saw that the countess began to suffer from thirst, as the poison worked through her system. I hastened to the supper-room, where the servants were already revelling, in anticipation of the death of their mistress, and procured a goblet of water and wine, and then returned and wet the lips of the dying woman.

"Who are you?" she asked, as her eyes rested on my face.

"An American, and a man who really pities you."

"Ah, you are not a Frenchman, a tiger, fierce for human blood, like the whole race."

"No, I am not a Frenchman," I replied.

She raised her head a little, and pressed her hands on her bosom, as if she already felt the pains of death.

"It burns," she murmured, "as though fire was consuming me. Give me a drink of water, and something to hasten my death."

She emptied the goblet, and just at that moment a doctor entered the room. I made way for him. He knelt down and felt the pulse of the countess, and opened her eyes and examined them.

Then he arose, and, in answer to an inquiry, said, —

"She has taken some of the new vegetable poison discovered by Shafler, and all the surgeons of Paris could not save her or prolong her life."

"Can't you give her something to relieve the intense pain under which she is now suffering?" I asked.

"Yes; but she will suffer only for a short time longer. A confessor should be called at once, even if it is not now too late."

One of the gendarmes started in search of a priest, while the physician mixed an opiate with a little water, and compelled the dying woman to open her mouth and receive it upon her tongue.

"It is useless," she whispered. "I go;" and with a gasp she died, and her spirit was relieved of its earthly troubles.

"Cover the face of the corpse, and call a commissioner," Dupont said, and then turned to the company present, many of them speechless with horror at what they had seen.

"Messieurs," the detective remarked, "you can retire to your homes if so disposed, all excepting the three gentlemen who have so kindly won the prince's money. They will either refund it or go with the gendarmes to prison. Be quick with your choice, for we have no time to lose."

"We will take the prison," was the reply; and off the fellows were marched without a word.

"Prince," said Dupont, as the gamblers disappeared, "you shall have your money in the course of a day or two. Those fellows will not hold out a great while. They prefer the gayeties of Paris to its prisons. I feel safe in saying that you can count on again handling your two hundred thousand francs."

The prince bowed, but said not a word in the way of gratitude for what the detectives had done for him. He left the house as soon as possible, and shuddered as he passed the dead body of the countess.

In a few minutes the drawing-rooms were emptied, with the exception of the two secret officers, one of the gendarmes, Fred, and myself. I had no desire longer to remain in a room where so sad a tragedy had occurred, and intimated to Farenti that Fred and I would leave for our lodgings, if he had no objections.

"Wait one moment," was the reply. "As soon as a commissioner arrives we will start." And he was as good as his word; for as soon as the official had entered the room, Dupont promised to finish the work of explanations, and thus relieve his comrade of further duty for the night.

We left the house and called a carriage, and by three o'clock in the morning Farenti had set us down at our door.

"Here," he said, as he thurst cards into our hands, "take these. If you should want to see me again, on duty or off, don't fail to call. The cards will tell you where to find me, and if you have no objection, I will drop in on you once in a while, and hope that our next adventure will not be a tragical one. Good night."

He squeezed our hands and was gone; and we entered the house, after rousing the porter, to find Murden and Hopeful sound asleep on the lounges, instead of beds, as we expected.

We awakened them, and were greeted with a shower of reproaches, and one or two profane words.

"What did yer want to keep us up here all night for?" growled Hez. "Yer said yer would be home in an hour or two, and here it's daylight. I ain't got no patience with sich people, I ain't."

"Ah, Hez," replied Fred, "you wouldn't scold if you knew that we have made arrangements for to-morrow night for your especial benefit."

"What's that?" was the question.

"Why, we will all go to the Jardin Mabille, where we shall see lots of pretty French girls and some wonderful dancing. How does that strike you?"

"Wait till I see 'em," was the reply; and off to bed Hez went, but in a modified humor, for the idea appeared to please him.

We told Murden our adventures of the night; but they did not seem to surprise him. He was prepared for most anything after his arrest by the police. He said it was a clumsy piece of business letting the countess take the poison, and if he had had charge of the affair, he would have prevented it; and so satisfied in his own mind he went to bed, and after Fred and I had smoked a cigar, we followed suit.

We slept late the next morning, and could hardly realize the facts of the night past, while dressing. The dead face of the countess was still before us, and we could not drive it away, hard as we tried.

But a cup of coffee and a light breakfast aided in restoring us, and then I dressed for a visit to Miss Goldthwaite, for I recollected that I had not seen her since our arrival in Paris, and I feared that she would consider me neglectful if I remained away much longer; and I don't hesitate to state that I desired her favorable consideration above all persons in the world.

I left my friends at the restaurant, and hurried to Miss Josie's residence, and sent up my card. The young lady was at home, so the porter informed me; and without waiting to see if she was disengaged, I ran up stairs and entered the drawing-room, the door of which stood open.

The young lady was standing at a window with her back towards me. I stole forward, and before she was aware of my presence, I had my arm around her waist; and when she started back, astonished at the liberty, I saw that her eyes were filled with tears.

"Josie," I asked, as she twisted herself from my embrace, "tell me, what is the matter?"

"Nothing," was the reply; and then a fresh shower of tears started to her eyes.

This was something that required an investigation; so I made her take a seat while I did the same. I determined to have a long and confidential chat with the lady.

CHAPTER XXXIV.

THE EMPEROR NAPOLEON AND FAMILY. — A KIND RECEPTION. — AN EXPLANATION. — THE LEAVE-TAKING.

As I took a seat by Miss Josie's side, I stole a look at her face, and saw that it seemed perplexed, and a little indignant at the same time. She noticed that I was looking at her, and became angry in a moment.

"How dare you insult me so much as to put your arm around my waist, without my permission?" she asked, with as much indignation as she could manifest.

I sighed, for I saw that she was bound to quarrel with

me at any rate, and I knew that I had done nothing deserving her anger.

"Is your father at home?" I asked; for I thought that I would see Mr. Goldthwaite for a moment, and then retire, and return some other time, when she was in a more agreeable humor.

"No, he is not at home; and if he were, I do not believe that he would remain quiet and see his daughter insulted."

This was a little too much; so I instantly arose and pretended that I was about to take my leave.

"Miss Josie," I said, as calm as I could be under the circumstances, "if you really think that I meant to insult you, I beg you to alter your mind, for I had no such intention."

"Why did you put your arm around my waist?" she demanded, in a tone that was a little modified.

"Because nature prompted me to do so, and I could not resist."

"Yet nature did not prompt you to visit me all yesterday;" and the young lady looked her indignation.

I began to see light. It was dawning on me in the most mysterious manner.

"Josie," I said, "don't you know that all day yesterday I was at work to obtain some information of your sister, who is supposed to be confined in a convent in this city?"

"No; I was not aware of it. O, how cruel I have been to you! and what an opinion you must have of me!"

"I have the best opinion of you, Josie," I said, as I kissed her hand; "but you know that at times you are a little unreasonable and impetuous, and then you do love to quarrel."

"I fear that all you say is too true; but I don't know how I can cure myself of the habit," was the little darling's answer.

I was just about to put an arm around the best proportioned waist in all France, and to whisper in her ear that if she would but love me, all such trifling imperfections would be overlooked and laughed at, when I heard a door open.

I turned and saw Mr. Goldthwaite, Josie's father. I had an immense amount of respect for him, because I really loved his daughter, and hoped that he would act as a father towards me at some distant day; but his presence just at that moment was very disagreeable, and for the time I thought him rather meddlesome.

"Bless me," cried the old gentleman, coming forward, with an eager, outstretched hand, "I had no idea that you were in the house, my dear boy."

"I supposed that the servant would tell you," I answered; but I had not supposed anything of the kind, for the porter alone knew that I was a caller.

"Always send me word, my dear boy," replied Mr. Goldthwaite, "when you call. You must not leave the house without seeing me. We think too much of you for that — don't we, Josie?"

"As you say, papa," replied the young lady, without turning her head; but at the same time she drummed on the window-pane, as though she felt a little annoyed at the presence of her respected father, just at that particular moment, when she had anticipated so much and been disappointed.

"We missed you very much all day, yesterday," Mr. Goldthwaite said. "I didn't leave the house but for a short time, for fear you would call and I should lose the pleasure of seeing you. Even Josie would not go out, for she said that she knew you would be here."

I gave Miss Josie a glance of approval, but the young lady did not seem to notice it, for she turned from the window and faced her father.

"I do wish, papa, that you would think twice before you speak of me to gentlemen. You place me in the most embarrassing of positions."

Mr. Goldthwaite looked astonished, and could not comprehend how he had offended the little beauty; but I could understand her feelings, and sympathized with her.

"Sit down," said Mr. Goldthwaite, "and let us have a

short conversation on the topic that brought us to Paris. Have you heard a single word of Susie?"

Josie came and sat down by her father, and seemed interested in the question. I remembered what I had told the young lady, so was careful in my reply. They were satisfied with it, and the zeal that I promised to bring to bear in the search.

"I have heard but a rumor," the father said, "and it came from an old friend. I will not tell you what it is at the present time, for it is too cruel to repeat. In a few days I shall be better informed."

I saw that the subject was a painful one to Mr. Goldthwaite and his daughter; so it was dropped for more congenial topics; and thus we passed the forenoon in a pleasant manner, until it was time for me to take my departure, for I remembered that Hez had an interview with the emperor for the purpose of exhibiting the model of his gun, and it was desirable that he should be prompt.

"You will call this evening?" Josie asked, as she extended her hand.

"It will be impossible to see you to-night, but to-morrow I will call."

The young lady, like the spoiled child that she was, pouted a little, and then turned to the window and looked into the street, while I hurried to our lodgings, and found my friends all ready to start for the Tuileries with the model of the gun which Hopeful thought so much of.

"You don't s'pose the emperor would be mean enough to steal the thing — do yer?" asked Hez, as we entered the carriage that was to take us to the palace.

We assured Hez that we did not think Napoleon was the man to do any such thing; and this pacified him somewhat, but he declared that he would keep his eye on the emperor and watch all his motions.

"Where shall I go, messieurs?" asked the driver.

"To the Tuileries," we answered.

The coachman was a Frenchman; so he bowed, smiled, and stroked his mustache, and then hesitated.

"Well," we said, "what is the matter?"

"Pardon, messieurs," the man said, "but you are strangers in Paris, or I would not have told you that you could not enter the grounds of the Tuileries while the emperor is there."

"We go by appointment," I answered.

"Pardon," muttered the man, "I did not know that; monsieur did not trust me with his confidence."

He touched his cap with the air of a prince, and then mounted his box and drove us to the palace.

A sentinel prevented us from entering the gate, as we expected. The driver looked at us, and shrugged his shoulders, as much as to say, "You see — what I told you is true."

"We come by orders of the emperor," I said to the soldier.

"Are you Americans, with the model of a gun?" was asked.

"Yes."

"Pardon, messieurs, I have orders to admit you. Pass on."

We entered, and in a moment an under aid of the emperor met us.

"His majesty is ready to receive you," this person said. "Will you please to follow me?"

He conducted us to the palace, up one flight of stairs, — where we saw an abundance of servants, — and then gave us in charge of an aid who seemed to be in attendance on his majesty.

To this latter aid we were presented in due form.

"One of you," said the aid, "has a model which his majesty is to look at this morning."

"Yes."

"You will be kind enough to let me see it for a moment;" and the officer led the way to a small side room.

This was a precaution, so that no accident should happen to the emperor.

The aid examined the model with a critical eye.

"It is not loaded?" he said.

"No; we can show the workings of the gun without the aid of powder or ball," was Hez's reply.

"Good," said the aid. "Please follow me."

We did follow him, and found ourselves crossing several large halls, the walls of which were hung with paintings and engravings. We were not allowed to stop and admire anything that we saw, much as we wanted to, for an emperor was waiting for us, and an emperor's time is valuable.

Presently we came to some heavy silk curtains, where we found a page in attendance. The boy gave us a nod of welcome and a bright smile, and then drew aside the curtains, and we found ourselves in the presence of the emperor.

He was seated at a round table, which was covered with maps, books, and models, pen and paper. He wore a dark frock coat, buttoned around his stout form, and had on white linen trousers, loose and long, for they covered his boots, which were of patent leather.

Napoleon looked up from a book as the curtains were drawn aside, and when he saw us a smile passed over his face. It was a peculiar smile, and showed me that the man had a heart even if his enemies said he was destitute of such an organ.

"I am glad to see you, gentlemen," the emperor said, in excellent English, which pleased Hez so much he rushed forward and shook Napoleon's hand.

"Now," cried our impulsive friend from New Hampshire, "we can understand one another jist like brothers. I can't talk the French lingo, and it's no use for me to attempt it. It puts my tongue out of jint to try."

Napoleon smiled and motioned us to seats, and after we had sat down intimated that he was ready to look at the model of the gun.

In an instant Hez had produced it, and was deep in mysteries of springs, range, muzzle, loads, rapid firing, &c., &c.

I will give Hopeful the credit of saying that he understood machinery most thoroughly, and while talking about it, could make himself quite interesting. This time he did his best, for he considered his revolving gun the triumph of his genius. He showed the emperor how easy it was to load the weapon, how rapidly it could be fired, and with what accuracy, even by the most careless of marksmen.

His majesty listened most attentively, and said but little, yet I could see that he comprehended all that was placed before him. He asked a few questions, but they were not of a trifling nature, as Hez needed all of his intelligence to answer them.

While Hopeful was explaining some point that the emperor appeared doubtful of, the curtains were drawn aside, and a lady, leading a child by the hand, entered the room. A glance was sufficient to assure us that it was the empress and the prince imperial. We were on our feet in an instant and bowing most profoundly, which the empress acknowledged with a smile that was as sweet as ever played over the face of woman, while the prince accepted our courtesy with all the grave dignity of a king.

"I did not know that you gave an audience this morning, Louis?" the empress said, uncertain whether to advance or retreat.

"These are some Americans who wanted me to examine the model of a gun," returned the emperor. "Come and look at it. Here, mon prince, is something that will interest you."

The prince left his mother's side and passed over to his father.

"Ah," cried the empress, with an expression of horror on her fine classical face, "more models of murderous weapons?"

"Yes, Eugenie, more models. It is necessary for the safety of France that the empire should have the best and most destructive."

"And is it necessary that our child should look at such? Consider his tender years."

"I do; but if he is to rule France some day, he must understand all subjects that interest a Frenchman."

The emperor spoke in so significant a manner that the empress could not fail to understand him. An expression of regret and weariness passed over the lady's face, and she turned to leave the room, but suddenly recollected us, and prepared a smile for our benefit.

I will confess that I never saw so sweet a smile upon woman's face, or so much grace in woman's movements, in my life, as the empress displayed on that eventful day.

"You are Americans?" she asked. "I like the Americans, and Paris is honored by the visits of so many. We are always happy to see them."

"If they do not bring the model of guns to the palace," suggested Fred.

The empress smiled, but replied, —

"The emperor is interested in everything that appertains to the glory and power of France."

"And France repays the love which he bears her, because through his aid she has been placed in the front rank of nations," was Fred's reply. And quite a delicate little piece of flattery it was, as I afterwards told him; but my friend assured me that he was serious and in earnest in what he said.

The emperor heard the words, and suspended his examination of the model, much to Hez's disgust. He took the little prince by the hand, and came towards us.

"You compliment France and me," the emperor said, "and I thank you for it, and wish that all your countrymen had as favorable an opinion. America has suspected me of being hostile; but there is no warmer friend to the United States in Europe than myself."

We said that we were glad to hear it; but Fred suggested that the Mexican expedition was the principal thing that had caused our people to look at France and her ruler with suspicion.

The emperor glanced at the empress, and smiled; but whether it was at our frankness, or some secret thought, I could not tell.

"My motive for the Mexican expedition will one day be more apparent than at present," the emperor said. "History will do me justice on that point, if history is ever correctly written. Why, just look at the matter in a clear light. You know how the country was distracted with revolutions and bloodshed. It owed millions of dollars to my people, and they wanted their money, but could not obtain a dollar — only promises. Then England and Spain proposed a joint alliance for the purpose of obtaining debts and peace. I joined the alliance, and the result is before the world. I was deserted by my allies in the earliest stages of the conflict, and single-handed I carried on the project. The United States complained, yet I did not make a move until I had consulted with your authorities at Washington, and obtained assurances that I should meet with no opposition on your part; but after a while the politicians thought that they saw danger in a reliable kingdom instead of a distracted republic, and the cry was raised for intervention. That cry strengthened and encouraged the Mexicans, and at last I withdrew my soldiers from the country, and told Maximilian that I could no longer keep him on his throne. He did not heed my warning, and so lost his life; and for that I am blamed, but most unjustly."

During the time the emperor was speaking, the young prince listened to every word that his father uttered, as though to retain the thoughts upon his mind, while the empress paid the same attention that her son did. Of course we were surprised at the revelations and at the frankness with which Napoleon spoke, and I had no doubt at the time that he was uttering the truth; but we could not slap him on the back and tell him as much; so we simply bowed and looked profound, until Hez — confound him — broke the silence by saying, —

"I'll tell yer what it is, Mr. Napoleon, if you had had a

lot of my guns in yer fellers' hands, and they had knowed how to use 'em, all the Mexicans in the country could not have driv yer out; you may jist bet yer pile on that."

The emperor smiled, and replied,—

"Perhaps so; but now we will resume our examination of the weapon, if you have no objections."

Hez was delighted to do so. He did not care for Mexico. All that he wanted was to talk of guns and machinery.

"Perhaps, gentlemen," the empress said, "you would like to look over the palace while you are waiting for your companion."

We said that we should be delighted to do so, and the tinkle of a small bell summoned a page.

"Victor," said the lady, "show the gentlemen the palace and gardens, and then return with them to this room."

We bowed, and followed the page.

"Was there ever such a gracious lady?" demanded Murden, who was running over with enthusiasm for the empress and her husband and child. "I could die for her, and think nothing of it."

We were nearly as enthusiastic as our friend, and we could hardly realize that we were not dreaming, the whole thing seemed so strange; but when we returned to the palace, after an examination of the gardens, we were conducted to a room where we found an excellent collation that had been laid for us by the emperor's order, with some of the best champagne that I tasted while in France.

As soon as we had satisfied the cravings of our appetite, we once more returned to the emperor's private cabinet, and there took leave of those who had entertained us so handsomely.

"You shall hear from me in the course of a few days," Napoleon said, speaking to Hez, and alluding to the gun model. "I must study over it a little longer."

"Send for me any time, Mr. Napoleon," replied the son of New Hampshire. And then we left the palace for our rooms, and to get ready for the ball at the garden Mabille, where we expected to see some fun.

CHAPTER XXXV.

THE GARDEN MABILLE. — A PRETTY GIRL. — A FLIRTATION. — A DANCE. — AN INVITATION. — A GRAYBEARD. — THE IRON GATE.

In dressing for the visit to the Garden Mabille we were more particular than we had been while in Paris. We cast aside all the clothes which we had worn from the United States, and put on some which we had purchased in France, because we knew the kind of place we were going to, and were not disposed to give the people whom we were to meet an opportunity to pick us to pieces by the way of ridicule, as they would be likely to do if our clothing afforded the least evidence of an anti-Parisian character.

At ten o'clock we entered the Mabille, and were soon mingling with the crowd. At first we had some apprehension of Hopeful; but he told us that he could take care of himself without our aid; and, sure enough, the next moment he was attempting to galop with a black-eyed damsel, who held on to the son of New Hampshire as though she had got hold of a prize, and determined to retain it if smiles and blandishments could succeed, although they could not understand a word that each said to the other.

"Be careful, Hez," I said, "and don't get into trouble. Mind, the eyes of France are upon you."

"Don't you bother yer head about me," was the reply. "I kin take care of myself, I guess, without yer assistance. If France wants somethin' to look at, she may find lots of people besides me."

By the time the speech was finished, the young lady, his partner, had whirled him to the music of the band, some distance from me; and the next time I caught a glimpse of him and his flame, they were in one of the stalls drink ing iced champagne and eating ice cream as though they liked it and each other's company.

Fred and Murden soon separated from me — one to chat with a laughing girl, who could not keep her feet still while the music was playing, and the other to drink a bottle of wine and smoke a cigar in some part of the garden where he could be more retired, and run some chance of falling in with a countryman.

I was leaning against one of the stalls, quietly smoking a cigar, and almost wishing that some girl would come along and challenge me for a galop, when a female touched my elbow; but whether by design or accident I could not tell.

I said nothing, but continued smoking. Once in a while, however, I stole a glance at the lady, and saw that she was remarkably handsome, and resembled some one whom I had seen, but who I could not just remember at that time.

She remained standing at my side, and seemed to be interested in the dancing, but did not once look at me, although she must have known that I was watching her.

For ten minutes we stood side by side without speaking. I longed to have a chat with her, but feared that she was of a different class from those who surrounded her, or that she was under the protection of some of the wild students who were in the garden in large numbers, drinking and dancing, and quick to take offence in case one of their protégées was interfered with.

At last I moved to another part of the grounds; for I feared that temptation would be too much for me. The girl's handsome face was not to be resisted for any length of time by a sensitive man like myself.

I lighted a fresh cigar in my new quarters, and once more looked at the dancers. I saw Hez overturning all with whom he came in contact as he galoped in company with a nimble-footed nymph of a hundred and fifty pounds' weight. I heard the many curses that were hurled at his head by the grumbling Englishman, or the more polite

Frenchman, or the impulsive American. I saw Fred enjoying himself with a petite grisette, and caught sight of Murden drinking champagne with a burly Englishman with a red face, and then I turned around and saw —

Well, I was a little surprised and pleased withal; for as turned I saw the handsome face and dark eyes of the lady who had stood by my side so long in the other part of the garden.

I looked at her long and earnestly, and then she raised her eyes and met my glance with one so full of fun that I could no longer keep silent. I laughed outright, and said, in French, —

"Is this good fortune or accident? If it is my fortune to meet and become acquainted with you, I shall bless my luck for the remainder of my life. If our meeting is the result of accident, I shall also bless all such accidents in the future."

"You may call it what you will," replied the lady, with a smile that rippled into a laugh, hearty and cheerful; and then she glanced up at me with a pair of eyes that were only excelled by those of Miss Goldthwaite, so clear, so bright and large were they.

"Then let me call this second meeting by design," I said. "If you will, I shall consider myself a happy man."

"Second meeting! What do you mean?" she asked, with a look of pretended surprise.

"I have seen you once before this evening — have I not?"

"Who can tell? I have been here for some time. It would be singular if we had not seen each other."

"And now that I have spoken, is there any need of our separating for the present?"

She stole a look at me from those glorious black eyes, and then I saw a smile once more appear on her face.

"Can I trust you?" she asked.

"I am a man," and bowed before her.

"I suppose that you are, and that is the reason I want to know if I can trust you," she said, a little pettishly.

"Try me and see."

"I am almost inclined to;" and once more those black eyes were raised to my face, and seemed to read my thoughts.

"It shall be for your happiness if you do," was my fervent reply.

"You are not a Frenchman?" she asked, after a moment's thought.

"No; I am an American."

She started as though I had touched a topic that was disagreeable to her. Then she sighed, and murmured,—

"I thought so."

"Why did you think so?" I asked; and taking her hand, I placed it on my arm, and moved to a more retired part of the garden, where there was less confusion and more comfort.

"The moment I looked on you I was sure that you were an American," the lady said, as we moved along.

"You are an expert in reading nationalities, for I am proud to acknowledge myself an American, and I wish that you were one also."

"Why?" and she held down her head as though looking for something that was lost on the ground.

"Because I think that so much beauty should belong to my country. We Americans worship female loveliness."

"Do you?"

She looked up and laughed, and gave me a glance that was quite tantalizing. I began to feel quite interested in her, considering that I was in love with another lady, who was equally if not more beautiful.

"Let me offer you some refreshments," I said. "A glass of wine."

"No; I never drink wine with a stranger."

"And you call me a stranger?"

"Yes; I never saw you before this evening."

"But I have seen one just like you," I added, "and I am acquainted with her, so should be on the same friendly footing with you."

"Is the lady a native of France?"

"No; she belongs to my country."

"Tell me her name — won't you?" demanded the lady; and I was just about to refuse, when some one blundered against us, and I saw that it was Hez and his partner.

He was off in a moment, only just taking time to say, "Come on like me," when he was banging at some one else, in another part of the grounds.

"Will you dance?" I asked, "or do you decline on the same ground that you refuse wine with me?"

"I will dance with you if you wish," she said; and as she spoke she threw part of her lace shawl over her face, so that more than half her features were concealed. Then she put one of her small hands on my shoulder, and while my arm encircled her plump waist, away we went to the voluptuous movements and music of a waltz.

I found my companion an excellent dancer, light and easy; so I did not soon tire of the amusement; but when we were both pretty well blown, we stopped and edged away from the crowd.

"You dance well," the lady said, as soon she could find breath to speak.

"Thank you. I find you charming, either in the dance or the promenade. There is one more character in which I should like to test you."

"Name it;" and she laughed as though she liked the compliment.

"Let me see if you can partake of some refreshments with the same grace that you can dance."

For a moment she hesitated. Then she turned square around, and looked me full in the face, with an expression of her large black eyes that showed she was in earnest.

"First," she said, "tell me what you think of me."

"I think that you are the most charming lady that I have met in Paris."

"Pshaw! that is flattery, and rather gross at that. What I want to know is, do you believe me honest?"

Now, I did not believe her to be any better than the

rest of the girls who were rollicking on every side of us; but still it would have been extremely impolite for me to have said so, consequently I adopted the manly suggestion, that I thought she was one of the best women in Paris, and as pure as the driven snow, and as handsome as Venus.

She listened to my protestations in silence; but I could see by the curl of her handsome lips that she did not believe what I said came from my heart.

"One more question," she said. "Can you afford to pay for what refreshments we order?"

"Yes; but the question is a strange one."

"Perhaps it is; but this is not the first time that I have been in the gardens, or the first time that I have been asked to partake of refreshments."

"You are candor itself," I murmured.

"Don't be a fool," the lady replied, as I attempted to kiss one of her neatly-gloved hands.

I told her that I would not, for my next attempt would be nearer her lips, which I preferred to her hand.

She frowned, and continued:—

"Once or twice I have seen gentlemen reduced to despair because they could not pay for what I had ordered; and then they have blamed me."

"My dear girl," I said, "you can't be a Frenchwoman, you are so considerate of people's pockets."

She blushed, and said that she was French, and would be nothing else.

"Then, my conscientious little angel in petticoats, don't be alarmed, for I assure you that I have, at the present time, a thousand francs in my pocket, a diamond pin and a diamond ring, besides a gold watch, and an account at my banker's that will last me a long time, even if I am rather fast and extravagant."

"You are speaking the truth?" she asked.

"Yes; I could not tell an untruth to so charming a person."

"Don't be an ass," she remarked, in an impatient tone. "I don't like compliments from strangers."

"I've known you for an hour or more, and some one like you for some weeks."

"Tell me the name of the person who is like me. Is she French or American?"

"You just told me not to be an ass, and I shall take your advice," I replied, in a light, jesting tone; for I had no idea of mentioning Miss Josie's name in the presence of strangers, and in the midst of the wild revels of the Mabille.

She did not appear to be offended at my frankness, neither did she press her question, but motioned towards one of the stalls, as if she desired to be seated.

I complied with her motions, and called for ices and wine. She ate the former, but refused to touch the latter, although I pressed her to join me in a social glass. She was firm in her declination, and while I was arguing and jesting, some one stopped at the entrance of the stall and looked in. I just glanced at him, and saw that he had a gray beard and a pair of black, twinkling eyes.

"*Allons*," the stranger said, "don't have too much fun all alone by yourselves."

Then the fellow with the beard laughed and vanished from sight. I was too familiar with the Garden Mabille manners to pay the slightest attention to the fellow, for I knew it was one of the customs of the place to poke fun at all those who were in the least inclined to be spoony.

"Don't mind the fellow," I said to my companion, turning to look at her face as soon as the gray beard had disappeared; but to my surprise I saw that she was suddenly affected, and in a most extraordinary manner.

There were tears in her eyes, and her cheeks were without color, while her hands trembled so much that she was compelled to lay down the spoon which she held.

"Halloo!" I said; "what is up? Do you know that man?"

She did not answer, but took up a glass of wine and drank it.

"Did that man mean to threaten you?" I asked, still laughing at her agitation.

"I don't know."

"Is he a friend of yours?"

"No."

"You have seen him before?"

"Yes."

"Where?"

"Here in the gardens."

I was about to question her more, when she intimated that it was time for her to leave the gardens for home.

"Tell me the hour," she said.

I looked at my watch and saw that it was half past twelve, and so informed her.

"Yes," she remarked, with a sigh, "it is time for me to go home."

"And you will let me accompany you?" I asked.

She did not answer me, but remained in deep thought, as though pondering on the question.

"You consent," I continued, and kissed her hand.

"You had better remain here," was her reply. "Take my advice and remain here. Do not ask to accompany me home."

"Why not? I should esteem it an honor to do so."

"Take my advice and remain here. Come, be reasonable, and do not seek to accompany me from the gardens."

"No, I will go with you," I replied, in a decided tone, for my curiosity was excited. "I must escort you home, just out of politeness."

"Again I repeat that you had better remain here. You are an American, and I would spare you, for I don't believe that you are vile and dishonest."

"Thank you. I am no better than I should be; but I'm not vile or dishonest. Rest assured of that."

"Then why do you wish to follow me?"

"On account of your pretty face. It is enough to draw a man of stone; so how can I help being moved by it?"

She sighed and left the stall. I followed her, and drew her arm through mine. She did not resist, and did not speak a word as we passed through the crowd. At some distance I saw the man with the gray beard, but he did not appear to notice us. He did not even glance in our direction; yet I felt that the fellow knew we were on the move, and that he was taking notice of all our actions.

We left the garden and found several carriages waiting in the Grande Avenue des Champs Elysées.

"Shall we ride home?" I asked.

"No," was the reply. "If you will go with me you must walk."

"Is your home far from here?"

"Yes."

"Then let us ride. You must be fatigued with the evening's amusements."

"No, I shall walk. You can do as you please."

"You are unkind, and yet I am doing all that I can to be gallant and polite to you."

"I am aware of it."

"And yet you can treat me in so cruel a manner."

"Yes, for I have the will to drive you from my side and never see you more."

"Now you talk at random," I said, as I drew her arm within mine and walked along the avenue.

She sighed, but made no resistance; so we strolled along for a mile or more, I striving with all my might to make her chat and be cheerful; but only occasionally could I induce her to smile or to appear merry. She listened to all that I had to say, and sometimes asked questions respecting the United States, and was quite particular, when she did so, to talk about Boston, which city she seemed to have heard of in some manner through a relative.

I know I was telling her about the bombardment of Fort Sumter, and my duties on board a steam frigate, when we stopped for a moment on the corner of the avenue and a cross street. Just then I happened to glance around, and saw close to us the old gray-bearded fellow whom we noticed in the garden.

"Halloo!" I said; "do you recollect that old man? We saw him in the garden."

"Yes, I recollect him," she responded, in a low tone, and then hurried me along as though anxious to reach her home without delay.

I kept pace with her until she was tired, and then resumed my ordinary walk. Suddenly she stopped and looked me full in the face.

"I wish that you would leave me and go your own way," she said. "It would be better for you."

"I shall see you home," I remarked. "I can't leave so handsome a face in the streets of Paris at this time of night."

She stamped her little foot with impatience, and once more we resumed our walk.

We turned down the Rue Rivoli, crossed it, and plunged into a street that was narrow and poorly lighted. Then we came to a high wall that enclosed a dark, sombre looking building, with not a light to be seen in it. My conductor stopped at a small iron gate, and unlocked it with a key which she carried in her pocket.

I began to think that I was meeting with an adventure, and considered for a moment whether it was not best for me to retire while there was a chance; but pride and Australian experience came to my aid, and there was a handsome face to toll me on; so, man-like, I passed through the gate, and it was closed after me with a spring.

CHAPTER XXXVI.

IN A CONVENT. — A DANGEROUS POSITION. — A CONFESSION. — THE EFFECT OF A SNEEZE. — FACE TO FACE.

THE iron gate closed with a snap; not loud, but with enough force to convince me that it was locked, and that I should find some trouble in unfastening it in case I should wish to do so in a hurry. I am a man who always desires to secure a retreat in case one is necessary, for I don't believe in being over-confident and blind to one's strength.

I glanced around and saw that I was in a large garden, well laid out with flower-beds and shrubs, and that the wall that shut it off from the street was about twenty feet high, and on the top of it was a row of sharp spikes, suggestive of torn flesh and bruised limbs, should any one attempt to scale it without the use of long ladders.

It took me but a moment to notice all this, and to further observe that no tree of any size was growing near the wall, so that escaping by the aid of a friendly branch, in case I desired to, was out of the question.

After I had seen all this, my eyes finally settled on the face of the young lady who had conducted me thither. She was watching me in silence, yet I could see that her countenance was anxious and that her hand trembled.

I knew that her hand trembled, for I had taken it for a moment in the hope that she would just let me kiss those lips which looked so tempting. But she had started back and refused the favor I demanded, and then it struck me that I had made a ninny of myself, in thus escorting the lady to a place that looked more like a tomb, — so silent and sombre was it, — than a dwelling-house or fashionable hotel.

I had pursued the adventure thus far from the most simple curiosity, and not with the evil intentions of some men whom I numbered among my acquaintances. My love for Miss Josie was more than sufficient to keep me pure and refined; and now that I had escorted my strange companion to her home, I began to think that the joke had gone far enough, and that it was time for me to find my own rooms, and retire for the night.

"Come, my dear," I said, in a light and joking tone, "let me have a kiss, and then I will bid you good night."

I attempted to put an arm around her waist, but she was like an eel in movements, and slipped from my embrace, and held me at a most respectful distance.

"Hands off," she said. "I'm not your property, that you should treat me like one of the most common girls of the street."

"Very well," I replied, with a laugh, "be as virtuous as you please, only let us part friends, and promise to meet me to-morrow night at the Mabille, and I swear to you that I will not offer to accompany you home unless you desire my escort. Come, shake hands, and let me kiss your fingers; and then good night and pleasant dreams."

Slowly she extended her hand, as though she was thinking of the matter, and had not yet made up her mind what to do.

Just as our fingers met I heard a slight noise at the gate, as though some one, not quite sober, was attempting to insert a key in the lock.

My handsome companion caught the sound as soon as myself. She withdrew her hand with a jerk, and then muttered, loud enough for me to hear, —

"I must and will save him. Come," she whispered, seizing me by the arm, "follow me, and make not the least noise, or you are lost."

"What in the devil's name do you mean?" I demanded, for all my Australian bushranging experience began to revive, and I thought that I was in for an adventure that would do to relate to my companions at the breakfast table in the morning.

I put my hand on a certain pocket in my coat, and then felt reassured, for I was not without a friend, one that had seen service, and stood me in need many and many a time when I was in a tight place in Victoria, or in the blockade service on the southern coast.

Did I feel afraid at the prospect before me? No; I can't say that I did. My head was as cool and my pulse much firmer than when I had attempted to steal a kiss on our first entrance to the garden.

She did not respond to my question, but laid her hand on my arm and forced me along towards the dark and gloomy building, the lower windows of which I saw were grated with iron bars.

I could hear the noise at the gate, as though some person found it extremely difficult to discover the keyhole, and thus enter the garden; and it struck me that too much wine had rendered the fellow's hands rather tremulous. I did not see that there was anything to fear on his part; but the lady seemed to be apprehensive, for as soon as she reached a door, she opened it with a key and motioned me to pass in.

"But how am I to get out, and when?" I asked, as I hesitated.

"God only knows," was the low response. "Enter and be saved if I can save you."

"It would be hard to find a handsomer savior," I responded, but still remained on the threshold of the door, for I did not like the appearance of things.

Just at this moment I heard the street gate open. The lady heard it also, for she gave me a sudden push, and into the building I went, and the door was closed behind us.

"Give me your hand," she whispered, "and don't make noise enough to disturb a mouse."

"Here is my hand," I replied, and put it around her waist, and drew the girl towards me and kissed her on the lips, and, to my surprise, she did not make the least resistance.

"Now that you have acted like a fool, see that you behave like a sensible man," was the stern admonition. "You are in danger, and need all your coolness and courage to save yourself. Do you understand me?"

"Yes, and shall like you better if you will give me another kiss."

"Take it, and be quick about it."

I took not only one, but half a dozen, and she remained quiet while I did so.

"Have you finished?" she demanded, in a tone that was quite cool.

"No."

"Well, it is time, for I must again warn you that you are in danger, and that I will do the best I can to save you. I told you not to accompany me home, but you would."

"To be sure I did; but you did not mention that there was so much danger as to imperil my life. That is one of the things you forgot."

She seemed conscious that such was the case, for she remained silent.

"Tell me," I continued, "where I am, and in what part of the city. You can let me know so much."

"You are in the Convent of the Blessed Pilgrims," was the whispered response, "and it is situated on the banks of the Seine."

"Thank you for the information. It is quite consoling to know that I am in such sacred quarters. The Blessed Pilgrims must not belie their name, and prove cursed Pilgrims."

"Hush," she said, still whispering. "Do not jest, for you never were in more danger than at the present time. But if it is a possible thing, I will save you."

"Thank you; I don't think you can do less, after leading me into temptation and danger. But perhaps I can take care of myself, as I am of age, and have seen something of life in my time."

"I did not lead you into temptation," she said; "your own evil passions did that. I warned you not to follow me, or to insist upon seeing me home."

"It appears to me that you have changed your tune in a wonderful manner since we placed a stone wall between ourselves and the street. If you had but intimated that evil consequences would have resulted from an act of admiration, I should have seen you home just the same, for I may as well tell you, in case this is a bluff for my especial benefit, that I am not easily frightened; and so you may tell the sacred Pilgrims as soon as you like."

"You will not understand me. You will misunderstand me, speak as I will; and yet I would be your friend, for I may as well tell you that I like the looks of your face, it seems so honest."

I caught her in my arms at the end of this confession, and covered her face and neck with kisses; and while I was thus pleasantly engaged, some one tried the door through which we had just entered.

She tore herself from my embrace, although it was no easy work, and dragging me to a closet, opened it, and then entered, and made me do the same. She closed the door after us, and waited for some result which I did not comprehend or care for.

I could hear the girl's heart beat, so agitated was she; and to calm her fears, I put my arm around her waist, and pressed her form so firmly that she was forced to speak.

"O, my God," she exclaimed, "what a man you are! If death was at your elbow, I believe that you would waste the last moments of your life in an idle manner."

To my surprise the girl uttered this remarkable and wise sentiment in English — the first that she had spoken since we had met.

I was so astonished that I could only hold her in a firmer embrace, and try to reach the lips that allowed such wonderful sentiments to escape. In justice to myself, I must state that I was successful.

"Where in the name of wonder did you learn to speak such excellent English?" I whispered, with a squeeze that should have forced the truth from her.

"Be still," was her response. "Can't you see that life is at stake, and that a movement may destroy us?"

"But tell me where you learned to speak such pure English."

The closing of the door and the sound of heavy footsteps once more compelled me to be silent. I longed to take a look at the new comer, and half made an attempt to open the closet door for that purpose; but the young lady at my side prevented me by taking my hands in her own, and holding them most firmly.

"Susie!," cried the new comer, "where are you?"

"Keep quiet, and remain where you are," whispered the young girl, her lips close to my ear, so that no sound should go beyond the closet. "Do not move until I come back. Promise me."

"Yes, I promise."

She opened the closet door and glided into the room; and so light did she step, that I could not hear her movements.

"Is this Francisco?" she asked.

"The devil! yes. Where have you been all this time?"

"In the next room, waiting for you and Dieteli."

"And where is the stranger?" demanded the man whom she called Francisco.

"What stranger?"

"Why, the one I saw you with, and signalized you to entrap."

"O, he became faint-hearted, and left me in the street."

"Susie! you do not speak the truth. I followed you, and saw you both enter the garden gate. I am not so drunk, child, that I see double."

"I think that you did, father, for no one entered the gate with me. The stranger fled at the sight of the convent. He suspected something."

"Child, you will have no more opportunities to leave the convent, if this is the manner in which you serve us. You have made promises, and yet they have not availed us in the least. With your beauty and grace the convent should be enriched; but you do not work your cards like some of the sisters. You have no heart for the labor."

"Alas, I have done the best that I could, and yet you blame me," sobbed the girl.

I had a great inclination to go out and punch the fellow's head, but restrained myself, for the purpose of hearing more.

"I blame you because you do nothing. We thought you were just suited for the work that the brethren laid out for you. We said to you, There is so much to do, and will you go forth and help do it, thus benefiting the convent and the Lord, and removing vanities from the pockets of the world's people, or will you remain in the house and see nothing but the hard faces of your aunt and sister Alex, who have bitter words for all who are handsomer than themselves?"

My pretty little Susie! did not answer this reproach; so Father Francisco continued:—

"You cannot deny my words."

"No," was the response.

"You know that you have lured no one to the convent."

"I know that I have not."

"So you must not hope to go to the gardens again."

"I have no longer a desire to go there. To-night's work has shown me that I am unsuited for such business. I have looked my last upon the world, if I can obtain freedom only at the expense of my innocence."

"Isn't here a chance for you to do a little job in the gallantry line?" I asked myself. "It seems hard that one so handsome and young should be forever buried in a convent."

"As you please," returned the priest, in response to the girl's plaintive appeal. "We have others who can work with a will and for the success of the convent. Now go to your cell, and I'll see that bread and water is your portion for the next week for letting a promising subject escape through your hands. He was rich, and would have made a good night's work. His diamond pin alone was worth ten thousand francs, and his watch half as much again. Ah, I have no patience with you!"

Just at that moment a confounded fly or bug of some kind alighted on my nose, and tickled it so badly that I was compelled to sneeze. I tried not to. I covered my head with my coat, and almost strangled myself in the attempt to suppress it. But all was in vain. The insect had tickled my nostril before being driven off, and the sternutation would come.

"Te-he-te-h-e-te-h-e," I sneezed, three times, loud and long.

"*Mon Dieu*, what was that?" asked the priest.

"I know not," was the trembling response, although the lady knew quite well what the sound was, and where it came from.

There was an ominous silence for a moment — a silence that was painful.

"Quick," cried the priest — "a light; we must see where that noise comes from. If you have deceived me, so much the worse for you."

"There is no need of a light," was the response. "One of the brethren is asleep on the benches. Do not disturb him."

"We will see, sister, if your words are correct."

There was a sharp scraping sound, and then the flaring of a match light. The next instant the gas was illuminating the room. I peeped out and saw that the priest was the old gray-bearded fellow who had stuck so close to me in the gardens, and whom we had encountered on the Boulevards.

He was a tall, powerful-looking priest, but rather too fleshy to be active; so I thought, as I took his measure, supposing that perhaps we might have a struggle in case my retreat was discovered.

"I think," I said to myself, "that I can double you up in a few rounds in case there is occasion for it. He is not so tough a subject as I have seen in the bush in Australia."

In the mean time the priest was glancing around the room, an apartment that was used, it seemed to me, for the reception of visitors, while the girl was cowering in one corner of the place, nearly insensible from terror.

Brother Francisco smiled in a manner that I did not think looked amiable, as he saw the girl's position. He glanced from one end of the apartment to the other, and then remarked, —

"You see, sister, there is no brother here; so either you or I must have sneezed. It was not me, I am sure. Was it you?"

She did not answer him. She was too much affected to speak. The priest smiled; and then I saw his eyes go towards the closet in which I was secreted. I knew that the fellow suspected I was there; so I prepared to meet him face to face.

The priest took one step towards the closet, and then

paused and considered. He looked at Susiel, and seemed to enjoy her distress.

Then the man made up his mind. He strode towards the closet, and threw open the door. The priest and I stood face to face.

CHAPTER XXXVII.

A FALLEN PRIEST. — A RE-ENFORCEMENT. — AN ADVANCE. — A RETREAT. — A DEADLY AGENT. — A SURPRISE AND A RESCUE.

FOR one moment the priest and I looked at each other in some such manner as two dogs regard one another when about to dispute over a very promising bone.

Neither of us spoke; but there was no friendly feeling in our eyes as they met and measured each other's strength. At length the priest said, —

"Come out of the closet. I would speak to the person who hides when he hears the voice of a man."

I left the closet and stood before the fellow, so that he could not take me at a disadvantage. Miss Susiel arose and looked on with clasped hands and a terrified face. I made her a sign to keep quiet; but I don't know whether she understood me or not. At any rate, she did not utter a word until she thought her voice would have some weight.

"I am out of the closet; now, what do you intend to do with me?" I asked.

"Do you know why you were brought here?" the priest demanded.

"No."

"Then I will let you know."

He turned and crossed to the other side of the room. I knew what his intentions were, and sprang to his side just before he could lay his hand on a bell-rope that communicated with other parts of the convent.

"Don't do that," I said, and laid a heavy hand on his shoulder.

He attempted to shake off my grasp, but when he found that I was obstinate, turned on me like a famished wolf, and sought to tear my neck with his claws, and long, dirty finger-nails.

"Gently," I said, as I eluded his first furious onset. "Don't be impatient, most reverend father. There is time enough for us to talk, without taking each other by the throat. Let us reason, if you please."

"Viper, I will crush thee," hissed the holy father, whose passion began to be boundless. "Thou wilt wish that thou hadst never been born. If I lay hands on thee, thou wilt mourn for it."

"Thank you, holy father, for your warnings. Now we will understand each other. You mean mischief, and I am prepared for it."

"Do not let him touch the bell," suddenly cried Miss Susie. "He will call the whole of the convent to his aid, and then you are, indeed, lost."

The priest had intended to make a sudden rush for the bell-rope and sound an alarm before I could stop him. The girl warned me, and on her head he poured some of his rage.

Instead of rushing for the bell-rope, he turned towards the girl, and his heavy hand would have fallen upon her sweet, upturned face, if I had not interfered in time.

I caught his arm and saved her the blow; but this made the fellow more enraged.

"Ah," he said, as he wheeled suddenly, "*mon enfant*, you would interfere — would you? Then look out for yourself."

He aimed a blow at my head, as he spoke; but it was not the blow of a scientific pugilist. It was just such a blow as all Frenchmen aim at each other, the fist half closed, and not delivered from the shoulder.

I had no difficulty in turning the blow aside, so that it did not touch me.

The priest looked a little surprised at the result, and muttered something that sounded like a curse instead of a prayer.

"My friend," I said, "I would not advise you to do that again. You had much better keep your temper."

"*Ah*, devil, then you defy me — do you?" the holy father muttered, and once more he swung his ponderous and dirty fist around his head and let fly at me.

I saw the movement and stepped one side. The blow passed clear of me, but with so much force that the priest staggered a little; and this I seized upon.

Before he could recover, or put up his arms as a guard, I let him have a hot one right between his eyes, and down he fell as though struck by a pole-axe.

The holy father did not move for a moment after he touched the floor. He was all in a heap; and the blood was pouring from his face and nose in such a rapid manner that it dyed the floor and the old fellow's beard until he really looked a most pitiable object.

Then the heart of the young lady was touched, and she came towards me wringing her hands.

"O," she sobbed, "you have killed the holy father, and what will become of you?"

"Holy be — hanged," I responded. "If he wants to die under such punishment as this, why, let him. He has not got half as much as he deserves. The wretch! I have a good mind to kick him while he is down."

"Do not touch him again. He has been punished enough."

"I will promise if you will leave the place and go with me. Now is your time to escape."

"Alas, I cannot!" was the response.

"Give me your reason," I demanded, eagerly, for the old fellow began to move.

"I am an inmate of this convent, and can't leave it without the permission of superiors."

"I am superior to every one here, and I give you permission to go. Fly with me and be free. You are too lovely for a convent."

"Do not tempt me. I fear that they would curse me if I left without permission."

"And you pretend that you are happy here?" I asked.

"Happy! alas, no. I have been sorry that I entered the convent ever since I took the novitiate's vow. It was done in a moment of rashness, and has been bitterly repented of. A relative, a devout Catholic, persuaded me."

"I am here in Paris," I said, "to bring the dead to life. Let me rescue you from this living tomb, and add you to my list of triumphs in the great art of resurrection."

"Flee, Satan, and tempt the maid no more," cried the priest, raising himself on his elbow and speaking for the first time.

"Shut your mouth, you old goose, or I'll cram something into it," was my response; and then I turned to Miss Susiel once more.

"Listen to me, my dear little girl," I said, as soon as the priest had subsided. "I know of a kind and tender father who had two daughters, both of them as lovely as angels. He doted on them, for he had no wife to love. He was alone in the world with the exception of his children."

The young lady covered her face with her hands and sobbed. I was producing an impression with my eloquence, it was quite evident. I advanced a step and reverentially laid one hand on her head, while I put an arm around her waist and drew her towards me. She did not resist, which I considered quite sensible on her part.

"Tell me more of the person you speak of," she said.

"A few months since business called the gentleman to his native country. He left his eldest child in Paris, in charge of his sister, so that she could pursue her studies without interruption. Imagine that fond father's grief when he received information that daughter and sister had entered a convent, and were lost to the world forever, as they had left no trace of their retreat."

The young lady was now sobbing quite hysterically, and I applied myself to the task of composing her.

"Do you know the name of the daughter who so cruelly deserted her father?" asked my young charge.

"Yes."

"Tell it to me, please;" and the lady raised her head from my bosom and looked up with tears in her eyes; but still with an expression upon her sweet face that I could not understand.

"Susie Goldthwaite was her name," I replied. "Her father and sister are now in Paris, and anxiously looking for the lost one."

"And Josie," murmured the lady, whose voice was now tremulous, "does she mourn for her sister?"

"How! You know her name?"

"Alas, do I not? for I am her sister."

I was so surprised that my arms tightened around the lady's waist, and not until she intimated that I was suffocating her did I realize what I was about.

"Thank God," I managed to articulate, "that I have found you at last. I will never leave you till I see you restored to the arms of your father."

"O Heavens, can so much happiness await me?" cried Miss Susie, her face radiant with anticipation.

"Yes, I promise you. A fond father and a dear sister await you beyond the walls of this accursed institution."

"Can I leave with you?" she asked. "Can I be free?"

"Yes; and I would like to see the priest that will dare oppose me. Come, I'll protect you."

I was a little elated and spoke without thought, for I imagined that no one but the priest whom I had doubled up, and who was still on the floor, would oppose me; but I was a little premature in my boasting, for hardly had I finished speaking, when the door that led into the garden — the one that I had entered, and which the priest had neglected to secure on his entrance — opened, and in walked two companion priests, fellows who had been out on an expedition like that in which Father Francisco had been engaged. The new comers were astonished at the sight that met their gaze, as well they might be. But they comprehended all in a moment, and one of them remarked, in a quiet way, —

"Well, Father Francisco, you have been wrecked, by the looks of things."

The brother who was addressed now arose to his feet, and wiped away some of the blood from his face.

"I have been foully dealt with, and by the love of God I demand vengeance," cried the priest.

"Thou shalt have it," was the reply. "Thy face looks as though some one had injured thee. There is enough blood on thy beard to make a man swear a life away. Who has struck thee, brother?"

"That viper," was the reply, and I was pointed at.

"Then he suffers for his crime. No one can strike a priest and not be damned."

"He is damned already; but he shall be damned still more, for he has not only ill-used me, but he has tampered with Sister Susiel, and she has listened to him."

The priests uttered a groan of horror, and then all three men advanced two or three steps towards me with frowning looks. I saw that death awaited me at their hands, unless I could make a successful resistance.

"Do not approach me," I said, "or the worse for you. I am a desperate man, and will not die like a rat in a trap."

The three priests exchanged looks and then advanced once more. I retreated until my back was to the wall.

"Leave the room, sister," one of the priests said, speaking to Susiel.

She was so terrified that she did not heed him.

"Remain here," I said, addressing the lady in English. "Do not quit the apartment unless they kill me."

"Heaven forbid!" was the exclamation. "How can I aid you?"

"By remaining quiet. I will not leave the convent without you."

Once more the holy fathers advanced a step, and then drew from beneath their clothes long, narrow knives.

"You mean to use those knives — do you?" I asked.

"Yes," was the reply. "We will cut you into small pieces and feed the fishes of the Seine."

IN THE FRENCH CONVENT.—Page 373.

"Can't we compromise? Let me have the lady and I'll give you ten thousand francs."

The priests laughed.

"No," they said, "no compromise. You have come to your death."

They came towards me, and I saw that they were in earnest. I put my hand in my pocket, and to the surprise of the priests, produced an old friend, in the shape of a revolver.

At the sight of this weapon the priests stopped, and looked at each other in surprise.

They no longer advanced towards me.

"Back to your dens," I shouted, "or I'll shoot you like dogs." Then I moved forward and the priests backward.

Suddenly one of them put his hand in his pocket and threw something at my feet.

It exploded with a loud hiss, and in an instant I was enveloped in a cloud of smoke, so dense and stifling that I could not breathe. My strength was gone in a moment. I was disarmed, for I could not use my pistol without the risk of injuring the lady, much as I wanted to hurt the priests.

"We have tamed the game-cock," was the cry; and I could hear my enemies laugh in triumph at the thought.

I had no longer strength to stand on my feet, and now I sank upon the floor; but just as I fell I heard a crash, as though some one had broken into the room, and then there was a rush of pure air, a hum of voices, the tread of many feet, and lastly a struggle and fierce oaths uttered in English, that never sounded so sweet in spite of the profanity.

"Give 'em h—, consarn their picters," cried a familiar voice; and I had sense enough to recognize that it belonged to Hopeful.

The smoke cleared away, and I saw Fred, Murden, and Hopeful all astride of the three priests and holding them to the floor, while Dupont and Farenti, the French detectives, were standing near a smashed window, looking on, with much complacency, at the scene before them.

I staggered to my feet and reeled towards the air, which was entering the broken window.

"Well, *mon cher*," cried the French detectives, coming forward and lending me the aid of their arms, "you have had a narrow escape!" And after a moment continued,—

"The rascals exploded one of their balls of deadly gas at your feet, and in five minutes you would have been a corpse. We were just in time."

"Yes; but how came you here?" I asked, gaining strength at every moment.

"One of your companions, the Englishman, followed you here, and then went back to the gardens, where he met us. He told us what he had seen, and we suspected mischief. We found the rest of your friends, scaled the walls together, and stood for some time at the window, looking on and admiring the method which you took to convince the priests that you were their master."

"And he would have succeeded if it had not been for the shell of gas," cried Dupont. "I saw shoot in his eyes."

"Thank God, you came in time to save me," I said; "I was nearly exhausted."

"Yes; the good fathers make no mistakes when they fill the glass globes with their deadly gas; stronger men than you have been overcome with it in a few seconds. But look at that droll companion of yours. He is funny."

Hopeful was spanking the priest whom he had captured, because the father would not be still and submit to his humiliation.

"Gol darn yer," Hez was saying, "do ye want to come some more of yer games on my friend, what can be led anywhere by a handsome woman? Ye knew he could not resist 'em, like me. Why don't yer try it on me, and not take advantage of his weakness?"

Just at this moment Fred and Murden arose from the prostrate forms of the priests whom they had overcome and bound, and advanced to congratulate me, and also, at the same moment, Miss Susie rushed into my arms with an hysterical sob of joy at my escape.

CHAPTER XXXVIII.

SAFE ADVICE. — A SURPRISED FATHER. — A PROPOSAL. — OFF FOR ENGLAND. — WEDDINGS. — FINISHING UP. — THE END.

I MUST confess that I felt a thrill of joy at the warm embrace which Miss Susie gave me, but at the same time I knew that her actions would be misconstrued by my companions unless I was discreet, so I gently released myself from her arms and then led her to Fred, whom I was desirous of impressing, and formally introduced her as the daughter of our friend Mr. Goldthwaite.

"Ah," said Fred, in reply to the introduction, "I would have given half that I am worth to have been the first in restoring a daughter to a father. But my friend was always a lucky fellow, and I can only envy him."

Hez and Murden were also complimentary in their remarks, and then I explained to the two detectives the position in which the lady stood. They listened to me in silence, but with no expression of wonder upon their faces, and not until I had concluded did they speak.

"You don't know the law of France in regard to convents — do you?" Dupont asked.

"No."

"It is very strict. There is but one course to be pursued in obtaining the release of a nun. The process is a tedious one, and perhaps would not suit you."

"Not if it is slow."

"It is slow."

"Then we will make as quick work of it as you did when you entered through that window."

"What would you do?" asked the Frenchman.

"Take the lady with us. We will never leave the convent without her."

"Spoken like a brave American, but do you know the danger that you encounter by such a course?"

"No."

"We thought not. Stealing a nun from a convent is punished, by the laws of France, by hard labor in the docks of Toulon. You have no desire to go there?"

"No; and we don't intend to leave the lady in such a den as this."

"*Mon Dieu*, we don't blame you. This is a den, and the holy rascals whom you see lying on the floor, have been up to all kinds of crime for the past six months, and yet, *sacre*, we have had no idea of it. The disappearance of many strangers is now accounted for. The priests have induced some of the nuns to frequent the public places, and bring home men. Then the latter were robbed, and their bodies tumbled into the Seine. *Mon Dieu*, but it is terrible to think of."

I knew it was terrible, and I trembled for a question which I saw was to come, for Dupont turned to Susie, and asked,—

"How many times have these unworthy priests prevailed on you to go to the gardens?"

"Three times in all."

"And did you have company home each time?"

"No; my heart failed me each time until to-night. I was threatened with a cell and starvation unless I obeyed the will of the priests; so when the father with the gray beard told me to throw myself in the way of this gentleman" (pointing to me), "I did so because I had some hope of escape through his means."

"It is wonderful," muttered the detectives. "It might have gone on for a year, and we should never have suspected. Now, what shall we do?"

"Take the rascals to the nearest prison, and thus expose the Blessed Pilgrims to the world," I answered.

The detectives shook their heads, as they replied,—

"You don't know what you ask. If we should arrest these men and prefer charges against them, the whole of religious France would rise up and defend them, and denounce us as perjurers and assassins."

"And the rest of France would sustain you."

"No; it would do nothing, and we should be sacrificed, instead of the priests, for bringing scandal on the church."

"Then what shall we do? The lady must go with us. We cannot leave her here."

The detectives looked puzzled, and then they retired to a corner of the room and consulted together for a few minutes. The result of the conference they communicated to us in a few words.

"The laws of France," they said, "as we told you before, are very strict in regard to its convents and inmates; but if you take the lady, and no trace can be found of you or your charge, it don't seem to us that the vengeance of the law can be satisfied."

"By that you mean that the lady and those who take her must leave France as soon as possible," I said.

The officers bowed. I had comprehended them.

"In the name of Heaven, don't leave me here," the lady said, in the wildest alarm, for fear we should desert her. "Take me to my father and sister, and I will bless you."

"Do not be alarmed," replied Fred, who appeared to take a wonderful interest in Susie's welfare. "We swear to you that nothing shall induce us to leave the convent unless you accompany us."

The young girl gave him a look of gratitude, and then Fred ranged alongside of her, as though he constituted himself her champion.

"If she leaves the convent, will you quit France in less than twenty-four hours?" asked the detectives.

"Yes."

"Don't think," the officers said, "that we want you to go. Far from it; but it is your safety that we are looking after. We don't want you brought back and tried, and then have all this scandal exposed. It would be disagreeable — would it not?"

We thought that it would.

"Then take the lady, and leave the convent as soon as you please."

"And these bad priests! What will you do with them?" I asked.

"We shall report to the prefect, and he can order further investigations or not, just as he pleases. At any rate, the history of this night's work will be related, and the officials can probe the matter to the bottom, or leave it just where we found it. But of one thing be assured: the business of robbery in which the fathers have been engaged, is ended forever. Now go, for we shall soon have daylight."

"And you?" I asked.

"We shall remain here on the watch until you have left Paris. Then we shall make our report, and not before."

We wrung the detectives' hands, and after a last look at the prostrate and bound priests, left the convent as soon as possible. Fred offered his arm to Miss Susie, and she accepted it, while Murden and I took the lead, and prepared to answer all questions which the gendarmes might put in case they met us.

At the corner of the Place Concorde, we found two carriages with the drivers fast asleep on the boxes. They were night birds, and waiting in the hope of picking up a few francs before daylight.

I aroused the drivers and engaged both carriages. My friends looked on in silence, not knowing what I intended.

"Murden," I said, "you and Hez must go to our rooms and pack our trunks at once. At six o'clock we start for England. It is now three. There is time enough."

"But the model of my gun," cried Hopeful. "Gol darn it, you know Louis has it."

"You must leave it for the present, or else write to the emperor, and tell him that you are ready to make terms when he is satisfied that it is a good thing."

"Yes, and lots I'll make out of that kind of game — now snan't I? You know jist as well as I does, that the emperor will forget me, and claim all the merit of the thing — now don't you?"

"Let us hope for better things."

"It ain't no use to hope for better things from them crowned heads. If they can only show themselves smart off other people's ideas, they think they can keep on the throne forever. My gun is worth —"

"But think, Hez, how much the life and liberty of this young lady are worth."

"I know; but it won't be worth much to me, 'coz you know she wouldn't look at a freckle-faced feller like me, even if I has more brains than the rest of yer all put together."

"We won't discuss that question at the present time," I said, in a low tone, for I feared that Miss Susie would hear him. "If you want to do me a favor, just acquiesce in my wishes."

"'Cos you are in love with her sister, I 'spose. It is wonderful how much a man will do for a gal's relations when he's in love, and how quick he gets tired of doing for 'em arter he's married. There was my wife's aunts —"

"We'll hear the rest on the train," I cried, and bundled Hez into the carriage.

"Look ahere," said Hez, from the carriage window, "my shirts is at the washerwoman's, and I has but two left, and I'd like to know what I'm to do for clean ones."

Murden gave the signal to the driver, and the carriage dashed off.

"Where shall we go with the lady?" asked Fred.

"There is but one place for her — to her father's."

"And it is necessary that you should go with her, I suppose," Fred said with a sly look, for he understood my case.

"Yes; the sooner he understands that the *dead is alive*, the better he will feel."

I assisted Susie to enter the carriage, while the driver looked on and wondered what we were up to, but knew too much of Parisian life to ask questions, as long as there was a good fee to be obtained.

"You are ready and anxious to see your father and sister?" I whispered.

The young girl responded with a pressure of her hand, but was too much agitated to speak.

We gave the driver his orders and off we went, over the smooth streets, the wheels of the vehicle hardly making the least noise.

In ten minutes we were in front of Mr. Goldthwaite's house. It was just daylight, or a little before four o'clock I went to the lodge, and attempted to rouse the porter, but it required time to get him out of bed, and when he opened the door he grumbled like an old French soldier.

"*Sacre*," he muttered, "what is the meaning of this? Do you want me to call the police, that you make such a noise in the morning, before it is time to leave one's bed?" And then he appeared to recollect me, and a grim smile passed over his face as he pulled off his night-cap and bowed.

"Pardon, monsieur; I did not know that it was you, it is so early."

I slipped a five-franc piece into his hand, and then another smile passed over his face. He was ready to obey monsieur in all things.

"Go to Mr. Goldthwaite's room," I said, "and tell him that I must see him without delay. Do you understand?"

"Yes, monsieur, he shall sleep no more this morning;" and with a military salute he left me.

"Remain here with the lady, Fred, until I give the signal for you to escort her up stairs. I must prepare her friends to receive her."

Then I followed the porter to Mr. Goldthwaite's sitting-room, and waited for the old gentleman to appear. I did not have to wait long. In a few minutes Mr. Goldthwaite entered the apartment with one slipper on and a dressing-gown thrown over his shoulders.

"God bless me!" he cried, "what can have induced this early visit? All well — ain't you?"

"Yes, we are all well," I answered; "and I can assure you that I have my reasons for disturbing you at this unseasonable hour."

"You have news —"

Mr. Goldthwaite hesitated, and did not dare to finish the sentence.

Just at this moment I heard the door of Miss Josie's apartment open, and turning I saw the young lady enter the room, dressed as if to receive morning callers.

"What has happened?" she asked, and came towards me and extended her hands, looking anxious and a little frightened.

"Can you bear good or ill news?" I asked.

"Yes; I can bear anything now," was the reply. "I hoped that something had happened to you; but now I know you are safe —"

She suddenly recollected what she had said, and to whom she was talking. Then she paused and blushed, and withdrew her hands from mine.

Her father looked on, and seemed quite dumb under the influence of my early visit. He could not comprehend it as yet. He knew that something had happened, and hoped that it was some matter that concerned his own family.

I looked at the father and then at the daughter, to see if they were prepared for my revelations, for I knew they would astonish them.

"Can you bear all that I have to say?" I asked.

Miss Josie put one of her little hands in mine in order to show that she was quite composed.

"We are calm," she said. "Trust us."

"The dead is alive," I cried in a low tone.

Mr. Goldthwaite started forward with a wild cry, while Josie dropped my hand and covered her face.

They knew what I meant without asking a question.

"Where is she?" demanded the father, after a moment's time to recover his self-possession.

"She is near us."

"In a convent?"

"She has been in one."

"Is she still in one?"

"No."

"Where is she?"

"At the door. In one moment she will be in your arms."

"Thank God!"

"But listen to me for a moment," I said. "I have stolen her from a convent. In a few hours her loss will be known. We have but a short time to spare."

"Tell me what to do and I'll do it, but let me see my child," cried the father.

"We must leave Paris in an hour's time. Tell your servants to pack your trunks without delay. Josie, set your maid to work. There is no safety for us outside of England and the United States."

"We will do as you direct us," father and daughter both said.

I stepped to the window and gave the signal to Fred, and up the stairs he assisted his agitated charge. The door was thrown open, and then father and daughters were soon in each other's arms.

Fred and I left them alone for a short time, or until we concluded that the first transport had passed away, and all were ready to hear reason. Then I ventured to knock at the door, and was told to enter.

I found father and daughters clasping each other's hands.

"We must be moving," I said. "You can talk on board the cars."

"We will be ready in half an hour," answered Josie. "Our trunks are most packed."

I passed into the next room, and Josie followed me.

"I must take time to talk to you for what you have done," she said. "Susie has told us all. Can we ever be grateful enough?"

"Yes."

"How?"

"Josie," I said, and stole an arm around her waist, "you know that I love you."

"I know that I have not got time to finish packing," she said.

"But you will give me one moment?"

"How can I?"

She did not offer to move, although she pretended to be in such a hurry.

"Do you love me?" I asked, and held her firm, in spite of her little struggles.

"Well, I suppose that I must answer yes, or have my life squeezed out of me."

"And you will marry me?"

"Well, I think that I shall have to some time or other."

"And on the strength of that promise I may have a kiss?"

"Yes, just one."

I took a dozen or two, and wanted more, but could not get them.

"I admire your impudence," she said, and ran to her own room.

Then Mr. Goldthwaite came to me.

"How can I thank you for what you have done?" he asked.

"By giving me Josie," I said.

"I couldn't give her to one whom I like better," he replied. "But are you sure that you love her well enough for a wife?"

"Yes, for I have just told her that such is the case."

"Hem! And what answer did she return?"

"Like a dutiful daughter she referred me to you."

This was not quite correct, for Josie had not mentioned the old gentleman's name; but then it does no harm to let our elders see that we pay them some respect.

"Ah," said the gratified father, "Josie always was a good girl. I hope she will make you as good a wife as she has me a child. Take her, my son, and be kind to her."

I promised, and faithfully have I kept my word. And now I have but little more to write. We escaped from France without the least detention, thanks to the care of the two Paris detectives. They wrote us, in London, that the priests of the Blessed Pilgrims had been punished by being sent to Rome, and that was the last heard of them.

Josie's aunt preferred a life in the convent to freedom; so she still remains in the Pilgrims, where she has time enough to repent of her sins.

Hopeful never heard from Napoleon about the model gun; but some time ago the emperor invented a weapon which he called the Chassepot. Hez, in his rage, declares that the Chassepot and his Hopper Gun are one and the same thing, and that Louis stole his invention; but it don't seem possible that such could be the case. Hopeful is now in Hillsboro' County, New Hampshire; and when he is not talking of Martha or a new wife, he is planning fresh expeditions or great inventions.

While we were in London, Fred and Miss Susie were often thrown together, and the result was just what I hoped for — a warm attachment on their part; and the *finale* was a double wedding, for Fred and I were married on the same day, in the presence of a few friends, in the city of London.

We passed a few weeks with the Earl of Buckland, at his country seat, and a few weeks with my father-in-law, Sir William, before we sailed for the United States. I will give Sir William and his lady the credit of doing all that they could do to render our visit agreeable; and not a word did they say to prove that they regretted the step which I had taken.

My son and Rover gave us a welcome that proved how sincere they were in their affections; and the dog is with us at the present time, but the boy is with his grandparents on a visit.

As for honest Murden, we applied ourselves so closely to his business that the English cabinet granted all he desired, and he went back to Australia the most popular man in the colony. He was immediately made minister of the interior, and has held that position ever since. He is immensely wealthy, and still a widower. I hope that I have not seen the last of him.

And now, dear readers, a long farewell; and may you be as happy as the parties who have so often afforded you amusement through these pages.

www.ingramcontent.com/pod-product-compliance
Lightning Source LLC
Chambersburg PA
CBHW032026220426
43664CB00006B/376